A PROSPECT OF SOUTHWELL

D1514642

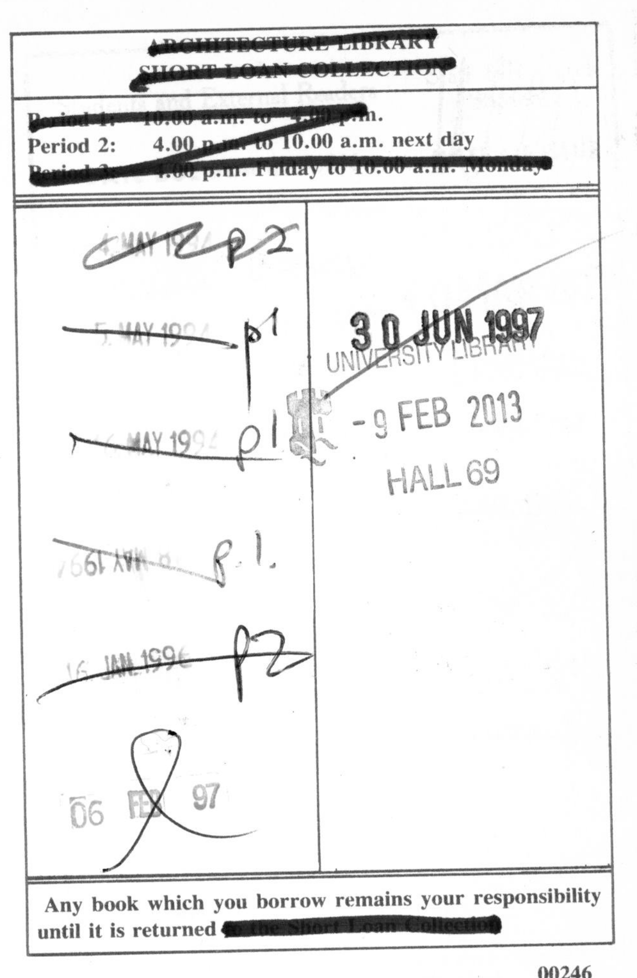
ARCHITECTURE LIBRARY
SHORT LOAN COLLECTION
Period 1: 10.00 a.m. to 4.00 p.m.
Period 2: 4.00 p.m. to 10.00 a.m. next day
Period 3: 4.00 p.m. Friday to 10.00 a.m. Monday
30 JUN 1997
UNIVERSITY LIBRARY
- 9 FEB 2013
HALL 69
06 FEB 97
Any book which you borrow remains your responsibility until it is returned to the Short Loan Collection
00246

UNIVERSITY OF NOTTINGHAM
WITHDRAWN FROM THE LIBRARY
66 0001157 X
TELEPEN

A Prospect of Southwell

An architectural history of the church and domestic buildings of the collegiate foundation

by

Norman Summers

Phillimore

1974

Published by
PHILLIMORE & CO. LTD.
London and Chichester

Head Office: Shopwyke Hall,
Chichester, Sussex, England

© Norman Summers, 1974

ISBN 0 85033 181 1

*Thanks are due to the generous help of
the University of Nottingham and of
the Marc Fitch Fund in enabling
this volume to be published*

Text set in 11/13pt. Baskerville
Printed in Great Britain by Eyre and Spottiswoode Ltd.,
Her Majesty's Printers at Grosvenor Press, Portsmouth

Contents

List of Plates

(between pages 88 and 89)

List of Figures

Acknowledgments

Samuel Hieronymus Grimm (1734-94), a topographical artist of great skill and accuracy, and Swiss by birth, came to London in 1769. The large number of drawings he subsequently executed in ink and wash included many views of Nottinghamshire, commissioned by Sir Richard Kaye, Dean of Lincoln and, amongst his other appointments, Prebendary of North Muskham in Southwell. I am indebted to the Trustees of the British Museum for permission to reproduce the Grimm drawings in the Kaye Collection (ref: Add. MSS 15543 and 44); and to the Keeper of the Western MSS at the Bodleian Library, Oxford, for the reproductions from the Gough Collection of Maps and Drawings, vol. 26.

Another record of Southwell of historical interest, although from more modern times, is in the work of Alfred J. Loughton (1865-1953). He was a man of great versatility, of a type seen more frequently in the 18th century. He was a local man who made bicycles in the days before their manufacture became exclusively big business; he made violins; he became interested in photography first as a hobby, and then as another commercial enterprise. His large collection of prints and negatives (mostly on glass plates) of general views and sculptural details of the Minster was donated by his family to the library at his death, and was placed at my disposal by the Provost of Southwell and the Minster Librarian. Messrs. Keith Harris and Philip Sharrocks, and Mrs. Susan Ward, of the MSS. Department of Nottingham University library undertook the difficult task of printing from the negatives which have inevitably suffered some deterioration from long storage; they also made many of the prints from other sources. Mr. Keith Oliff of the University Department of Architecture has been responsible for photographs taken specially for the book.

Mr. John Cater redrew the plan of the Minster used in Fig. 8. Figs. 1, 2 and 3 are based on the Ordnance Survey maps and are reproduced with the sanction of the Controller of H.M. Stationery Office, Crown Copyright reserved.

I am also indebted to the following for permission to use transcripts and reproductions from original documents; the Trustees of the British Museum ('The Case of Southwell', Add. MSS 28088 f.46 of Index of 1854-75, in chapter 5); the Provost of Southwell (Appendices A to D, and F, and plates in chapter 5, from the Minster Library); the Borthwick Institute of Historical Research, York, by permission of the Controller of H.M. Stationery Office (Appendices E and K, Chancery Rolls 1628 and Prog. Mar. 1732/33); the County Archivist, Notts. County Record Office (Appendices G, H, and J, PRSW/97/17B, 116/106, and PRSW 122/17).

I am particularly grateful for stimulus and help from Professor M. W. Barley, of the University of Nottingham, and Mr. K. S. S. Train, formerly Hon. Secretary of the Thoroton Society of Nottinghamshire, both of whom also read the draft of the text; their detailed and valuable comments have been incorporated in its final form. Mr. R. M. Beaumont, Librarian of Southwell Minster, has drawn on his deep knowledge of chapter records innumerable times on my behalf. The Very Revd. J. F. Pratt, Provost of Southwell, has given me every encouragement, and access to records and church property of all kinds. Mrs. Hazel Cotter, of the Department of Architecture, University of Nottingham, has coped with all the typing of drafts, and with the large volume of correspondence necessary for my research, and my daughter helped in checking the text. The people of Southwell, private householders and those in official positions, too numerous to mention individually have, without exception, given permission to examine private documents and to survey and record their houses and other buildings. Finally, and not least, I am grateful to my wife, who so often sees the wood when I can see only trees.

Southwell,
February 1974. *Norman Summers*

Thanks are due to the following for contributing illustrations:
K.F. Oliff (Plates 1, 3, 4, 5, 17, 28-34, 56, 58, 60-62); A.J. Loughton (Plates 14, 15, 18-27, 36, 37); British Museum (Plates 6, 16, 38, 40-44, 48, 52, 55, 57, 59); Bodleian Library, Oxford (Plates 11, 12, 35); Southwell Minster Library (Plates 45-47); Notts. County Record Office (Plate 49).

Preface

Some years ago, having a particular interest in domestic building, I was impressed by the number of houses in Southwell which were obviously of historical and architectural value, and I set out to study them to find out more about their origins. I soon discovered a complex of interwoven threads of history which stemmed from the very special form of organisation which developed from the foundation of the church just over 1,000 years ago. A proper understanding of these houses – mostly the mansions of former prebendaries of the church – could only be achieved by putting them in the context of the history of the church, of the houses of the other clergy serving it, and of the town which grew up around it. This book is the result.

The pressures for change in our living environment today are greater than ever before and, more than this, the pace at which change is taking place accelerates with each new technical advance. One hastily-made decision can set into action a chain of events which, in a fraction of time, can sweep away everything around us which has been laboriously accumulated by our forefathers. In the process, with eagerness for new and perhaps untried forms of development, the human scale of man related to his natural surroundings, and the quality of living environments he has built up over a long period of time, are too often forgotten. Planning for the future must be based on an understanding of the present, and that in turn can only come from an appreciation of the past. Southwell reflects its unique history, and its essential character is worthy of careful preservation; future development should take account of this and be planned in sympathy with a living tradition. The second thousand years of the church in the town is now well under way; when that too is past let us hope that we shall be judged fit custodians of our time.

Foreword

Southwell is a hidden place, seen only when one overlooks it from the top of nearby hills. It is a small, midlands version of *Barchester*. It has never had a novelist, but it has certainly had a succession of historians, and it made a distinctive mark on the ideas of a great historian of this century, Sir Frank Stenton, whose home it was. The architecture of its Minster has been described by such authorities as A. Hamilton Thompson and Nicholas Pevsner. Nevertheless, no one has tried to write the history of Southwell as told by its buildings. The great merit of Dr. Summers' book is that it brings together two aspects of this unique institution, the collegiate church and the buildings which naturally sprang up round it. One aspect is the growth of the buildings, and their vicissitudes through many centuries as told by the stones and timbers themselves. Even if the few canons who kept the institution going were scrupulous about keeping records, most were destroyed when Parliamentary Soldiers in 1646 rifled the archbishop's palace where they were stored. With only the minimum of documents surviving, the story of Southwell in the middle ages must be read in its monuments. For the later centuries there are more documents, and the second aspect of Dr. Summers' work which is new, and valuable, is his account of the canons' dealings with their buildings in recent centuries. The story of a complex of medieval buildings does not end at 1500, and to bring it to recent times underlines the continuity of history.

Our great churches of the middle ages are usually admired in isolation, but just as every monastery had its refectory, dormitory and the rest, so a collegiate church had its own institutional aspect - the vicars' court and the college of chantry priests - as well as the private residences of the canons. The palace of the archbishops of York, though not essentially part of the institution, clearly gave Southwell added status, and Dr. Summers explains its character. Together these buildings give a *raison d'être* for Southwell - provided that one adds the rights and privileges of the canons, as ecclesiastics and as landlords. The people of Nottinghamshire journeyed to Southwell, either for their duties as Christians or their obligations as landholders, for over a thousand years.

Southwell has attracted artists as well as historians. Dr. Summers' book is enriched not only by photographs but also by the opportunity to reproduce hitherto unpublished drawings, such as those by S. H. Grimm. I hope that his work, for its research and for its wealth and variety of illustrations, will be widely appreciated.

M. W. Barley

I

Introduction

The Town

IN JUNE 1789 the diarist John Byng (later the 5th Viscount Torrington) was staying in Newark at the end of his tour of the Midlands. It was a warm, pleasant day when he set out on horseback, crossed the Trent by the ferry at Farndon, and rode via Rolleston, Fiskerton, Thurgarton, and Halloughton; 'Thence I soon came in sight of the pretty Town of Southwell, and of its superb Collegiate Church'. He dined well off cold beef, veal, and gooseberry tart, rounding it off with brandy, at the *Saracen's Head* Inn, and spent the afternoon visiting the church and chapter house, sketching the west gateway of the churchyard, and admiring the newly-built vicars' houses and the ruins of the archbishops' palace. He attended evensong in the Minster, flattered by being seated in a stall by the residentiary canon, and praised the vicar choral who read the prayers, the music by the organist, and the anthem sung by the four singing men and 11 choristers. Back at the inn he called for tea, paid his bill for the day – including hay and corn for his horse it came to only 2s. 5d. – and completed the round trip back to Newark via Upton and Kelham. Summing up the day later, he wrote 'Southwell is a well built, clean town, such a one as a quiet distressed family ought to retire to; coals, provisions, and religion to be had good and cheap'.[1]

The town visited by the Hon. John Byng was still a rural backwater, which had not grown appreciably since medieval times. It lay well off the established lines of communication; the Great North Road and the Roman Fosse Way met at the crossing of the river Trent in Newark, six miles to the east, and the old road from Leicester through Nottingham to Doncaster passed nearly five miles to the west. Lacking mineral resources such as stone, coal or iron, there was no incentive for industrial expansion, and its only river – the Greet – could only provide power for local mills. It had been the presence of the collegiate foundation which gave the town regional importance, and the palace of the archbishops of York which provided a convenient halting place for them on the long journey from York to the Court in London. When he first approached the town, cresting the hill a mile to the south, Byng would have looked down at the Minster, sheltered by rising ground to the west and north, with the ruins of the palace in front, and the red brick and stuccoed houses standing a respectful distance around (Pl. 1). In the years immediately following his visit the prebendal houses were mostly improved and enlarged; in modern times Bishop's Manor was built amongst the palace ruins. and suburban housing has spread over the fields and orchards outside the town centre, but if he could return today he would easily recognise most of the features he then admired.

The parish of Southwell lies on the Keuper Marls, which are fertile clays in a wide band running roughly north and south through the county, between the valley of the river Trent on the east, and the Bunter Sandstones of Sherwood Forest on the west. The parish area, of nearly 5,000 acres is large for villages on the marls, where most are between 2,000 and 3,000 acres; it is roughly triangular in shape, with a base over five miles long from east to west, and nearly three and a half miles from south to north, with the town sited near the centre of the parish (Fig. 1). Cultivation of the open fields in an extensive layout of this character could not have been managed easily from the centre of the town proper, and it is likely that the hamlets of Easthorpe, Westhorpe, and Normanton, lying conveniently as they do to the extremities of the parish, developed as the real centres of agricultural activity. The suffix 'thorp' was used in the Danelaw in the sense of an outlying farmstead or small hamlet dependent on a larger place, so that Easthorpe and Westhorpe were almost certainly secondary settlements following the Danish invasions of the 9th century.[2] There are working farms in Normanton and Westhorpe to this day, and the church records contain regular references to what were obviously farm units in all three hamlets. By the time of parliamentary enclosures in the 18th century the hamlets were dealt with separately.[3] The *Burgage*, a separate manor within the parish, adjoining the town to the north-east, was agricultural in character, but the *Prebendage* – the collegiate church and its property – developed on an urban plan and became the town (Fig. 2).

The English monastic church was planned with its refectory, dormitory, and other domestic buildings grouped around the cloister adjoining the church; Canterbury, Durham, and Ely were three such examples of cathedral status. In contrast, the secular cathedral was a collegiate church, i.e. one governed by a chapter of canons who were ordained priests. They did not lead the claustral life, and therefore had no need of communal domestic buildings; even so a cloister was generally built as a covered promenade. At Hereford and Exeter for example the cloisters adjoined the nave of the church with the chapter house off the eastern walk as in a monastery. The church was generally set within its own enclosure – the close, or minster yard – separated from the town immediately around it; the churchyard, reserved for burials, surrounded the church within the close; the episcopal palace occupied, or was accessible from, one side of the close, with the houses of the dignitaries and the lodgings for the vicars choral occupying the other two sides. This is the pattern of Salisbury and Wells, showing some similarity of layout with the organised grouping of the ancillary buildings of a monastic foundation, but at York and Lincoln the seclusion of the close has been marred for a present-day visitor by the encroachment of traffic. The definition of

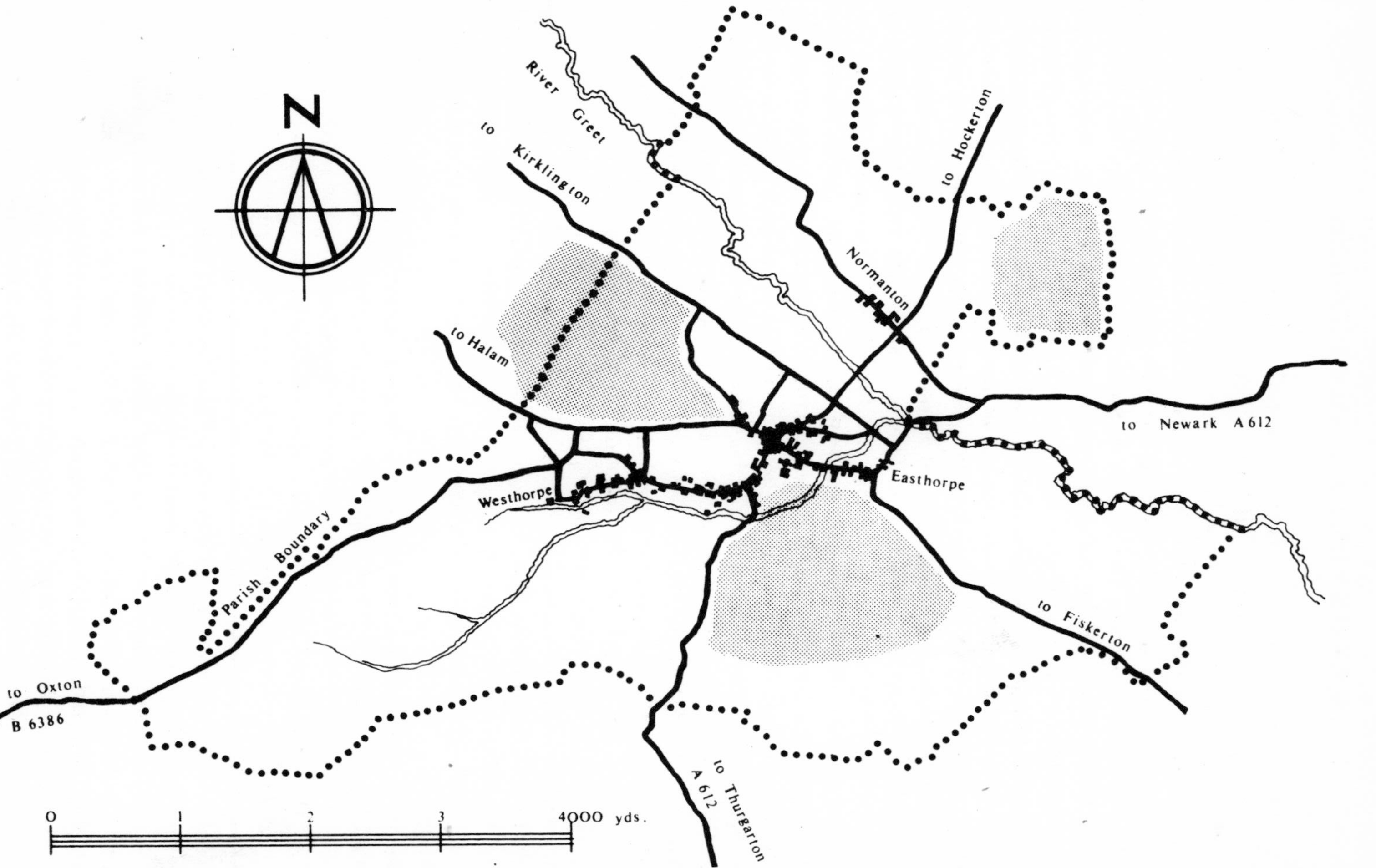

Fig 1: *The Parish of Southwell. Linear development along roads radiating from the town centre, to the hamlets of Easthorpe and Westhorpe. The three parks of the archbishops of York are shown shaded—Hockerwood Park on the north-east, Norwood Park on the west, and Southwell or New Park in the south of the parish adjoining the Palace. (Based on Ordnance Survey maps, and reproduced with the sanction of the Controller of H.M. Stationery Office. Crown copyright reserved.)*

the boundaries of the close was later found to be necessary; in 1285 the chapter of Lincoln applied for a licence to build an enclosing wall 12 feet high where necessary to give greater protection from undesirables at night, and similar rights were also granted at this period to Exeter, York, Lichfield and Wells. Gatehouses, which were locked at night, completed the protection, and the close became a form of fortified enclosure. The church at Southwell, although not of cathedral status, fulfilled some of the functions of a cathedral as mother church of all Nottinghamshire, and as a collegiate foundation of high standing. All the elements of a cathedral close were present, but the lack of a hierarchy in its government and of firm control at its head is reflected in the informality in the layout of its buildings. The palace at the south side of the church was a residence of the archbishops of York, and was part of a park of some 132 acres extending south-eastwards from the churchyard. This was Southwell Park, also known as Little, or New Park, and contained two large ponds which provided fish for the household on fast days. Although most of the land was let out as farms and plantations, and some of it was common pasture, the existence of the park may well have restrained development on the south side of the church and have been a factor militating against the siting of the collegiate buildings in a more formal layout. The lodgings and common hall for the vicars choral were first sited beyond the east end of the church and were later rebuilt at the north-east corner on land which had originally been part of the churchyard. The buildings to the north-west of the church, at the junction of Church Street and Westgate are encroachment on the churchyard, and a plan of 1819[4] shows that this was then a dense layout of houses and shops; the *Crown* Inn occupied the corner as now, and behind it, on Church Street, stood the medieval building of the chantry priests' house around a courtyard garden (Pl. VI). The latter was demolished soon after the plan was made, when Richard Ingleman built the new grammar school on the site.

The most remarkable feature of the collegiate layout is in the siting of the prebendal houses. They have no precinctual plan, but stand detached within their own grounds and are set back from the road frontages lining the north and west sides of the churchyard (Fig. 3). The present buildings are replacements on the same sites and are country mansions of a modest scale but in an urban setting (Pls. III, IV, & V). The pattern of site boundaries, however, has strong similarities with the layout of a medieval open-field village in which the farmhouses, with their byres and barns lined the roads from the centre; the crofts, or enclosures in which they stood extended behind to a back lane which gave easy access to arable and pasture for produce and animals. The sites on Westgate extend to a line marked by a public footpath today (an embryonic back lane) dividing them from land which was open pasture until recent years. The Church Street sites extend northwards in a similar way, but Burgage Lane was then the back lane and was so named on the Ordnance Survey of 1885, when it was already developed by cottage building resulting from town expansion (Fig. 2). The early prebendaries

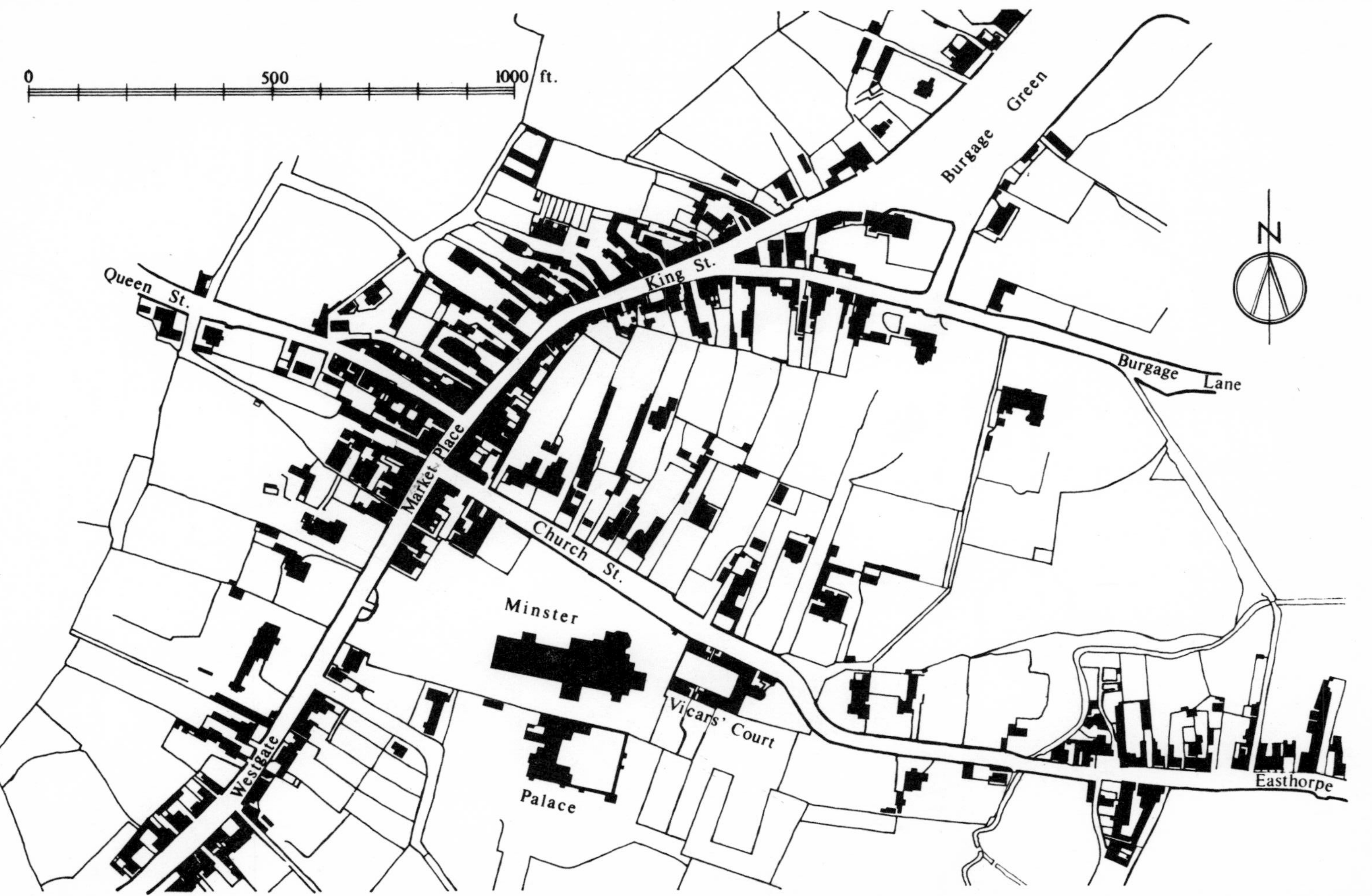

Fig 2: *The Town Centre. The buildings of the collegiate foundation, related to the other buildings of the prebendage. Compare with Fig 3. (Based on Ordnance Survey maps, 1938 revision, and reproduced with the sanction of the Controller of H.M. Stationery Office. Crown copyright reserved.)*

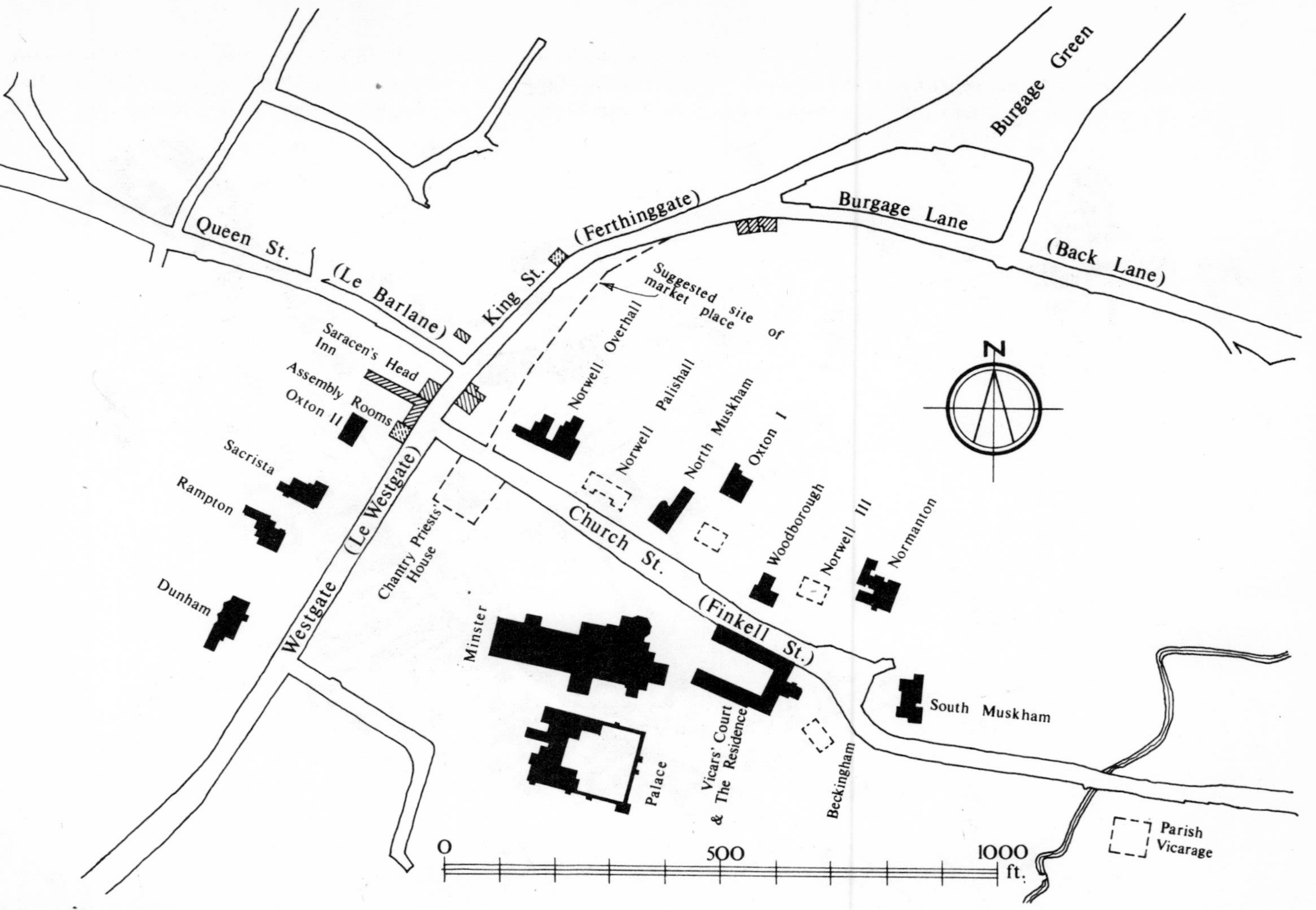

Fig 3: *The prebendal houses, related to the Minster, and other collegiate buildings; those shown in dotted lines have been sited only on documentary evidence. Other buildings of the prebendage, in which timber framing has been observed, are shown hatched. The earliest recorded street names are given in brackets. (Based on Ordnance Survey maps, and reproduced with the sanction of the Controller of H.M. Stationery Office. Crown copyright reserved.)*

would have been actively concerned in cultivation of the open fields, so that these similarities with a layout of crofts cannot be entirely accidental; even when the prebendary relied on produce brought in from his parochial manor, the back lane would have been a useful access for heavy waggons. There are references to barns attached to prebendal mansions in later leases, and the lease of the prebendal house of Dunham in the 18th century included *Lowes Wong*[5] a strip of pasture in the open land at the rear of the house. Had the estates not been so firmly in the hands of the individual prebendaries, the houses in Southwell might have been enclosed into one cohesive group with the other collegiate buildings, but the incentive and opportunity were not there in the formative days; by the time of the administrative reforms of the 16th century, and after the Restoration, it was too late to reorganise them into a precinctual layout.

Fig 4: *Buildings on the west side of Market Place. The house and shops on the left were built across the frontage of the prebend of Oxton II. Beyond are the Assembly Rooms, and the* Saracen's Head *Inn.*

The *Saracen's Head* Inn stands in a commanding position at the western termination of Church Street (Fig. 5). In 1646, King Charles I spent his last day of freedom there, arriving early in the morning of 5 May, and surrendering himself to the Scottish Commissioners later, in the afternoon; it was then the *King's Head,* but changed its name in the 18th century when the sign of the *Saracen's Head* was more popular in the county. That part of the main street which it fronts is still known as Market Place and contained the market cross, although its exact site has been lost (Fig. 4).[6] In 1805, Richard Ingleman was the architect for the assembly rooms which were built adjoining the south side of the inn, partly on the site of a derelict building known as the Market House, which obtruded across the road nearly one third of its width, so that on market days at that time only 10 feet was left for passing vehicles. This is not the generous provision for a market which one would expect to find associated with a church foundation of the importance of Southwell;[7] but northwards, the rear boundaries of the properties on the east side of King Street form a straight line against the prebendal mansion of Norwell Overhall (now the National Westminster Bank). Regarded as encroachments, these properties stand on the site of the early, triangular, market place, with the *Saracen's Head,* market cross, and market house at its base (Fig. 3). John Leland, making his itinerary in the 16th century, wrote that 'there is no market publike', and Robert Thoroton, the painstaking historian of Nottinghamshire in the 17th century, was silent on the subject. Encroachment on the original market must have taken place in the Middle Ages and in any case would have been a piecemeal process of replacement of temporary market stalls by more permanent structures. Not until the late 18th or early 19th century was a market re-established, and then in the restricted space left at the junction of roads by the *Saracen's Head.*

Southwell, therefore does not appear ever to have held an important place as a commercial centre for the villages around, Newark is only seven miles away, and is sited where the Fosse Way runs close to an arm of the river Trent; its market is probably pre-Conquest in origin, and the castle made it an important defensive position from Norman times. With all its advantages of siting, Newark has had a continuous history of commercial importance with which Southwell could not compete. Ripon and Beverley, the other great collegiate foundations in the diocese of York, by contrast were important agricultural centres and have retained their market functions into modern times.[8]

The west side of King Street presents a complete contrast in plan. Frontages on the street are again narrow, but the original plots, each with a house on the road, and with gardens, stables, or warehouses behind, have been filled in. At several points passages give entry to cottage development at right angles to the road (Fig. 2), a form of urban infill which was characteristic of town expansion from the 16th century onwards (Fig. 6).[9] The rear of the properties is open to a back lane which may have had its origins in essential movements between crofts and the open fields, but it was certainly retained and developed here for the servicing

Fig 5: *The* Saracen's Head *Inn, Market Place*

of shops which grew up along the old Farthingate in later periods. The establishment of the Ropewalk to the west, and the buildings on it, may have inhibited development on the back lane itself.

The manor of Burgage was also in the lordship of the archbishops of York; it extended from the Southern edge of Burgage Green to the river Greet in the north, and from Potwell Dyke westwards to the Ropewalk, and somewhat beyond at its north-west limit. It was therefore quite a small agricultural area within the parish. Dickinson asserted that the Burgage 'is certainly much reduced in size and population from what it has been in former times' but does not support this convincingly; nor is there evidence for the Roman station he postulates there. Burgage Green is an attractive open space of grass and trees enclosed by roads; detached houses stand in spacious grounds, but no building has any part earlier than the 18th century, and the central green is unenclosed common grazing within the manor. In 1622 James I made a grant of incorporation to the town of Southwell, with sundry privileges, but with a proviso against prejudice to the archbishop of York, and the chapter and prebends of Southwell collegiate church.[10] This is a late date for the grant of a borough charter. The layout of sites around Burgage Green have marked similarities with burgage tenements which may have been set out for a new market.[11] The commercial life of the town, however, had been long established in the prebendage, and the prebendaries may have decided that the new charter did prejudice their rights. Whatever the reason, the charter was not put into effect and Burgage Green remained rural in character. The lordship of the manor passed in 1840 to the Ecclesiastical Commissioners and the Deputy Steward, Mr. Waldo Dowson, holds the court when appropriate, but the business today is mainly confined to the lettings of grazing on the common land.

Outside the town centre, and beyond the prebendal houses of Church Street and Westgate, the town straggles along the roads in a linear pattern to Easthorpe and Westhorpe (Pl. III). The houses stand only one deep along the roads, their sites for the most part having narrow frontages in proportion to their depth, and

Fig 6: *Waterloo Yard. 18th-century cottages (now demolished) built on passage ways at right angles to the main street (King Street). Typical town growth of the 17th and 18th centuries.*

the pattern of site boundaries is that of the strips of open field cultivation which were very little changed in the process of enclosure.

The Buildings of the Prebendage; the Vernacular Tradition

The college at Southwell was already in being by the time of the Norman Conquest, and this would have included the refectory and communal buildings for the canons who were by then probably seven in number. The archbishop also had established a residence. Although we have no knowledge of the nature of these early buildings, it is likely that the Saxon church was built of stone, and that the domestic accommodation was timber-framed with walls of mud and roofs of thatch. The village community within the area under control of the church must already have become more than a purely agricultural settlement, but its buildings would have been primitive in materials and construction. In the 14th century stone was employed for the new lodgings of the vicars choral and for the palace but, apart from the one fragment of the prebendal house of Norwell Overhall described later, there is no evidence of stone being used at any period for the lesser buildings of the prebendage. Brickwork did not begin to replace timber-framing techniques for these until the late 16th and the 17th centuries. As time went on the pace of rebuilding accelerated and reached its peak in the late 18th century.

In 1818, Shilton wrote,

> very few inland places, not favoured with that powerful auxiliary, a navigable river or canal, have made such rapid progress within the last thirty years as Southwell; in that time have been erected not many less than twenty substantial houses, the greater part of which are in the occupation of the owners; persons of very respectable, if not affluent fortunes.

He had seen three new houses established around Burgage Green; then Hill House by John Thomas Becher, and Burgage Court, both on Back Lane, and three more (No. 17 Kelham House, No. 21 Stenton House, and No. 23 Clyde House all on Westgate); Hardwick House in Queen Street, and Park House on the Nottingham Road. The greatest activity, however, was not in new building, but in the additions and improvements to the houses on prebendal sites in Westgate and Church Street, some of which still show parts which are probably of the 17th century. Together, all these include every substantial house in Southwell; with the new vicars' houses, and the improvements to the residence house; and with the new frontages and re-building in King Street and Queen Street of a host of smaller properties, the changes in the town in that period were dramatic, and Shilton's eulogy understandable.

The predominant architectural character of Southwell is set by its buildings of red brick with red-pantiled (and the later blue Welsh-slated) roofs. To the newcomer accustomed to the more mellow, multicoloured bricks from the clays of south and east of England, the harshness and uniformity of colour here may appear unsympathetic to the informality of design in traditional building, but with familiarity, the warmth of the red Nottinghamshire brick enlivens the greyer skies and heavy green of the vegetation so often seen in the Trent valley.

The earliest medieval brickwork in England is almost completely contained in the eastern and south-eastern counties and it is surprising that, in a county so deficient in building stones as Nottinghamshire, no brickwork can be positively identified of an earlier date than the 16th century. Even then its use was confined to a few outstanding examples such as Holme Pierrepont Hall, the gatehouse to Hodsock Priory (not a priory, but the home of the Clifton family), and the basement service rooms of Wollaton Hall; the earliest examples of lesser buildings are Old Hall Farm, Kneesall,[12] and the prebendal house of Oxton II in Southwell. Decoration in rubbed or moulded brickwork is not a Nottinghamshire tradition, although the Kneesall house had terracotta dressings to doors and windows. Decorated brickwork in the county is limited to rustication formed by projecting bricks in quoins, pediments, and modillioned string courses, examples of which are in the grammar school at Bulwell (1667), Old Hall, North Wheatley (1673), and No. 143 Main Street, Sutton Bonington (c.1675). Substantial brick farmhouses and lesser manor houses of the late 17th century occur frequently throughout the county, and by the 18th and 19th centuries brick was used almost exclusively even for farm buildings and the smallest cottages. Brickwork was not only fashionable but economical in use in the later periods; houses are characteristically lofty, having floor-to-ceiling heights on the main two floors between 9 ft. and 10 ft. 6 in., with attics which are only partly in the roof space (i.e. the attic floors are below the eaves level, so that extra headroom is provided by projecting the external walls above first floor ceiling levels). Window and door openings, of Georgian proportions, are plain, but are often headed with flat arches of cut and rubbed bricks. The front range of the prebendal house of North Muskham, in Southwell is an example of this type. Brick was also commonly used to re-face timber frames and earth walls of earlier structures, examples of which still remain in Nos. 28 and 40 Westhorpe, Southwell. Most of the evidence of 17th-century brick building in the town was submerged in the re-building of the later 18th century, but a moulded brick label over a window remaining in the gable end of the former theatre in Queen Street, is c.1630 in date; No. 58 King Street, and the *Wheatsheaf* Inn opposite have plain window openings, but the steep gabled roofs, and the plain string courses, are typical of the late 17th century.

The only local building stone available was the sandy-limestone known locally as *skerry,* found in thin beds in the clay of the Keuper Marls. The stone is coarsely stratified and sometimes current-bedded, and in weathering this becomes more apparent as the softer, clay-like parts erode away; it can be roughly cut into squared blocks, but breaks away erratically at any attempt at accurate dressing, and its use has been confined at best to squared-rubble walling. It can be seen used in this way in the fragment of the early house of Norwell Overhall (now built into Minster Lodge), although the best example to be seen in the locality is the tower house of the 13th-century manor house of the prebendary in the village of Halloughton one and a half miles to the south of the town (Pl. X). Dressed and carved work for building, therefore, has had to be in the magnesian limestones from the Mansfield area on the Notts.-Derbyshire border, or in the lias and oolitic limestones from Lincolnshire.

The material which is perhaps more characteristic than any other in the region, is gypsum. As a rock, gypsum weathers too easily for external use, and has very little structural strength, but massive gypsum, or alabaster, is smooth in texture and so easily carved and brought to a polished surface that it has been used continuously since medieval times for church monuments, effigies, and decorative interior features. The best quality alabaster was mined at Tutbury, Staffs., and at Chellaston, Derbyshire, but Nottinghamshire deposits at Red Hill at the junction of the rivers Soar and Trent, and at Kingston and Gotham, were also probable sources in medieval times; Nottingham became one of the principal centres of the trade, and its workshops exported throughout the country, and even abroad. Fibrous gypsum, a coarser variety composed of needle-like crystals, and unsuitable for carving and polishing, is found extensively from Kneesall to Clarborough, and from Cropwell Bishop to Newark.

In traditional building, gypsum plasters produced by burning the rock in a kiln are harder than normal lime plasters, and were used locally for the infilling panels of a timber frame, in preference to mud used more frequently elsewhere. Plain roofing tiles, thin slabs of skerry, and even large pebbles, were bonded with plaster and wedged between studding to form partitions, and even externally; when protected by regular coats of lime wash they formed walls of surprising permanence and strength. The application of gypsum which is seen throughout the region wherever the mineral was easily obtained, was in the construction of upper floors of houses. Reeds were laid across joists and a layer of plaster 2 in. to 2½ in. thick, mixed with an aggregate of ashes, sand or fine stone, and even crushed unburnt gypsum, was cast on top and brought to a smooth, almost glazed, finish. The reeds were underdrawn with plaster between the joists, or often in later times a ceiling of plaster was applied to split laths nailed below the joists to produce a flush surface. These floors are heavy, and frequently develop cracks along the lines of the main supporting beams owing to the springing of the timbers, but they are solid, fire-resisting, and more sound-proof than boarded floors, besides being more economical in timber. This application of gypsum can be traced back at least into the 16th century,[13] and occurs locally into the mid-19th century, although in later periods the construction was reserved for inferior upper rooms, and attics. Timber framing, with an infill of plaster, or mud bound with hay, is the construction seen most frequently in early buildings, although rarely with the elaboration of structure or decoration to be found in the more heavily wooded areas of the country, such as the West Midlands, and parts of East Anglia. The densely settled marls of Nottinghamshire would have been early clearance for cultivation, and the oaks of Sherwood Forest were in royal hands until the enclosure and clearance of the 17th and 18th centuries. The Minster records frequently show that the episcopal parks of Norwood and Hexgreave, and the chapter estate of Warsop Wood, yielded timber for building as well as for sale to finance projects, but there was no great surplus. William Mompesson's accounts for the building of the first residence house in 1689, contain several references to re-use of old materials from demolished buildings, and the chapter was alert to the possibilities of making economies in this way; in 1707 they were giving permission to Samuel Lowe for the demolition of a barn he had leased, on condition that the timber was given to the building of a new house for the parish vicar; and at the same time ordered that the Free Grammar School be demolished and the materials be used to convert Booth's chapel into a school and library. It is therefore not surprising that when widespread rebuilding occurred in the late 17th and the 18th centuries it was carried out in the brickwork which had then become both economical and fashionable to use. The character and distribution of earlier, and timber-framed, buildings in the town, therefore, is restricted to the few remaining fragments which escaped demolition. Timber roofs and floors were often retained when the framing to walls was replaced, and these provide the clues for historical interpretation.

In the prebendal houses, surviving timber framing is confined to the roof structure in South Muskham, and in the re-used timbers in Dunham; added to these, the first floor beams and roof structure recorded in Oxton II, and the Grimm drawing of Norwell Palishall made just before its demolition, all indicate a high quality of structure and decoration. The 14th century building of the vicars' lodgings was also, according to Dickinson, very elaborate indeed, the head of every beam terminating in the head or body of an angel, and every other place which admitted of an ornamental piece of carving having the two emblematic roses of the houses of York and Lancaster.

The other town buildings were soundly constructed but lacked fine detail. The *Saracen's Head* Inn today has double-hung sash windows inserted in the jettied facade in Market Place, and although the walls are stuccoed over the framing, much of the timber is exposed internally, and in the yard behind. The house adjoining it on the north side (now a stationer's shop) was provided with a brick facade and sash windows in the 18th century, the wall rising to a parapet in front of the roof, but the frame of an earlier structure is behind the facade, and exposed inside the upper floors. Almost opposite, Nos. 1 and 3 Market Place retain framing timbers in later brickwork, and are the only certain survivals of pre-18th-century building on the area of suggested encroachment on the original Market Place. None of these have details indicating a date before 1600, but one small building on the west side of King Street, in the yard behind No. 5 may be earlier; it has timber posts remaining in later brick walls, a roof structure of a 16th-century type, and parts of a mud and wattle partition in the roof space; the plan is only two bays long and it lies at right angles to the street. This is probably a rear wing of the *Bull* Inn which stood on the site.

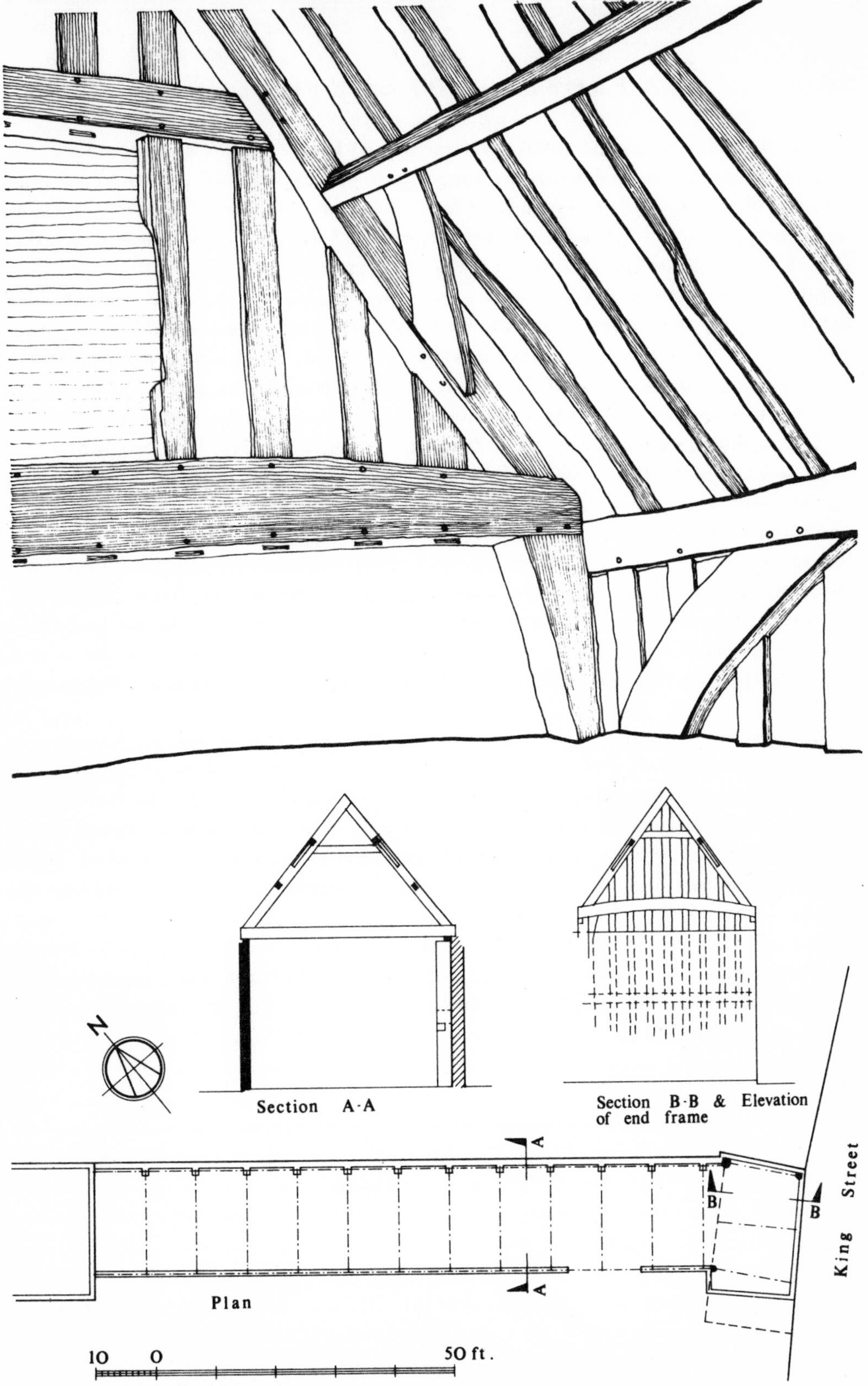

Fig 7: *Market building with maltings behind, in King Street.*
(a) *Sketch of timber construction in the roof at the south end of the King Street frontage.* **(b)** *Survey of buildings before demolition.*

One building, mid-way down the west side of King Street, was indicative of the type of more substantial town building one would expect in the prebendage until the middle of the 17th century. It was unfortunately demolished in 1967, to make way for redevelopment of the site and the building of the new supermarket (Pls. VII, VIII, and IX, and Fig. 7). Behind a small office/shop with a plate-glass window on the street frontage was a long range of workshops; the site extended behind to give rear access from the back lane, and the premises had been a garage and workshops with all the appearance of makeshift adaptation common in the early days of the motor car. The whole building was in very poor condition and not until the roof was exposed and the structure partly demolished was it apparent that a much earlier structure lay underneath. The long workshop had been built as a malting, with brick side walls, a low first floor on heavy timber beams, and a late 17th-century roof in 12 bays. The front section was a late medieval framed structure, two and a half bays long, the half bay being left by partial reduction of its length; the ridge line ran parallel with the road. One gable end and the side walls contained parts of a substantial timber frame with studs, the infilling panels being of plain roofing tiles and pieces of sandstone bonded in gypsum plaster. Nothing is recorded of its original use, but its form was characteristic of market buildings with living accommodation over the ground floor.

In general, it cannot be said that the vernacular tradition of building in Nottinghamshire is of very high quality. The roof of Holme Pierrepont Hall which has been recently exposed, uncovering arched principals with cusped wind braces, and the decorative 15th-century front of the *White Hart* Inn in Newark, are outstanding. This quality is matched in Southwell, only by the best work in the prebendal houses and in the medieval vicars' lodgings, fitting the status of the higher ranks of the clergy. Possibly because of the difficulties of the college during the Civil War of the 17th Century, new buildings of brickwork in Southwell lagged behind the county generally, and did not reach large numbers until the building boom of the later 18th and the early 19th centuries.

Notes to Chapter One

1. The Hon. John Byng (ed. by C. Bruyn Andrews), *The Torrington Diaries* (1938), vol. IV, pp. 140-43.
2. Kenneth Cameron, 'Scandinavian Settlement in the Territory of the Five Boroughs', in *Medieval Scandinavia,* vol. III (1971).
3. W.E. Tate, *Parliamentary Land Enclosures in the County of Nottingham* (Thoroton Society, Record Series, vol. V, 1935 pp. 51 and 172).
4. The original of this survey, by Richard Ingleman, Architect to the Chapter, has been lost, but a copy made in 1925 is in the possession of the Headmaster of the Minster Grammar School.
5. The origin of 'wong' is the Old Scand. 'vangr', a piece of meadow land, especially a piece of unenclosed land in the openfield system (*Place Names of Nottinghamshire,* p. 292).
6. W.P.W. Phillimore and T.M. Blagg, *Nottinghamshire Parish Registers* (1912), The Registers for 1657-58 include several references to Banns 'published at ye Markett Cross'. also: Land Tax Assessments for 1780 (in Notts. C.R.O.) point to the Cross being at the junction of the present Church Street and Market Place.
7. Alan Everitt, 'The Marketing of Agricultural Produce', in *Agrarian History of England and Wales* (1966), vol. IV, Joan Thirsk ed., p. 466 et seq.
8. G.H. Martin, 'The Town as palimpsest', in *The Study of Urban History* (1968), H.J. Dyos ed., p. 164.
9. M.W. Barley, *House and Home* (1963), p. 29.
10. H.M.S.O., *State Papers Domestic 1619-23* (1958), p. 422.
11. It is possible that these are much earlier in date. The early 13th-century charters in the White Book of Southwell contain references to *burgagium.* Presumably the archbishop was taking the initiative in encouraging the development of a town by making some of his own land available on burgage tenure (i.e. money rent, rather than the payment by labour services usually required for agricultural land); the canons would probably have lacked the initiative to do this within the prebendage.
12. N. Summers, 'Old Hall Farm, Kneesall', *Thoroton Society Transactions,* vol. LXXVI (1972).
13. Joseph Hunter, *History of Hallamshire* (1819), p. 78. Letter by Bess of Hardwick to her servant at Chatsworth, 14 Nov. 1552 '. . . cause the flore yn my bedchamber to be made even, ether w^{t} plaster, claye, or lyme . . .'.

II

The collegiate foundation

1. The Early Church

IT WAS IN 1956 that the collegiate church of St. Mary the Virgin at Southwell celebrated the thousandth anniversary of its foundation. Its origins, as with so many of our great churches, lie in Saxon times, but its subsequent history is unique in that, in spite of periods of growth and change, of church reforms throughout the centuries, and the vicissitudes of the Reformation, and of the Civil War of the 17th century, the college at Southwell retained the essentials of its Saxon foundation until its final dissolution in the 19th century. Although the town which developed around it was almost certainly pre-Christian in its first settlement, it owed much of its later form and character to the powerful and distinctive presence of the church, and reflects its individuality.

To explain the origins of the collegiate church one must first ask why it was founded at that time, and in that place. As it happens, neither history nor archaeology can tell us anything of Christian churches or monasteries in the county between the age of St. Augustine (597-604 A.D.) and the Viking raids in which so many churches were pillaged and destroyed. Speculation has inevitably turned on the possible existence of an earlier church on the site, and therefore of any connection between the minster and the Roman villa which is known to have existed nearby. Remains of walls and tesselated floors have been found between about 150 ft. and 300 ft. east of the Minster. Excavation has revealed traces of what was really a country house of some pretension, with buildings around a courtyard.[1] It seems to have been abandoned before 400 A.D., though a group of Saxon settlers squatted in the ruins for a time c.500 A.D. It is possible that the spring or stream which eventually gave its name to Southwell had a religious significance in pagan Roman times, which was retained in early Saxon times. It is also possible that the estate belonging to the Roman villa was acquired intact by some immigrant Saxon and so remained through the five centuries and more from c.400 to 956 A.D. There is no evidence to support either of these suggestions, but it may still be more than a coincidence that this important Saxon church should have been planted so close to the site of a large Roman villa, whose ruined walls and floors were to serve as a quarry for the new buildings which after 956 began to be erected.

The foundation of a minster church is fortunately recorded in the Great White

Book of York, into which a 14th-century clerk copied, as best he could, the charter of c.956 which has now disappeared. This was the grant of Southwell to Archbishop Oskytel by Eadwig, King of the English. Even at that time it was by no means certain that England would ever settle down peacefully as a single kingdom, but Oskytel almost certainly established a church at Southwell with a body of clergy to serve it. by the early years of the 11th century Southwell was the resting place of the remains of St. Eadburh, daughter of a king of the Angles and Abbess of Repton in the 7th century. Later Archbishop Cynesige (1050-60)[2] gave bells to Southwell, and his successor Ealdred enriched the three minsters of York, Beverley, and Southwell. At York and Southwell Ealdred established refectories where the canons might take meals in common, but at Beverley he is said to have completed the refectory and dormitory begun by his predecessors Aelfric and Cynesige during the period from 1023 to 1051. It is clear that, by the Norman Conquest, a collegiate body was firmly established at Southwell. This was not a cathedral; that is a title reserved for the see or headquarters of a bishop, and is the church in which his *cathedra* or throne is set up. Southwell was in the diocese of York, and did not achieve the status of the head church of its own diocese until late in the 19th century.

The fundamental characteristic of a college of clergy was in being a body of secular canons, that is ordained priests, entrusted with duties in the maintenance of the services of the church and in the cure of souls. The canons were supported by the income from endowments of property and tithes, known as prebends, originally a provender, or daily distribution of food or money from a common source. The canons therefore were also known as prebendaries and together formed the chapter, which was the administrative council of the church. The receipt of a prebend did not, in itself, confer the right of a seat in the chapter, which was reserved for those holding the office of a canon, although both were normally vested in the same person. York, Salisbury, Lincoln and Wells were only a few of the great churches maintained by this form of administration.

The other dominant form of church organisation which developed in parallel with the colleges was the body of canons regular who lived communally under strict rule and thus were nearer to the monastic orders – Benedictine, Cistercian, Carthusian, Cluniac, and others – who were forsaking the world outside in religious devotion, and therefore without need for ordination. The largest order of canons regular was the Augustinian, many of whom, however, were ordained and served hospitals such as St. Bartholomew's, London. Both organisations of canons were, correctly, termed *collegia,* or collections of persons, and the name *monasterium,* monastery, or minster, was applicable to the churches and habitations of both, but over the years the title of *minster* has remained attached mainly to churches served by secular canons, and *monastery* to define the organisations of canons regular as well as the monastic orders. Indeed, in earliest times the differences of organisation were not so clearly defined. In the reforms of the church in the peaceful years of the mid-10th century, a monastic rule was imposed on many churches which were originally collegiate, although the midland and northern minsters escaped, and in time the differences of function caused a widening separation of the two forms of organisation. The canons secular, as missionary priests as well as assistants and advisers to the bishop in his cathedral were free to go out into the world; they were not barred from marriage until some years after the Norman Conquest, and were landlords responsible for the management of their individual prebendal estates. All this militated against the ideals of the communal life, and even excused non-residence, eventually leading to a life nearer to that of the parish priest than to the asceticism of the monastery. By the time that celibacy was imposed on the clergy, the collegiate churches were too well established to revert to a communal form of organisation.

The diocese of York was a very large one, and at an early date the three great collegiate foundations of Ripon, Beverley, and Southwell were established with particular responsibility for the western, eastern, and southern parts respectively; Beverley was re-formed in 928 from an earlier monastic house which had been destroyed by the Danes c.866, and Ripon, also monastic in origin, was re-formed about the time of the Conquest after devastation c.930. Southwell, sited away from the main lines of communication and remote from so much political strife, enjoyed a security and independence normally held by a church of full cathedral status. Its sheltered site, three miles from the river Trent, was a pleasant place for retirement temporarily, and occasionally permanently, by successive archbishops of York. How many of the prebends were established in this early period is not known, but it seems likely to have been seven as at York, Beverley, and probably also at Ripon. By the end of the 13th century the full number of 16 prebends had been endowed at Southwell, and the college remained at that number until the 19th century. In comparison, the college at Beverley rose ultimately only to nine, but York, as befitted its full cathedral status, held the impressive number of 36.

The Norman Conquest led to an overall rationalisation of ecclesiastical institutions, both monastic and secular. Thomas I, also known as Thomas of Bayeux, who became Archbishop of York in 1070, found the canons there dispersed and their properties devastated after William's punitive advance through the north of England. He encouraged them to return, and set the chapter under a dean, an arrangement which was Norman in origin and which became general later in collegiate churches in this country. The other dignitaries, whose offices developed from the increasing formality imposed on the colleges were: the precentor, responsible for ordering the services and music; the treasurer, who kept the treasure, vestments, plate, and relics; and the chancellor who was secretary to the chapter and who kept the common seal. The chancellor also normally had duties as *theologus,* in arranging for theological lectures, and *scolasticus,* as master of the school for clerks.

Southwell never achieved the maturity of this form of organisation, whether by neglect or by active opposition on the part of the chapter. Beverley had its provost, who was not necessarily a canon, and a chancellor, precentor, and treasurer, who were officers ranking below members of the chapter, and even Ripon recognised the supremacy of the prebend of Stanwick. Southwell acknowledged no senior official as head of the chapter, the senior canon in residence carrying out the duties in rotation, and no officers were nominated as such. The prebendary of Sacrista may be equated to the treasurer; there are also documentary references to a precentor but the duties do not seem to be linked to any particular prebend; and although the duties of chancellor were carried out by the prebendary of Normanton the title was never applied to the appointment. We have therefore in Southwell a unique case of arrested development. Communal residence of the canons was discontinued quite early in its history as in other collegiate churches, but the college retained its communal form of government against the tide of sophisticated organisation which affected all the major ecclesiastical institutions in the Middle Ages and even against the drastic re-modelling after the Reformation elsewhere.

It was Thomas II, Archbishop of York 1108-14, who turned his attentions particularly to Southwell. He raised it to the dignity of mother church for all Nottinghamshire, founding further prebends and encouraging the complete re-building of the church on a larger scale. In a letter addressed to all his parishioners in the county he begged them to assist the building by almsgiving, and clergy and laity were allowed to make the Whitsuntide procession to Southwell in lieu of the more onerous journey to York. The earliest record of the privileges of the church and canons of Southwell is found in a Bull of Pope Alexander III in 1171. This confirmed the endowments and possessions of the college, and the same customs and liberties 'which the church of York is known to have had and still to have'. It granted the chapter independence of spiritual or temporal jurisdiction, whether from the archbishops of York or the king, owing allegiance to none but the pope. The headless chapter became, in effect, an independent self-governing republic beside the monarchical form of other collegiate foundations.

Within the diocese of York, the archdeaconry of Nottingham comprised most parishes of the county; incumbents to these were instituted by the archbishop, and the parishes were subject to visitations by the archdeacon who held courts to try ecclesiastical offences, The peculiar of Southwell, however, was a separate ecclesiastical district within the county, covering 28 parishes and townships in Nottinghamshire, mostly near Southwell. It was under the jurisdiction of the chapter of Southwell which had many privileges, the chief ones being the right to institute vicars to the parishes in the peculiar, to prove wills, to hold visitations, and to try offenders against ecclesiastical laws. Ecclesiastical offences included absence from church, slander, and immorality. The peculiar was exempt from control by the archdeacon of Nottingham, and was abolished in the dissolution of the chapter in 1840. Within the peculiar, the chapter exercised all the powers equivalent to those of a bishop of a diocese in an ecclesiastical court, and the canons in turn, in their prebendal manors, were exempt from spiritual and temporal jurisdiction. The archbishops of York, as papal representatives, successively filled the role of official visitor; they held what were, in reality, courts at their visitations, their main function being to ensure the proper observation of the statutes. But the statutes could only be made in chapter with the consent of the canons assembled, so that the archbishop's control was rather by means of restraint than by initiative. Even so, it appears to have been an effective arrangement because, as seen in the records of visitations, Southwell fared no worse and sometimes better than Ripon and elsewhere. Although their power had been seriously undermined as a result of the Bull of 1171, the archbishops still had the privilege of appointing to the prebends (i.e. were their patrons), by right of having endowed them; they also had civil jurisdiction in the liberty of Southwell and Scrooby, as great landowners in the county. The liberty extended over about 20 parishes, some of which were near Scrooby, so that the area of the liberty was not wholly contained within the peculiar. Within the liberty, the archbishops independently appointed justices of the peace, and held quarter sessions, either at Southwell or Scrooby until it was abolished in 1836.

The 16 prebends were, with two exceptions, named after their prebendal estates. There was no prebend of Southwell, but the prebendary of Normanton, a hamlet in the north of the parish, had the presentation of the vicarage of Southwell and was entitled to most of the parish tithes. The prebend of Sacrista, or Segeston, holding the office of Sacristan in the church, was not a prebend in the true sense since it had no lands except the prebendal house and garden in Southwell, the income being mostly from church offerings. There were two prebends of Oxton, Oxton and Crophyll (i.e. Cropwell Bishop), and Oxton Second Part; Norwell contained three prebends, Norwell Overhall, Norwell Palishall, and Norwell Third Part. The foundations of all these, together with North Muskham and Woodborough, are not recorded, and it is probable that all were early foundations made by, or soon after, the Norman Conquest. The later endowments, made by the archbishops out of personal or archiepiscopal estates, and recorded in the White Book of Southwell, were: South Muskham (by Thomas II 1108-14); Beckingham and Dunham (By Thurstan 1119-35); Halloughton or Halton (by Roger of Bishopsbridge 1160); Rampton (by Pavia and Robert Malluvel her son c.1200); Eaton (1290); and North Leverton (made out of Beckingham 1291), both by John Le Romaine.

The dual character of the responsibilities of secular canons generally in collegiate foundations was, from the beginning, a cause of breakdown in the organisation imposed on them. As well as the duties in the maintenance of services in the mother church, the canons were parish priests in the churches around, and their prebends were, generally speaking, the profits of the lands allotted to these parish churches. Of the estates, manors and churches granted to the chapter, a portion would be retained as a common fund to be distributed amongst the canons actually in residence, and the remainder formed the endowments of separate prebends and was set apart for individual revenues. This custom was that established by Thomas I at York, and was followed throughout the country; at York the prebendaries had particular houses allotted to them for residence, but at Lincoln, Wells and Hereford, houses as they became vacant were allotted to canons wishing to take up residence. As the custom of residence declined, the chapter leased unoccupied properties to augment the common fund. Beverley had its provost, as did York for a time, who was the official specifically charged with responsibility for the management of chapter estates.

At Southwell, the endowments were managed with characteristic disregard of accepted practice elsewhere. There were certain estates which were managed by the chapter to provide the common fund, but the prebendal estates were left in the hands of the prebendaries to administer individually, whether resident or not. It could be argued, therefore, that no provost was necessary, and although the prebendal leases were required to be registered with the chapter and copied into the chapter lease book, only a comparatively small proportion were ever so recorded. Each prebendary had his mansion at Southwell as well as his parochial manor or parsonage, and the leasing of the town mansions became both the effect and a cause of increasing non-residence amongst the canons.

The impossibility of being in two places at once soon led the canons into being resident at neither, and the custom developed of maintaining deputies or vicars – vicars choral and vicars parochial at the mother church and in the outlying parishes respectively – which was recognised and approved of officially. The Bull of 1171, declaring the churches of the prebends and those of the chapter to be free of episcopal jurisdiction, added 'that they might institute fit vicars in them without any contradiction, as the said archbishops and chapters of York ever suffered them and their predecessors to do'. The foundations of the prebends of Eaton and Leverton made specific provision in the endowments for vicars choral; in 1291, Archbishop John Le Romaine, completing the numbers of the prebends to 16 by the creation of North Leverton as a separate prebend out of Beckingham of which it had previously been a part, declared 'the prebend to have his stall in the quire on the north side next to that of the Sacrist, and his place in the chapter house duely assigned by the chapter, and to have and pay his vicar choral, as the other canons used'. The establishment of vicars choral therefore was, as with the prebends, eventually fixed at 16.

Apart from the one 11th-century reference to the building of a refectory, there is no later record of communal living by the canons of Southwell. A much stricter rule of conformity was, however, imposed on the vicars choral, and provision made for lodgings and a common hall. After the Reformation, when the clergy were permitted to marry, this group of buildings was altered to accommodate the reduced number of married clergy then in the college, and in the present buildings of Vicars' Court, dating from the 18th century, we see the vestiges of communal residence translated into more modern terms. Each canon was required to make some contribution towards the maintenance of his vicar choral, but this was never an adequate stipend in itself, and endowments were made from time to time to the chapter in trust for their support. In this respect Southwell yet again demonstrated the immaturity of its development, and the commons of the vicars choral remained in the trusteeship of the chapter throughout its history. The vicars had their own statutes, bylaws and commons, but never achieved their own seal and were never in strict law a corporate body. Incorporation elsewhere was the means of achieving better endowments and a stricter life; the vicars of York, Lincoln, Ripon, Wells, Salisbury, Hereford, Lichfield and Exeter all achieved corporate status in the hundred years 1350-1450, but the movement passed Southwell by.

The chantry priests, the third major group in the church were, in a sense, formed out of the body of vicars choral. The latter were charged with the duty of prayers for the souls of the founders and benefactors of the church, but the endowments of the chantries were also directed more specifically to the persons and families of those who established them. The first chantry at Southwell was endowed by a canon of the church and judge in the King's Bench, Robert of Lexington, in 1241. Eventually, at the time of their dissolution, there were 13. The chantry priests each celebrated mass daily at altars in chapels formed by screens at the west ends of nave and choir aisles, and in the transepts; nine such chapels were recorded, dedicated to the saints, although the exact siting of most of them individually has been lost. The distinction between chantry priests and vicars choral was at times obscure; vicars choral were recorded also as holding chantries, and recruitment to vacancies amongst the vicars was occasionally made from the body of chantry priests. The latter were also required to augment the choir, as were the vicars choral. The chantry priests had their own statutes, and a house of their own for living in common, which must have contained a hall, kitchen, service rooms and dormitory and was situated at the north-west corner of the churchyard, on the site behind the *Crown* Inn where the grammar school was built in the 19th century. Under similar circumstances at York and Wells and elsewhere in the 15th century, chantry priests, as vicars choral, were incorporated into colleges and given greater independence of control of their own affairs, but the canons of Southwell retained even this aspect of the church organisation firmly in their own hands. The endowments of land made to provide a common fund for their maintenance were held by the chapter in trust.

The certificates of the Chantry Commissioners set up under the Act of Henry VIII in 1545 provide a survey of the complete establishment at Southwell at that time. Three canons were in residence, with the 16 vicars choral and 13 chantry priests; there were four deacons, and sub-deacons, six choristers, two thuribulers or incense bearers, and two clerks. The parish vicar is listed separately although it appears from other records that he was normally one of the vicars choral. The offices of registrar, master of the grammar school, master of the song school, bursars (guardians of the fabric and common funds) and wardens were probably filled by vicars choral or chantry priests, but with vergers and other minor officials some 50 persons actively served the church in residence.

The values of individual prebends and the revenues which could be expected from them are difficult to establish with any accuracy of detail. Valuations made at different times were not always made on the same basis, and deductions and allowances not always consistently included. Comparative values between prebends, however, are maintained in the separate lists. The surveys made in the reign of Henry VIII provide the most complete documentation. Norwell Overhall was the wealthiest endowment with an income approaching £50 a year in money of the time; North Muskham £30; Norwell Palishall, Oxton II, Dunham, Oxton I and Normanton ranged between £20 and £30. Beckingham, Rampton, and South Muskham ranged between £20 and £10. Woodborough, Halloughton, Norwell III, North Leverton, Eaton and Sacrista were all below £10 a year. Eaton and Sacrista were the poorest endowments at approximately £2 a year, although the Chantry Commissioners recorded Sacrista at £7 5s. 7d., which must have included perquisites not allowed for in other valuations. These figures are residues after deductions had been made; each prebendary paid his vicar choral £4 a year, and the prebendary of Normanton was also required to pay £2 a year to the master of the grammar school, and 20s. to the parish vicar of Southwell. Added to his income from the prebendal estate, each canon would receive his share from the common fund during his period of residence, but the total common fund amounted to only £45 a year in the 16th century and would not amount to much if more than the three prebendaries had been in residence at one time. Occasional but irregular sums could be expected in fines on the renewal of leases of prebendal properties, in gifts for presentations of chapter livings and other patronage. The average income from these estates was only £18, nine of the 16 prebends being valued at less than £20, but the wealthier ones compared well with similar endowments elsewhere.

The eight prebends of Beverley at the valuation of 1545 ranged from £48 a year down to £11, but averaged £38. Apart from these the provostship was valued highly at £109, but the chancellorship at only £18 and the precentorship at only £13. At the same date the seven prebends of Ripon averaged £52, but this included the prebend of Stanwyge at £40, and the prebend of Anwyke at the remarkable figure of £221; without these the remainder averaged only £20 each.

Further comparisons are to be made in the list of preferments held by William of Wykeham in 1366. He was Prebendary of Dunham at Southwell with a total income from the estate estimated at £36 a year. With other church appointments he held nine similar prebends elsewhere; that of Sutton at Lincoln was outstandingly valuable at £172 year, and that of Totenhall at St. Paul's the poorest at £10. The average value of his prebends was £46 a year, but excluding Sutton the average was £32. William of Wykeham was an exceptional case of plurality of livings, Keeper of the Privy Seal, and prominent in church and state.

Few churchmen ever attained such a range of appointments, the total of all being worth £866 a year, but it is clear that even the best endowments at Southwell could not in themselves attract the most ambitious and able men to take up permanent residence here. The prebends could however offer substantial rewards when plurality of livings and non-residence were the accepted practice, and in time the custom grew to award such preferments to clergy who were, in effect, high-ranking civil servants, without any expectation of their ever taking up residence. A country parson might live tolerably well at the time of the Reformation on £5 a year, and the vicars choral, even with the additions from their common fund could not expect more than £7 to £8 a year; the chantries also varied in value, being worth from £5 to £10 a year.

The total income of the college at Southwell in 1545 was some £500 per annum, including the revenues of its prebends, vicars choral, chantries and common and fabric lands. York and Lincoln were valued at just over four times as much, as befitted their larger establishments and full cathedral status; the Augustinian priories at Worksop, Newstead, and Thurgarton, and the Praemonstratensian abbey of Welbeck, were the richest in the country, and were all in the range of £210 to £280. The college, although it could not compete in wealth and size with the great cathedrals, both monastic and secular, ranked high amongst secondary ecclesiastical establishments in medieval England.

2. The Reformation, and later history

The rough surgery administered by Henry VIII on church establishments was often not entirely undeserved, and in many quarters not unpopular. Frustrated by problems over the dissolution of his marriage to Catherine, Henry saw the solution of his personal and financial difficulties in reforms made under the guise of the furtherance of Protestantism. The changes he made were sweeping, but not entirely inhuman. In an Act of 1536, the lesser monasteries with incomes below £200 were dissolved and their possessions passed to the King. In a further Act of 1539, the larger monasteries were persuaded to follow suit. Ultimately, the cathedrals served by colleges of secular canons survived, although some of the richer prebends passed to the Crown, and the number of vicars choral was reduced. Other collegiate churches, however, were mostly dissolved, some being retained as parish churches under vicars appointed from the previous canons. Most of the monastic churches which had been cathedrals were also saved, being reformed on the basis of the colleges under a dean and chapter of canons, but many fine churches were lost which were not so fortunately placed. New sees were planned, although eventually only six were made with former abbey churches as their cathedrals. Wherever possible the former canons and vicars were appointed into the new establishments, and many who could not be so employed were pensioned off.

In 1540, anticipating the dissolution which had overtaken so many similar foundations, the Archbishop of York, with the canons vicars choral and chantry priests of Southwell jointly and formally surrendered their property to the King. Surprisingly, the practical effect was negligible; the canons appear to have carried on just as before, until in 1543 a private Act restored the property to the chapter, and the college was re-formed with the King named as founder, having the right to appoint to the prebends instead of the archbishops as before. The threat of redundancy over the heads of most of the priests serving the Minster was thus deferred. Henry's intention was to make Southwell the see of a new diocese, but either because of shortage of funds or weakness of purpose, this was never carried out. Why Southwell should not only be reprieved but firmly re-founded is inexplicable unless it was possibly through the intervention of Cranmer, himself a native of Nottinghamshire. Beverley, with a history even longer than Southwell, was dissolved and was purchased by the inhabitants to become a parish church, and Ripon was re-founded only in 1604 by James I who placed the seven prebendaries under a dean and endowed the church with a modest income of £274 a year.

The Chantries Act, passed in 1547 in the first year of Edward VI's reign, was the effective instrument of the dissolution of the Southwell chapter. The Act applied to all remaining chantries and colleges, and this time the protection afforded Southwell under Henry VIII was no longer powerful enough; the chapter property passed to the Crown and the church was reduced to parochial status; the former prebendary of Sacrista was appointed vicar at a stipend of £20, with two assistant priests at £5 a year each. The other clergy of the college were pensioned, and this was the position for nearly 10 years. Much of the property was granted to William Neville, steward of the Duke of Northumberland, in 1549, including nine of the prebendal mansions in Southwell with their orchards and gardens, the vicars' college, the chantry priests' house, and a number of chantries and other lands and messuages.[3] He in turn conveyed a substantial part to John Beaumont, Master of the Rolls. When Beaumont confessed to charges of dishonesty and corruption before the Court of Star Chamber in 1552, his property reverted to the Crown and was regranted in 1553, together with the parks in Southwell (Hexgrave, Norwood, and the New Park), to Sir Henry Sydneye, one of the four principal gentlemen of the Privy Chamber.[4] In 1557, Queen Mary, anxious to restore the old religion, re-established the chapter in a Charter of Exemplification, but restoration of the Southwell endowments was not so easily achieved. Property still in possession of the Crown could give practical effect to Mary's intention; Archbishop Nicholas regained further estates by purchase and exchange in 1557,[5] but a series of court actions was necessary to regain possessions from those who were loath to part with them. It was not until 1585, when Queen Elizabeth granted a new set of statutes to the chapter, that the college could be re-organised in a form which persisted for another 250 years. Intrigue against the legal status of the chapter, however, continued until a new charter of James I in 1604 confirmed them against any possible attack from outside.

The new statutes did much to establish the college on a basis of sound organisation, although the chapter was still left without a dean or other permanently-appointed dignitary at its head. The senior prebendary in residence presided at chapter meetings; the office of vicar general was created, elected from amongst the prebendaries to exercise episcopal functions (except ordination and confirmation) over the villages of the peculiar of Southwell, although he had no special function in the internal affairs of the chapter. An auditor, a receiver general, a registrar, and a custos of the fabric were new appointments as officials, but not necessarily from the prebendaries. The 16 prebends were retained, still with a great measure of independence in the administration of their estates, and there were to be at least six vicars choral, six choirmen, and six choristers in residence. One of the vicars was also to be parish vicar and another the schoolmaster. Non-residence of the canons must still have given rise to difficulties which were not finally resolved until 1693; then an Injunction of Archbishop John Sharpe, who did much to regularise the organisation which was again causing concern, decreed that the prebendaries should do quarterly residence by turns for the future according to seniority, although substitutes were permitted. Thus the duties of residentiary over the years began to assume the status of temporary rank.

The events of the 17th century were, outwardly at least, even more dramatic. Southwell appears to have had Parliamentary sympathies in a county which was predominantly Royalist, and the town was occupied by both sides in turn. Cromwell's troops stabled their horses in the church defacing monuments and sculpture, smashing the windows and destroying the records. Plans to demolish the nave of the church and retain only the chancel for parochial purposes were checked only by the intervention of Edward Cludd, a prominent parliamentarian in the county who had more moderate views and local sympathies than most of his party. Under the Commonwealth episcopacy was abolished and the property of the bishops vested in trustees, but at the Restoration in 1660, when the rights and property of the chapter were restored, the college resumed its status with remarkable smoothness and without any of the legal wrangling of the previous century. There was still much to be done, but the later years of the 17th century, from which time the records are much more complete, are distinguished by the vigour and thoroughness with which the restoration of the church and the re-organisation of the collegiate establishment were undertaken.

For nearly 200 years more the chapter at Southwell remained undisturbed by national events. Throughout the 18th century the chapter records reflect mainly a concern with the administration of its property, and with a considerable volume of building of great architectural interest – the restoration of the church after a disastrous fire in 1711, and with new houses for the vicars choral and the residentiary canons – but in other respects it sank into a comfortable lethargy. In the early years of the 19th century the chapter was stimulated into a new era of efficiency, by the work of the Rev. John Thomas Becher, prebendary of South Muskham and a man of great ability and wide interests. But the 19th century was one of church reform, and even the revived chapter of Southwell was not strong enough to resist the changes planned. By an Act of 1840, future appointments to prebends were suspended, and the church propeties vested in the Ecclesiastical

Commissioners; the more far-sighted politicians and churchmen could foresee the need for a new diocese in which Southwell could provide the see, and many wished the chapter to continue in existence until it could be effected, but they were in the minority. The chapter was allowed to decline, and the church reduced to parochial status again for the third time in its history. The collegiate chapter was finally extinguished with the death of the last prebendary in 1873, but within five years the Bishoprics Act of 1878 prepared the way for a new diocese of Nottinghamshire and Derbyshire, which was finally achieved by an Order in Council in 1884. Further re-organisation has since been undertaken, the major change being the creation of Derbyshire as a separate diocese. The former collegiate church of Southwell today fulfills the dual function of a parish church, and as the see of the bishop whose diocese embraces the county of Nottingham.

Notes to Chapter Two

1. C.M. Daniels, 'Excavations on the site of the Roman Villa at Southwell, 1959, *Thoroton Society Transactions*, vol. LXX (1966), pp. 13-33.
2. Later historians frequently used the latinised version of his names, *Kinsius.*
3. Calendar of Patent Rolls, 1549-51, p.38.
4. C.P.R., 1553, P. 60.
5. C.P.R., 1555-57, p. 264
   and 1557-58, pp. 116-17.

III
The Minster

The Minster

It is reasonable to assume that the lands granted to Archbishop Oskytel would have included a Christian settlement with some form of church, and that this would have been restored and enlarged, or even rebuilt, in the early days of the collegiate foundation. By the middle of the 11th century, Archbishop Cynesige's gift of bells to the Minster indicates that a building of considerable importance was by then in being, or under construction. Very little is known of the scale or plan of this church, but a number of remaining fragments support the assumption that, for its time, it was a building of high quality in materials and workmanship. Below the floor level of the present south transept lie the remains of a tesselated floor which is most likely to be Saxon in date; its level and position is consistent with it being the paving of a transept of a cruciform church.[1] Next is the lintel now built above the doorway in the west wall of the north transept; this was a tympanum, mutilated at one end to fit its present position, and is carved in low relief with a representation of St. Michael and the Dragon, and David rescuing the lamb from the lion (Pl.xxix a). The workmanship is Saxon, in the 'Urnes' style showing Viking influence, and is crude by later medieval standards; it cannot be later than mid-11th century in date.[2] Lastly there is the record in 1853, by the Rev. J.F. Dimock, of the finding of moulded and carved stones of late Saxon design during the repairs to the foundations of the piers to the central tower and the south wall of the nave, some years before. These had been re-used in the rubble work of the 12th-century reconstruction.

The Norman Church.

The stability brought to ecclesiastical institutions after the Norman Conquest resulted in the building of churches throughout the country on a scale never to be equalled in later times, and involved the wholesale destruction of so much earlier work that the Saxon achievement has often been underestimated. For nearly 100 years, however, development of the monasteries dominated activity within the church, and the magnificence of scale in the building of the monastic cathedral churches such as Ely, Peterborough, and Durham, in the 12th century could be matched amongst the secular foundations only by St. Paul's. The greatest accumulation of wealth and the multiplication of prebendal endowments in the

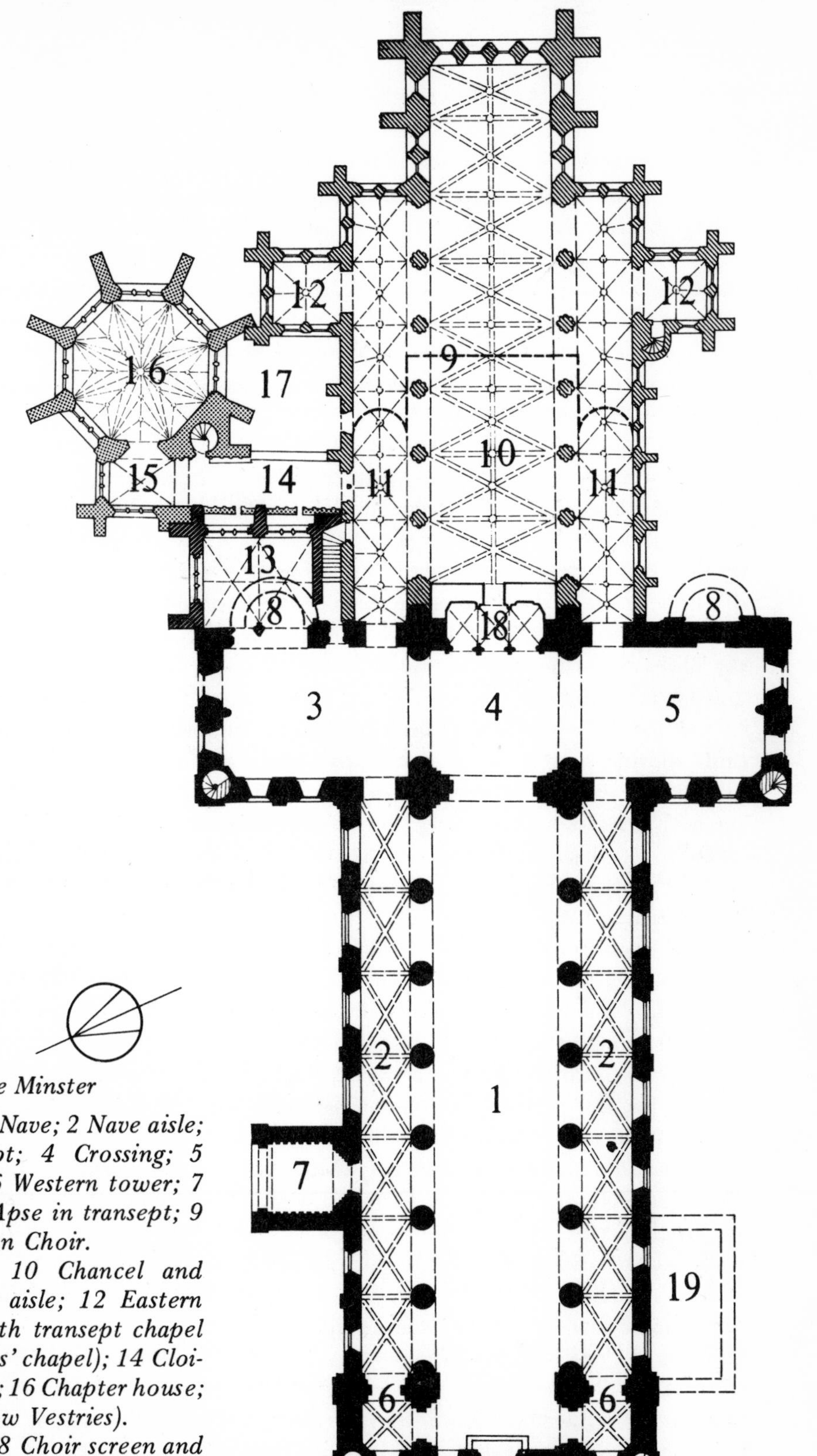

ig 8: *Plan of the Minster*

2th century: *1 Nave; 2 Nave aisle; North transept; 4 Crossing; 5 outh transept; 6 Western tower; 7 'orth Porch; 8 Apse in transept; 9 xtent of Norman Choir.*

3th century: *10 Chancel and 'hoir; 11 Choir aisle; 12 Eastern 'ansept; 13 North transept chapel ıow the Airmens' chapel); 14 Cloi- er; 15 Vestibule; 16 Chapter house; 7 Courtyard (now Vestries).*

4th century: *18 Choir screen and 'rgan loft; 19 Booth's Chapel.*

colleges came later, and it was in the 13th and 14th centuries that the churches of Lincoln and York, Beverley and Ripon, were more thoroughly rebuilt and enlarged, with the consequent loss of earlier Norman work. At Southwell in contrast, the nave and transepts, with the towers over the crossing and at the west end, remain substantially as the 12th-century builders left them; east of the crossing the choir was rebuilt on an enlarged plan in the 13th century, and the north transept chapel and chapter house added, but the clarity of the growth of the church is remarkable, and subsequent periods of Gothic building have done little to confuse the simplicity of its form.

Archbishop Thomas's letter of 1108 to the parishioners of Nottinghamshire marks the early stages of the reconstruction of the Saxon church. Building of the medieval churches customarily started at the eastern end to accommodate the altar and choir at an early stage for at least the basic needs in services, the transepts and nave being added later as further funds became available. The plan of the eastern end of this church has been established from excavations carried out during the 19th century; the chancel was short in proportion to the length of the nave and projected beyond its side aisles which terminated in semicircular, or apsidal, ends. Similar apses projected from the east walls of both transepts (Fig.8). In this form the Norman church has strong similarities with the English churches built in this period under continental influence such as Canterbury and Westminster; the difference at Southwell is that the projection of the chancel itself was squared instead of repeating the apsidal form of the aisles. The square ended chancel was a standard plan for Cistercian abbey churches; Southwell, however, was too early to have been influenced by Cistercian practice. The design was more likely to have stemmed from the northern Saxon churches, which in turn were derived from Celtic forms of Irish Origin [3] such as at Monkwearmouth [4] and Escomb, [5] both in County Durham. Later, it certainly became the accepted design for English churches, as distinct from the elaborations of apsidal plans retained and developed on the Continent.

Assuming that the span of 50 years for building a church on this scale would be normal for the period, the remaining parts west of the crossing may be safely dated as not earlier than 1120 to 1130. So much of Norman work is experimental in form and a striving after effect which was not always successful in the result. The great cylindrical piers at Gloucester soar in their height to be surmounted as an anticlimax by a triforium of small scale, but Southwell nave matches solid with void in a balance which is completely resolved. The nave arcading is low, and widely spreading for its height, the simple cylindrical drums of the piers having only simple scalloped capitals and square bases, the arches above being relieved by plain ridge and roll mouldings with one row of billet moulding on the faces (Pl.XXII). Its proportions may lack the lofty grandeur of Ely, Peterborough, or Durham, but the whole has a static quality, restful, and human in scale, and saved from overpowering weight by the open triforium above (PL.XIX). Each bay of the triforium follows the arcade below; each arch has corbels at the springing and the stump of a shaft at the crown, and was meant to be completed by a decorative infill of masonry. The only comparative example of this may be seen in the triforium of nave and choir at Romsey Abbey; [6] the solution adopted there is a design of sub-arches within the main span, resting at the centres on short intermediate shafts, and with secondary columns centrally within the main arches and reaching up to the crowns. It is a somewhat clumsy striving to relieve the spaces with sub-arches which anticipate later tracery developments. It is not known whether the Southwell masons, having made the preparatory corbels, omitted the sub-arches, because of shortage of resources, or second thoughts in design, but completion of the infill would have emphasised, to their detriment, the low proportions of the arcade below. At the topmost, clerestory, level, where the plain wall surfaces provide the necessary mass to give visual stability to the lower tiers of arches, the openings are unusual in design. A passageway runs within the thickness of the wall at this level throughout the length of the nave and transepts as is normal in great Romanesque churches; the windows externally are circular, but at the corresponding positions in the internal wall the openings are semicircular headed with short attached shafts at the jambs. In the nave and transepts there is little change in design throughout the period of construction, and the whole presents an effect of sophisticated accomplishment. The identity of the master mason who designed and superintended the work is, of course, unknown.

To appreciate the whole achievement of skill at Southwell against the rugged simplicity of earlier Norman work, one must go to the north-west of the county, to the abbey church of Blyth. Only the nave and the north aisle remain of the original cruciform plan, founded in 1088 and built in the last years of the 11th century, and now surviving as the parish church. The arcading is coarsely tooled stone, with arches in squared and unmoulded recessions; the piers are square, each with two attached, semicircular shafts in the line of the arcade, and one on the inside face taken above the arcading, although the vault above is 13th-century in date. The aisle bays at Blyth, as are those in the nave aisles at Ely, are roofed with groined vaults, and the difficulty of maintaining precision of form in this early type of Romanesque vault is apparent in the wavering lines of the diagonals. The nave aisles at Southwell, constructed perhaps some 20 years later, employ the much more sophisticated ribbed vault in which moulded arches define the curvature of transverse and diagonal lines, with plain panels filling in between. The parallel here is with Peterborough aisles, but both stem from the prototype at  Durham. Romanesque arch forms, however, are based on the semicircle and have limitations when applied to vaulting by the fact that in correct geometry, the height of rise is necessarily half the span and therefore governed by it. The controlling span of an aisle vault is in the longitudinal arch of the nave arcade, the transverse arches across the aisle normally being shorter, and the diagonals longer, in span. To arrive at a level ridge line down the length of the vault, therefore, the transverse arches must be stilted (i.e. raised on short vertical ribs), as they are at

Southwell and the diagonals depressed to a segment of a circle or an ellipse (PL.XXI). The grouped ribs springing from the nave piers and the wall corbels, each at widely differing curvatures, make a clumsy separation, and further development in technique could not be achieved until the pointed arch was adopted in the later years of the 12th century. In this form the arch is struck from two centres equidistant from the centre of each total span, and the height and rate of curvature may be adjusted between the varying spans of the different ribs. The constant striving after perfection of form to be seen throughout the development of architecture in the Gothic period, has its origins in such problems of solid geometry of building and was one of the major factors in the first adoption of the Gothic two-centred arch. The Norman vaults at Southwell may thus be seen as a great advance in skill from the more primitive forms at Blyth and Ely, but transitional into the 13th-century work seen in the choir.

The arches from the nave, choir, and transepts, into the crossing are in recessions of ridge and roll, cable and billet mouldings, coming down on the east and west sides to cushion capitals with three recessed orders of pilasters, and into the transepts they rest on semicircular columns repeating those of the nave arcade. All are lofty, reaching to triforium level in magnificent contrast with the slow movement of the low nave arcades (Pl.XX). Against the east crossing piers are the remains of the semi-circular pilasters and capitals which were part of the Norman chancel; they were partially obscured by walling when the chancel was rebuilt in the 13th century. At a higher level the capitals of piers between chancel and crossing, are carved with figurative scenes from the life of Christ: the Last Supper, the Entry into Jerusalem, the Adoration of the Shepherds, the Annunciation, and Christ washing Peter's feet (Pl.XXIXb). They have no comparison with the sophisticated nobility of nave and transepts; the workmanship is more advanced than in the Saxon tympanum described above, but is still crude.[7] If they, too, are not re-used material from the Saxon church, they are certainly the earliest remaining Norman work and imply an advance of style between the building of the original east end, and the nave and transepts which followed. The original apsidal chapels in the eastern walls of both transepts are still marked by the infilled arches which opened into them, and the spaces of transepts and crossing are more powerful in their simplicity than, for example, at Peterborough where aisles against the eastern walls accommodated chantry chapels, or at Gloucester where the choir occupies the space of the crossing.

The basic form of the church externally, with its tall nave against which stand the lower aisles, and the twin western and the crossing towers, reflects the simplicity of the interior, and is in the line of evolution from German Romanesque as seen at Spires (c.1030), through William the Conqueror's own church at Caen (St. Etienne, the Abbaye aux Hommes, c.1066) to the later and more complex forms of the Gothic period (Pl.XIV).[8] The flat buttresses add nothing to the strength of the walls, but with the zig-zag mouldings of the string course, and the corbel table at the eaves, they liven and modulate the solid masses of the masonry. The blind arcading on the upper stage of the north-western tower is a design of intersecting semicircular arches on short shafts; at the same level on the south-western tower only the centre parts of the intersections were used to produce a design of lancet arches, which anticipate the Early English style and therefore probably mark the last work in the completion of the Norman church. Church towers of the Romanesque period characteristically terminated in low, pyramidal spires, sometimes springing from gabled wall faces, as at Spires and in the earlier (Saxon) church at Sompting in Sussex. The modern spires at Southwell, therefore, although taller than desirable for strict historical accuracy, are nearer in spirit to their originals than the flat roofs of most Norman churches which still exist today, and would have been matched by a similar spire over the crossing.

The only original aisle window is that against the north-western tower, although the others of similar design are good 19th-century copies. The four windows at the eastern ends of each aisle are insertions of the late 14th century to improve the lighting within the church; the cills were lowered for these windows, and this necessitated breaking through the string course, but the moulding was then returned down at the sides and replaced at the lower levels in some concession to the continuity of the original work. The most dramatic and incongruous change made to the Norman building, however, was in the 15th century with the insertion of the great west window, and the castellated parapet above which masks the end of the nave between the western towers. Although a fine example of a seven-light window of the Perpendicular period, it destroyed all evidence of the original west facade of the nave. Reconstruction must be speculative, but again it was likely to have been based on the example of the Abbaye aux Hommes, where the steep nave roof is expressed as a gable between the western towers, which has two tiers each of three narrow round-headed windows. It is unfortunate that this comparison cannot be taken farther, because the spires above the level of the nave roof at Caen are additions of the 13th century.

Complete mastery of the Romanesque style is shown in the north porch perhaps more than anywhere else in the Norman church; there are no fumbling afterthoughts, and every detail is related to the whole (Pl.XVII). The zig-zag ornament in the string course of the main building continues on the outer walls of the porch, across the capitals of the pilasters supporting the wide outer arch, and above the blind arcading of the inner walls, to tie the whole composition together. The inner doorway into the north aisle of the church is the most elaborate of the early building, with six recessed arches, five of them on attached shafts (Pl.XVIII). It is unusual enough for a porch of this date to have survived; it is unique in having a barrel-vaulted roof which supports a heated upper room. This type of vault is a constant semicircle in its cross-section, resting evenly on the side walls, and is the earliest design of stone roofing attempted in the Romanesque period. (The vaults of Blyth were, in effect, intersecting barrel vaults which achieved groined intersections coming down on the four corners of the bay.) The upper room was probably that of the sacrist, who was required to sleep in the church to be available to ring the bells at the appointed hours; in the north-west corner are the remains of a fireplace which vented through the pierced pinnacle at the foot of the front gable. Although comparisons may be made they are perhaps in this case invidious; the south porch of Malmesbury Abbey, Wilts., possesses the most exquisite carving of the period, but the Perpendicular parapet and the modern (c.1905) ribbed vault destroy the purity of style of the whole. Ribbed vaults of late Norman type are at Bredon Church, Worcs., and Sherborne Abbey, Dorset; like Southwell they are two-storied, but both have suffered later changes.[9]

Porches giving access to the aisles were a common feature in medieval churches, but generally on the south side. The placing of the Southwell porch on the north side points to the fact that this was, even at that date, the main approach for the townspeople, and that it provided the easiest access for the canons who had already built their prebendal houses along the north side of the churchyard. The stone benches lining the inside walls of the porch show that it formed not only a protected entry into the aisle, but that it also played an integral part in the secondary function of the Minster as a parish church. The first parts of the services of Baptism, Holy Matrimony, and the Churching of Women, were customarily held at the door;[10] Chaucer in his *Canterbury Tales,* for example, describes the Wife of Bath

'She was a worthy womman al hir lyve:
Housbandes at chirche dore she hadde fyve'.[11]

Being external to the church proper, the porch was a meeting place also for secular occasions, and even for business transactions. An example of this at Southwell (by no means unique) is in a lease dated 30 May 1717; the Rev. Thomas Laybourne, Prebendary of North Muskham, granted his estate, with all houses, lands, etc., to the Right Hon. John, Lord Belasyse of Winchester, for a period of three lives, the rents to be paid on the Feasts of the Annunciation of the Blessed Virgin Mary, and St. Michael the Archangel, 'at the North Porch dore of the Sd. Collegiat Church of the Blessed Virgin Mary of Southwell . . .'.[12]

Doorways are always an important feature of Norman buildings, and even the humblest village church boasted some extra care lavished in their decoration. The west door at Southwell echoes that within the north porch, but is more restrained, with four attached shafts within the five recessions; and in the south transept is an unusual doorway with a segmental arch above, across which the string course in the walls continues unbroken. This south door, modest in scale, was not for ceremonial occasions, but provided a more private access from the palace only a few yards away; its placing supports the assumption that the archbishops maintained a residence at Southwell from an early date (Pl.XX).

The 13th-Century Choir

To judge from its style, the church at Southwell stood completed soon after the middle of the 12th century and there followed a long pause in building activity. Amongst the other collegiate foundations Bishop Hugh of Lincoln commenced rebuilding his great cathedral in the closing years of the century, after an earthquake had almost demolished the earlier building; the church at Ripon was almost wholly rebuilt under Archbishop Roger (1154-81), and that at Beverley in the first half of the 13th century. Southwell was not lagging behind in the size and importance of its establishment relative to its function in the diocese; most of its prebends were in existence by 1200 and by then the Norman choir must have been inadequate for the body of vicars choral, choristers, and others assisting in the services of the church. It was not until about 1233, however, that work was started to rebuild the Norman choir to an enlarged plan that more than doubled its length (Fig.8). The underlying reasons for the delay, and the restraint in the scope of the work – the remaining parts of the Norman church were left undisturbed in that period – can only be attributed to the peculiarities in its form of collegiate government, and to the lack of leadership in the chapter. It was Walter de Gray, Archbishop of York 1216-56, who provided the stimulus for the rebuilding; in 1234 he issued letters of indulgence for 30 days for those contributing to the fabric at Southwell 'lately begun', as the accepted means for augmenting the resources of the chapter which were quite inadequate for more than normal maintenance and repairs. In spite of the limitations on his authority over the Chapter, Gray also achieved a number of measures to improve discipline within the college; he pressed for more regularity in the appointment of vicars choral and parochial, and may have attempted to impose a dean as head of the chapter in permanent residence. There are references to 'Hugh, Dean of Southwell' in documents of the period, but Hugh's authority, if it was ever accepted, was short-lived. Gray had greater success at Ripon, where in 1230 he established the Prebendary of Stanwick as president of the chapter in permanent residence.

The new choir which was then built at Southwell has fortunately remained almost unchanged to the present day. It terminates at the east end in a squared chancel, and has side aisles, also with squared ends, which stop two bays short of the total length; side chapels off the aisles form little eastern transepts, and the scale of the whole is small in comparison with the ambitious projects at Lincoln which had anticipated it (Pl.XXIV). The two-centred lancet arches decorating the upper stages of the south-western tower had pointed the way to significant changes at the end of the Romanesque period, but these were not innovations; the pointed arch and the ribbed vault had appeared towards the end of the 11th century at Durham, although their structural potential had not been fully realised or explored. No other details of the early church at Southwell are transitional in style, and the break in architectural development is complete until the exquisite essay in the mature Early English of the choir.

The nave, aisles, and eastern transepts are vaulted, but the application of the pointed arch, in contrast with the semicircular forms employed in Norman work, enable the adaption of the curvature of ribs to the differing spans of transverse and diagonal arches. Mouldings are closely set and deeply undercut to produce fine lines of light and shade, and the clustered piers and composite, moulded, capitals combine to lighten the apparent weight of structural members. The whole effect is lightness and movement, in contrast with the impassive weight of the Norman nave (Pl.XXV). The more usual Gothic form for the bays of the arcading – a triforium at the level of the low aisle roofs, with a clerestorey above to light the nave – has been adapted to the smaller and more intimate scale of the choir; above the nave arcades, triforium and clerestorey are united behind a screen of lancet arches on the inside face, which tie the elements together in a pattern which simplifies the whole composition. The ridge rib which runs down the centre of each vault is another feature used consistently here, and is an innovation of the English builders which had appeared earlier at Lincoln, but which never found favour on the Continent.

The setting out of the extended plan of the choir enabled work to be started again from the east end, and the chancel and eastern transepts would have been completed before the earlier building was disturbed. Services could therefore be held in the new building without interruption, while the old choir was demolished to continue the work and join up with the crossing. Progress was good, and this stage was reached by c.1241; the foundation deed of the first chantry, by Robert de Lexington, a canon of the church at this time, directed that services were to be celebrated 'in the Chapel of St. Thomas the Martyr, in the new work', although the exact siting of this altar has not been identified.

Once the new choir had been carried westwards as far as the old building, it seems probable that the masons started again at the crossing and worked eastwards. At the point of junction in the fourth bay from the crossing some readjustment of levels became necessary, and the break can be seen in the string course below the cills of the windows in the south aisle: the crown of the arch in the south arcade is also lower than the rest, and the space between it and the string course above is made up with a carved medallion.

The significant references in the Chapter Acts throw light on the work of this period. In 1248 the *custos* of the fabric – the churchwarden responsible for the receipts and expenses concerning the church – was instructed to prepare a yearly account of his receipts; at the same time the canons were to pay one-fifteenth of their prebends for the next three years to the fabric fund. The building of the choir would then have been nearing completion and the chapter was clearly concerned with the necessary resources to do so. In 1260 the chapter decreed that the receipts and expenses of the custos of the fabric should be examined, and also that no further work should be undertaken without the consent of the chapter. Some disagreement amongst the canons existed at this date to make this decision necessary, and by its architectural character it was the chapel on the east side of the north transept which was the cause. This chapel replaced the original Norman apse there; its moulded arches and shafts are still 13th-century in type, and although there are strong similarities with work in the choir, they are somewhat later in date. By the descriptions of work in restoration carried out in the 19th century, it appears that some of the finishing details were then found to be incomplete. The original, tall, semicircular arch which had opened into the apse was filled by two, acutely-pointed arches of unequal span resting on a pier which was placed to allow two equal bays of vaulting internally. The double piscina points to its adaption for two chantries, but it seems unlikely to have been built for such a purpose, or the endowments would have financed its building without the restriction being necessary on the custos of the fabric. After the dissolution of chantries the chapel was successively the choir school, the library, and vicars' vestries; it is now the memorial chapel to airmen who lost their lives in the two World Wars. The windows are insertions of the 14th century, and an upper room over the chapel vault is the present library, reached by a stone stair from the north aisle of the choir.

The Chapter House

Archbishop Walter de Gray died in 1256. Soon after 1260 the church again stood complete, and for nearly 30 years no further work was undertaken. Then, in the closing years of the 13th century came the last major work of all, the building of the chapter house, with its entrance vestibule, and the passage way or cloister connecting it to the north aisle of the choir. Again small in scale compared with its contemporaries, the workmanship of this building ranks with the finest achievements in England during the whole of the Gothic period.

The chapter of Southwell had never acted with much initiative, except in maintaining its own independence, and its major works had always needed the stimulus from outside. John Le Romaine became Archbishop in 1286, and he acted with decision in reforms both at York and at Southwell; at York he began the work of rebuilding the nave and the chapter house, and the building of the chapter house at Southwell was almost certainly achieved only on his initiative. His decree issued at Southwell (that is, while he was staying at his palace there), and dated 25 January 1288[13] reads

> For the levying of the arrears of the subsidy appointed for the construction of the Chapter House at Southwell, and for the sequestration of the Prebends of those who do not pay. To the Chapter of Southwell. The proctors of your Church aforesaid have advised us that is is lawful for you, after a special meeting of you all, . . to ordain the levy of a fixed subsidy for the necessary construction of your Chapter House, which should be raised for this purpose, by general agreement of the colleagues, out of the established incomes of the different prebends, by a fixed date; some people, however, have not as yet paid the aforesaid subsidy according to the rate provided, though others promptly acquitted what they owed; and on this account they have humbly besought us to provide action against those who have not paid . . .

He then threatens sequestration against all defaulters who have not paid the subsidy by the following Easter.

The Bull of Pope Alexander III in 1171 had retained the appointment to prebends ultimately in his hands, and those of his successors, and some advantage had been taken of this to grant them to favoured foreigners, mostly Italians who enjoyed the revenues but contributed nothing to the service of the collegiate foundation. As a result the prebendal estates had been neglected, but Romaine corrected the abuse at least in part; in a decree dated 13 January 1294,[14] he ordered that the prebendal houses of the foreign canons which had fallen into ruin were to be properly repaired within a year; in default the chapter was empowered to exact heavy fines which were to be devoted to the construction of the new chapter house, and since the revenues of the estates were collected by local officials, this was an enactment easy to execute. It seems probable from these acts that in 1288 funds were being accumulated and preparations were being made for the building or, at most, the work was in its early stages, but by 1294 the work was well under way and all opportunities were being seized to augment resources to complete it.

The chapter house is octagonal in plan, buttressed at the angles, one of which abuts the north-east transept, so that with the vestibule and passage against the north transept chapel, it formed a small enclosed courtyard (Pl.XXIV). The low arcading on the east side of the passage way was originally open as a cloister, but in the 19th century it was partially walled up and the glazed panels were inserted in the arches to exclude the weather; then in modern times the courtyard was roofed over to make the present vestries. With these changes the contrasts have been lost between the low, airy, cloister, and the entrance from the dimly-lit aisle at one end, leading to the taller, more enclosed, and vaulted vestibule at the other; in the vestibule the entry turns at right angles to the climax in the lofty, clear space of the chapter house itself. At Lincoln the chapter house also stands on the north side of the church, but is entered from a cloister comparable in size with the larger monastic foundations; the Southwell cloister is, by contrast, intimate in scale, so that the concentration of effect is made on its exquisite detail (Pl.XXXI b).

It seems probable that the chapter house of Southwell preceded that of York by a few years,[15] and may have influenced the design of the latter. The diameter of the octagon is only 31 feet compared with 60 feet at York, but the arched ribs flow from wall to crown in one clear sweep of stone without support from the central pier found necessary at Wells and Lincoln (Pl.XXVIII).[16] It may be that the masons of York found the task too daunting, because the vault there was completed in timber, built in imitation of stone. Southwell therefore remained unique in its time.

The details of the arches and carving in the cloister are the earliest work of this great project, and lead up to the maturity of the Decorated Gothic in the chapter house, but every element in the design employs foliage carving in a bewildering variety of forms. Maple, oak, hawthorn, ranunculus, potentilla, vine, ivy, and hop are used on capitals, spandrels, and bosses, sometimes conventionally, but mostly in inspired naturalism which still remains subservient to the impressive clarity of structure expressed in the design. Marble,[17] which was popular for attached shafts to piers, and in window and door jambs in the 13th century, and which was used so profusely in the work at Lincoln, occurs at Southwell only in the doorway to the chapter house (Pl.XXVII), and in the entrance from the choir aisle into the cloister, but the leaf carving here in capitals and arches ranks with the finest work to be seen elsewhere in the period.[18]

The 14th and 15th Centuries

Reconstruction of the great collegiate churches continued into the 14th and 15th centuries. The three towers of Lincoln were rebuilt and raised in height in the 14th century, as were those of York, where reconstruction was carried much farther to almost a complete rebuilding of nave and choir lasting into the 15th century. In the other collegiate churches of the diocese of York, the rebuilding of the nave and west front at Beverley lasted into the early years of the 15th century, and at Ripon the building of the eastern bays to the choir and the reconstruction of the tower and nave extended even into the 16th century. In contrast the building of the church at Southwell occurred, at intervals, in three distinctive periods of activity; each was a self-contained project with a limited objective, and each required the stimulation and reforming zeal of an outstanding archbishop who was prepared to exceed, if necessary, the limited authority which he held over the chapter. After 1300 the church was finally complete; no major work of reconstruction or expansion in the church was ever again undertaken. Standing at the crossing, in the silent and empty church on a grey winter's day, we can now conjure up the scene as it was at that time. The nave, then still lit only dimly from the narrow windows of the Norman church, must have been sombre against the newly-built and enlarged choir and the light grace of the new chapter house. At the main offices of the day, and particularly at the greater festivals, the full assembly of the canons in residence, with the vicars choral and the chantry priests, the deacons, sub-deacons, clerks, choristers, vergers and other lay officials, filled the choir, the white of alb and surplice showing up the colours of silken copes in the flickering candle light. Candles, too, on the altars of the chantry priests against the piers of the nave and in the transepts, would have heightened the atmosphere of continual and busy use of the church.

Although the chapter did not emulate its sister churches of Beverley and Ripon in their scale of later reconstruction, a small body of masons was retained in a series of lesser improvements. A dispute with the king's foresters over tolls which were being exacted, was settled by a licence issued by Edward III in 1337 confirming to the chapter the right of free carriage through Sherwood Forest for carts carrying stone from quarries at Mansfield towards the fabric of the church. The work then in hand was certainly, by the evidence of its design, the new choir screen, or *pulpitum.* It is probable that the Norman choir extended into the crossing, as at Gloucester and Winchester, which would account for the shortness of its eastwards extension, also that a rood screen of timber was built into the eastern arch of the crossing when the choir was rebuilt. The 14th-century pulpitum is the most elaborately decorative element in the whole church, and its effect is heightened by contrast with the severity of the Norman work to the west and the classical Early English of the choir to the east. Three arches on the western side enclose a vestibule with a flat ceiling carried on flying ribs (Pl.XXI a); on the eastern side, the single arch giving entry into the choir is flanked by three stalls on each side. Little gables over the stalls are crocketted, ogee arches are cusped, and at every point sculptured heads and carved foliage are placed in a riot of disciplined decoration. The sedilia, on the south side of the chancel, is a rare type in having five seats, and is probably by the same masons; it became very dilapidated later and was faced up with an oak screen. In the early years of the 14th century this was removed, and the Bernasconi brothers restored much of the carving of the sedilia as well as some of the sculptured heads on the screen; they also built side stalls in the choir which have since been removed. Their work is easily distinguished by the religious sentimentality shown, which was characteristic of the period, compared with the more robust portraits and caricatures of the medieval carving.

The vaults over the choir must have given some cause for concern at this time because the flying buttresses, with their crocketed pinnacles are mid-14th-century in type. Had they been placed at every bay they would have been more easily integrated into the structure in a more impressive way, but placed as they are only over the centre bays they unhappily confuse the simple form of the Early English work (Pl.XXVI). Other work of that period was the insertion of the present windows in the north transept chapel, and windows in the lower stages of the western towers. The latter were filled with flamboyant tracery in the Decorated style but were replaced in the 19th century by copies of 12th-century types. Towards the end of the century, also, the present windows were inserted at the west end of the nave aisles.

Two views of the church, from the north-west and from the south-west, engraved by William Hollar, appeared in the first edition of Dugdale's *Monasticon Anglicanum* in 1673, and in Robert Thoroton's *Antiquities of Nottinghamshire* in 1677 (Pl.XII). The roofs of the nave, transepts, and choir shown are too low in pitch to be original 12th or 13th-century work; the ridge levels are also well below the blind arcading of the lower stage of the crossing tower, and the plain, semicircular-headed openings are exposed externally which would have been within the roof spaces of the original building. No record exists of this renewal of the external roof structures, but there is every reason to place it contemporary with the insertion of the west window in the mid-15th century. It is probable that the Norman roof of the nave covered a flat, painted, timber ceiling internally, on the pattern of Ely and Peterborough; removal of the ceiling would have been necessary, at least at the western end between the towers, to accommodate the height of the new west window, but a somewhat lower pitch of external roof was then possible, particularly if it rested on the line of the outside face of the wall as the eaves overhang shown in the prints. It has been suggested that the feet of the original rafters may have been decayed, and that the lowering of the roof pitch was an economical measure to re-use the same rafters in reduced lengths.[19]

The external roof of the choir has remained at a low pitch, and the lines of the Norman roof and of the steeper 13th-century roof are still marked on the east face of the crossing tower; the castellated parapet and clumsy four-light window in the gable at the east end indicate a 15th-century date for the alteration. The structure of this roof was again restored, probably at the same time in the 19th century, but a few of the sound oak timbers then retained may be from the earlier work.

The Church after the Middle Ages

Records of work carried out before the Restoration are scarce, but it is clear that in 1660 the fabric was in a very bad condition. Some repairs to the roof and windows had been necessary in the latter part of the 16th century, but the neglect and wilful damage of the Civil War was much more serious. In the three years, 1660-63, some £1,350 was expended by the receiver general on timber, lead, and tiles, glass from Lincoln, stone from Mansfield, and lime from Warsop, to render the building weatherproof again and to refurnish it appropriately.

In 1711 the church was again in danger. The spire of the south-western tower was struck by lightning and caught fire, which spread to the nave and crossing tower, destroying the roofs, the bells, clock and organ, and damaging the masonry, particularly the piers, arches, and upper stages of the crossing tower. Repairs were started immediately, but the estimated cost of nearly £4,000 was beyond the resources of the chapter. Queen Anne was petitioned for a grant of trees for the rebuilding and for sale towards the cost; a public subscription was started and the Duke of Newcastle donated £500, so that by 1714 the chapter could report to the archbishop at his visitation, 'The church in good repair before the lamentable fire, and is now very great forwardness towards the same'. Unfortunately the opportunity was not taken to restore the nave roof to its original steep pitch. The ridge of the new roof was so low that it was below the arch of the west window, and a raised section was necessary between the towers to retain the window within the outer shell of the building. Several drawings done in 1791 by Samuel Hieronymus Grimm and now in the Kaye Collection at the British Museum show the church as it was after the repairs of fire damage, and as it remained throughout the 18th century (Pl.XVI). One view from the north-east shows the higher construction of the nave roof between the towers, although the detail is insufficient to interpret its exact form; this could not have been necessary in the earlier roof or the construction of the west window to such a great height would have been pointless (Pl.LV). Drawings in Killpack's history of the church, published in 1839, include interiors of the nave; it then had a flat, panelled ceiling which, in spite of the raised western section, appeared to cut off the arch of the west window with a crude lack of sympathy with the 15th-century improvements. Engravings by John Coney, dated 1818, in the 1830 edition of Dugdale's *Monasticon,* show that the transepts were ceiled in a similar manner.

The efforts of restoration after the fire had sapped the resources of the chapter so much that in 1740 it was decreed

> that in consideration that the Fabrick has been lately put to great expense and being now very low in stock, that it is recommended to each residentary as the wish of this present chapter that nothing shall be laid out upon the Fabrick exceeding the sum of three pounds by the Residentary in being, without the approbation and consent of the chapter and that the same shall be observed with respect to the residence.

In 1744, however, the chapter, possibly with the earlier damage to the church in mind, donated £20 towards the purchase of a parish fire engine.

At that time there was a small chapel against the west end of the south side of the nave. This was originally the chantry founded by Henry le Vavasour, Prebendary of Norwell Palishall, about 1280; Archbishop William Booth (1452-65) had been buried there, and his brother Lawrence Booth (Archbishop 1476-80) founded two chantries and extended the chapel, finally being buried beside his brother. The building was afterwards known as Booth's Chapel, but was allowed to fall into decay after the dissolution of the chantries. It was later restored and used as the library and grammar school, but in 1784 the chapter demolished it on the grounds that it spoilt the symmetry of the church. The chapel is shown on an early Grimm drawing in the Gough Collection at the Bodleian Library, and it certainly appears to have had no architectural merit, and have been an incongruous addition to the Norman church (Pl.XI). The chapter authorised the residentiary, who was then Dr. Peckard, to apply the materials recovered to the building of a new library. He was also to hire a room in the prebendal house of Oxton II (the Red Prebend) for use as a schoolroom. The new library was an even clumsier structure, built in the angle formed by the south transept and the south aisle of the choir; it was a lean-to structure requiring the choir aisle windows being bricked up and a chimney being erected against the church wall, but fortunately the whole addition was removed again in 1825, and the choir and transept walls were restored as nearly as possible to their original state.

The status of the ordinary clergy of the church had risen considerably during the 18th century, and the buildings which had served the vicars and the resident canon were no longer considered adequate for their accommodation. In the last quarter of the century the chapter was heavily committed to the rebuilding of the vicars' houses and to the improvement and enlargement of the residence house, as well as altering the chantry priests' house for use by the grammar school, and improving the churchyard. They were also seeking professional advice on a more formal basis. In 1792 an approach was made to James Wyatt 'desiring him to inform the chapter of the sum of money he would require for his journey and inspection of the fabrick, and for a plan of future improvements in the new paving the choir of the church. . .'. Wyatt was a national figure, surveyor to Westminster Abbey and with a record of work already on the cathedrals of Salisbury, Hereford and Lichfield, but he was probably too busy or expensive for the scale of work then anticipated at Southwell, because there is no record of him ever working here. In 1801 Richard Ingleman, a local man, was appointed Surveyor to the Fabric at a salary of £10 p.a. This was the first appointment of its kind in the Minster, and although his salary was terminated in 1808, he continued to advise the chapter, presumably on a fee basis, for many years. Ingleman had already undertaken minor works in the church in 1791 in removing a screen and placing the altar farther back, but his first concern in 1801 was with the western towers. Cracks had developed in the walls of the north-west tower which were attributed to the excessive weight of the lead-covered spire, and Ingleman removed both spires, substituting very low pyramidal roofs behind parapets (Pl.XIII). Either the cause of the damage was misunderstood, or the repairs to the masonry were inadequate, because both towers had to be repaired again extensively in 1816 at a total cost of nearly £650. In 1803 the chapter, anxious to obtain further advice 'decreed that Mr. Wilkins (the Architect) be immediately consulted with respect to the state of the Fabric'. William Wilkins was an architect and builder of Norwich who had been trained by his father, a plasterer and stucco worker; his son, another William, was later a prominent architect in the Greek Revival style and, in 1821, architect for St. Paul's Church, Nottingham, now demolished. Wilkins's main contributions to Southwell were in repaving the choir and building a new roof to the chapter house; this roof is shown in Killpack and, like the new roofs on the western towers, was a low pyramid completely out of sympathy with the original building.

Other repairs carried out at this time were to the roofs of the church, the windows, doors, and seats, and to the structure of the south transept and the north porch. The raised section of the nave roof between the towers, which had been necessary after the fire of 1711, was also urgently in need of repairs; a plan for a pitched, slated, roof at this point was approved by the chapter in April 1808, but nothing was done. At the October meeting the instruction was peremptory, 'that it is absolutely requisite that the pitched roof on the bow between the western towers be immediately repaired by recasting the lead, and that the residentiary do see that this decree is attended to without further delay'. Altogether some £16,000 was laid out by the chapter in the first 10 years of the 19th century. Another public appeal was launched to augment the fabric fund, but part of the cost was defrayed by the sale of lead from the roof which raised £2,800, and £5,200 was borrowed at five per cent interest, although most of the outstanding loans were repaid by 1812.

This work of the chapter was most timely, and had it been delayed the structure of the church might well have deteriorated beyond repair. The reform of the collegiate foundation in the 19th century was slow in maturing, during which time little thought could have been given to the long term care of the fabric. But in 1880, Ewan Christian, architect to the Ecclesiastical Commissioners, who were by now responsible for its upkeep, carried out a number of projects of restoration with a sympathy not always shown at that time. He re-built the spires on the western towers to a design close to their pre-1711 form, and re-roofed the chapter house at its original pitch. He removed the roofs of nave and transepts, and renewed them as nearly as possible to their original form, leaving the raised section between the western towers untouched to accommodate the height of the west window. A flat ceiling would have been incongruous where it would abut the high western bay, and his solution of a waggon-type roof over the nave matches well, and is historically a very appropriate alternative. There has been little visible change since Christian's time, but maintenance of a building of this quality is a continuing process and the mason's scaffold can still be seen as craftsmen carry on with the work of replacing pinnacles or renewing decayed stone from wall surfaces. Although the student of architecture may see Southwell Minster as a medieval church, and may readily discern the three main phases of its building, we have now seen how much restoration has been necessary in recent centuries to preserve the achievements of medieval canons and the masons they employed.

Notes to Chapter Three.

1. I am indebted to Dr. C.A.R. Radford for this suggestion, made on his inspection in April 1970. Also, a coarse tesselated pavement discovered below the nave floor of Wimborne Minster is thought to have belonged to the 8th-century church there. (R.C.H.M., Dorset, V, forthcoming)
2. T.D. Kendrick, *Late Saxon and Viking Art* (1949), p. 121
3. T.D. Atkinson, *English Architecture* (1904), pp. 107-9
4. T.G. Jackson, *Byzantine and Romanesque Architecture* (1913), vol. 2, p. 184
5. Geoffrey Webb, *Architecture in Britain in the Middle Ages,* 2nd edn. (1965), p. 9
6. Rev. Thomas Perkins, *History and Description of Romsey Abbey* (1907)
7. Robert Stoll, *Architecture and Sculpture in Early Britain* (1966) p.534
8. K.J. Conant, *Carolingian and Romanesque Architecture* (1959), pp. 74 and 282
9. Malmesbury - see T.G. Jackson, *op.cit.*, p. 251
   Sherbourne - see Joseph Giratt, *An Encyclopaedia of Architecture* (1908), p. 998
   Bredon — see Nikolaus Pevsner, *Buildings of Worcestershire* (1968), p. 96
10. 'Manuale et Processionale ad usum insignis ecclesiae Eboracencis' (Surtees Society, vol. 63, 1875) pp 23 and 24
    and Appendix 'Manuale ad usum insignis ecclesiae Sarum'.
    also: W.H. Frere, *A History of the Book of Common Prayer* (1902) pp. 570, 617, and 639.
11. F.N. Robinson, ed., *The Works of Geoffrey Chaucer* (1966), Prologue to the Canterbury Tales, lines 459 and 60
12. Notts. C.R.O., DD/SP.38/2
13. 'The Register of Archbishop John le Romeyne' Part I, (Surtees Society, vol. 123, 1913) p. 370
14. *op.cit.* Part II
    (Surtees Society, vol. 128, 1916) p. 30
15. Nicola Coldstream, 'York Chapter House', *Journal of the British Archaeological Assn.*, vol. XXXV (1972)
16. Geoffrey Webb, *op.cit.*, pp 61, 62 and 153-56.
17. It seems probable that the marble used at Southwell is one of the Derbyshire limestones, and not that from the Isle of Purbeck, in Dorset, as employed at Lincoln.
18. Nikolaus Pevsner, *The Leaves of Southwell* (1945).
19. Rev. Arthur Dimock, *The Cathedral Church of Southwell* (1901), p. 42.

IV

The palace of the Archbishops of York

The Palace

On the south side of the church the modern residence of the bishops of Southwell, known as Bishop's Manor, stands within the ruins of the former palace of the archbishops of York (Pl.XXXII). Early records suggest that the archbishops had established a residence here soon after the foundation of the collegiate church. Aelfric Puttuc, Archbishop of York 1023-51, died at Southwell, though his body was taken to Peterborough for burial. In 1108 Archbishop Gerard was resident at Southwell until one day, wishing to rest in his garden after dinner, he dismissed his servants, who returned later only to find he had died in his sleep; under his pillow was a work by Julius Firmicus, on judicial astrology – a shocking discovery for those times when such studies were considered heretical – and his death without the last rites was interpreted by his enemies as divine judgment for his addiction to the magical and forbidden arts.

We have seen that the Norman church had an entrance provided in the south transept especially for the use of the archbishops. Nothing is known of the form of the early palace, but comparison with contemporary examples recorded elsewhere limits speculation to two possible types: the first floor hall, as its name implies, was raised on a basement or cellar, so that the living accommodation would achieve some security in defence in troubled times. Access was directly to the hall by an external flight of steps against the wall, and the basement was used as storage. King Harold's manor house at Bosham, Sussex, was of this form and is shown in the Bayeux Tapestry of c.1077, but the finest example still to be seen is in the East Midlands, in the manor house of Boothby Pagnell, Lincs., built in the late 12th century. This house has a fine vaulted undercroft; on the first floor is a small heated hall and an unheated chamber. First floor halls were built until the early 15th century, but all known examples were built in stone construction, none being recorded as timber frames. The other typical form of early medieval house was the aisled hall, a single storied building at ground level. The structural problems of roofing a wide span could be minimised by placing lines of posts to form a plan of nave with aisles; in domestic use the resultant interruption of floor space was an inconvenience only solved by the later design of more sophisticated forms of roof trusses spanning from wall to wall, but in churches where the demand for space for chantry altars could utilise the aisles effectively, and in barns where the aisles provided useful storage bays, such structures persisted into late medieval times. Aisled halls had been known since Saxon times at least, and examples have been recorded in both timber and stone construction. The hall of Oakham Castle, c.1190, has stone arcades on cylindrical stone piers, and in the ruins of the bishops' palace at Lincoln, c.1224, the bases of the two rows of piers can still be seen; the bishops' palace at Hereford, c.1160, is the prime example in timber framing.

Close examination of the ruins at Southwell reveals no evidence of any details which can be positively identified as earlier than 14th-century in date. The rubble walls average only 34in. in thickness, although the remaining cross wall in the south range is 41in. thick, and no early carving was incorporated in the rebuilding, as in the church. For the palace to have disappeared so completely, therefore, it must be concluded that the structure was of timber. Its likely form was that of an aisled hall with end service rooms.

The existing ruins are of the palace rebuilt in the 14th and 15th centuries and comprise the north, east, and south sides of the outer wall of a courtyard plan, which have been retained to form a walled garden attached to the modern house (Figs.9 & 10). The first floor room at the north-west corner of the old palace is the only complete structure left, erroneously described today as the Great Hall. This was the archbishop's parlour, or state chamber (a lesser hall for private occasions), and the great hall proper stood against it to the south, on the site almost exactly occupied by the present house, forming the west side of the palace courtyard. One jamb of one of the tall windows which once lit the great hall on the west side can still be seen against the state chamber. The jambs of the modern entrance porch are also original, and are part of the arched entrance to a cross passage at the south end of the great hall: three arches are still in the south wall; the outer ones were to service rooms, and the centre one to a service passage (Pl.XXXVI), the external door of which may be seen leading into the garden on the south side (Pl.XXXIX). Thus the western side of the palace was, in itself, a common form for a substantial manor house in the 14th century, comprising a great hall, with a state chamber over a low, ground floor room at one end, and with a cross passage at the other end which gave access to service rooms. The existence of a passage, between the service rooms and leading to the doorway in the south wall, implies that the kitchen was a detached building at that side as, for example, in the bishop's palace at Lincoln, and Haddon Hall, Derbyshire. It may have been an inferior structure in timber, so that its disappearance is understandable. The great hall was nearly 80 ft. long, between the state chamber and the service rooms, and 35 ft. wide, and compares with the halls at Dartington, Devon, (1388) at 69 ft. 9 in. by 37 ft. 6 in., and South Wingfield, Derbyshire, (1440) at 72 ft. by 37 ft.; presuming that the Southwell hall was a rebuild of an aisled plan on the same site, the equivalent example at Lincoln measured 84 ft. by 58 ft., and that at Hereford 69 ft. by 48 ft.

The south and east external walls of the courtyard are complete up to the level of the first floor window cills, and are sufficient to attempt some reconstruction of the plan. Where these walls meet – i.e. at the south-east corner – is a garderobe tower with a unique group of four closets around a central shaft (Pl.XXXV); the entrance to this is from the ground floor via a short flight of eight steps. Above the garderobe is an open chamber entered from the first floor, and containing a newel stair corbelled out from the internal corner and leading up to the roof of the tower (Pl.XXXIV).

Against the east wall, at first floor level, were ranged three major apartments. The northern one, indicated by a five light window, set in a gable crowned with the remnants of a carved cross, has an image bracket internally in the north-east corner, and the foundations of a bell turret externally against the north-east buttress; this was the archbishop's private chapel. At the south end of this range is a second gable with a four light window; this apartment has carved corbels set in the south wall for the support of the roof trusses, and a doorway to the chamber in the tower over the garderobe, showing a standard of workmanship and accommodation befitting the private hall of the archbishop. In the centre of the range are a single garderobe (Pl.XXXIII), and an elaborately carved fireplace surround; between these, a wide void, lined at the sides with the moulded stones of window reveals, is difficult to interpret in the advanced state of decay of the ruins. A single window at this point would have been at least of seven lights, and comparable in size only with the great west window of the church itself, but the gable which would have been necessary to accommodate a window of the height one would expect, is entirely absent; nor is there any sign of a cross range to which such a gable would be a logical termination. The alternative, and more likely arrangement, between garderobe and fireplace would have been two smaller, two light, windows, of which only the outer jambs remain, the other parts with the wall between having been removed, although this is the only part of the upper walls on the east side which has become ruined in this way. Whatever the original design at this point, it included an important chamber, with a fine fireplace, and with an inner chamber and garderobe adjoining it.[1]

The south wall contains another garderobe, of two closets at first floor level in the middle of its length, and two fireplaces, although none of the windows exceed two lights in width. This range therefore included other lodgings, probably on both first and ground floors, the latter having access to garderobes in the tower.

The north wall of the courtyard is very incomplete, and now only high enough to obtain privacy for the present garden (Pl.XXXVIII). The bases of two fireplace projections remain, but there are no garderobes, so that this range probably contained lesser accommodation below, and possibly the more important non-residential offices above, with the library, etc., between the archbishop's state chamber and chapel.

Some archbishops and bishops built castles and manor houses which called for a licence from the king to crenellate, i.e. to provide limited means for defence in troubled places. Provision for defence could not have been a prime consideration

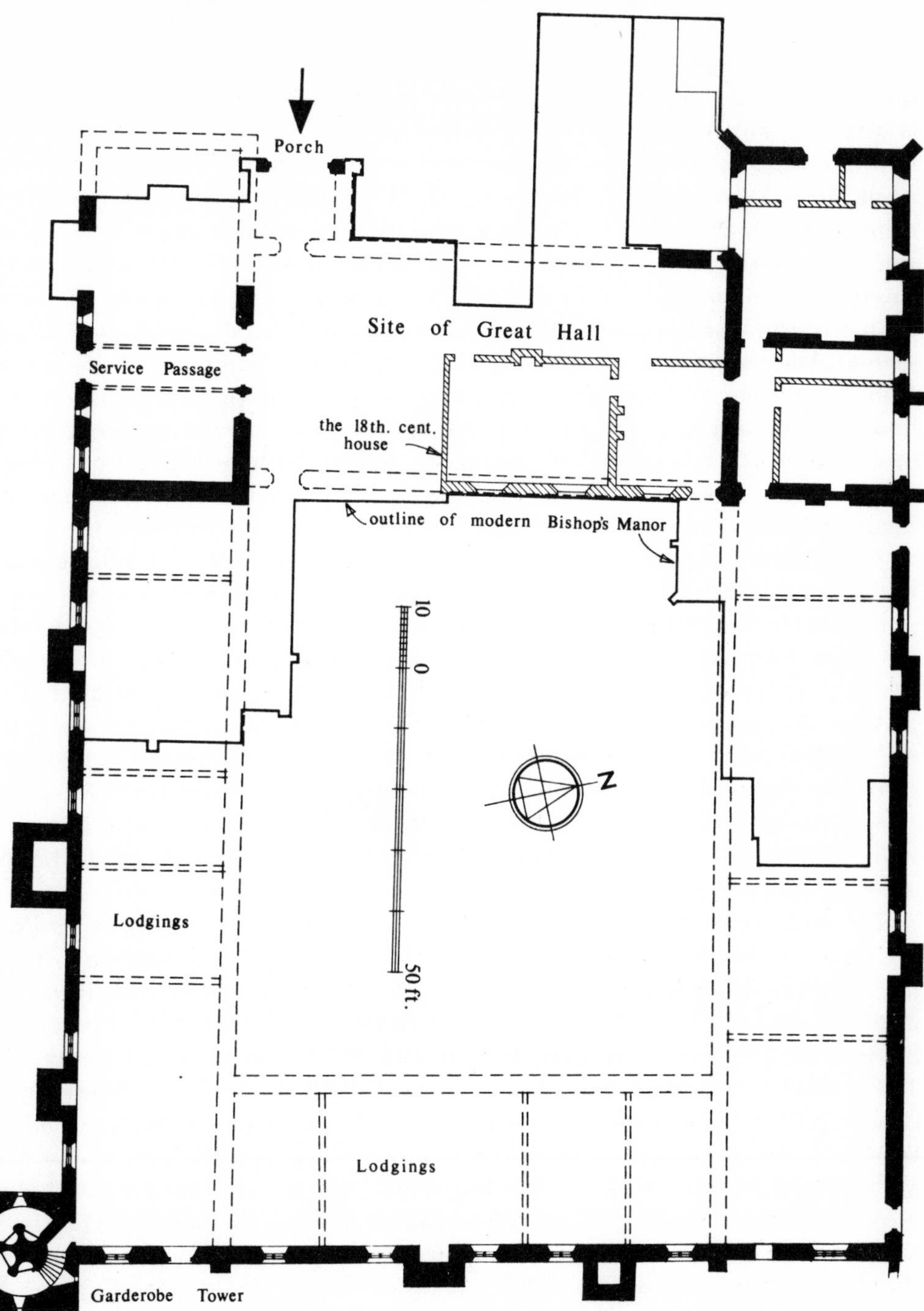

Fig 9: *Ground floor plan of The Archbishop's Palace. The remaining masonry walls are shown in black, and a reconstruction of the plan in dotted lines. The modern Bishop's Manor is within the heavy black lines at the west side of the courtyard.*

in the design of the palace at Southwell, so that the total requirements of the household would not have needed to be confined within the limits of a single courtyard plan. Apart from the detached kitchen, accommodation for a brewhouse, considerable storage, stabling, and lodgings for the archbishop's retinue would have been required. The siting of these cannot now be discerned in the ruins, but they may have been grouped to form an outer courtyard on the west side of the hall, with an entrance to the whole complex being controlled by a gatehouse. Double-courtyard plans were characteristic of great houses of the later 14th century, and the placing of the hall between outer and inner courts can be seen at Amberley Castle, Sussex (1377-83), Haddon Hall, and at Dartington. This form has the great advantage of separating the principal private apartments from lesser accommodation for the household, the cross passage of the great hall providing the link between the two parts. It is to be hoped that archaeological excavations will one day provide answers to some of these questions, and place Southwell palace firmly in the context of its time.

The present ruins show building of two periods. The form of the plinth around the external walls and of the lower parts of the chimney stacks, the jambs of the porch, and the doorways leading to service rooms and to the service passage from the great hall are stylistically of the latter half of the 14th century, but the remains of the windows shown in the jambs and tracery, the fireplaces internally, and the doorways in the south wall and in the south end of the east wall are of the 15th century. The windows in the state chamber fall within the two extremes of dating. Some of the later windows break into the plinth, and on the south side there is an interrupted string course at first floor level, but apart from these there is no evidence of major re-fenestration or structural alterations in the building during the 15th century.

The building of the earliest parts was attributed by Parker[2] to Thoresby, c.1360, but this was on the evidence of the mouldings and not supported by documentary records.[3] John Thoresby was Archbishop of York from 1353 until his death in 1373, but he had been connected with Southwell before this, holding the prebend of Norwell Overthall in 1329, and of South Muskham in 1340. During his episcopate he concentrated much of his energies on the completion of his church at York; he built the lady chapel at the east end, and laid the foundation stone of the new choir in 1360, demolishing his manor house at Sherburn to provide stone for the rebuilding; he also donated 100 marks initially, and a further £200 annually towards the cost of these works. It seems hardly likely, therefore, that if he completed a substantial palace at Southwell, it should have gone unrecorded.

Thoresby's successor, Alexander Neville, quarrelled with the canons of Ripon and Beverley, attempting to override their statutes; the building of the choir at York was suspended during his episcopate, and he was declared a traitor in 1387, fleeing the country to die in exile in Brabant in 1392. Although his episcopate was short and turbulent, however, other circumstantial evidence does point to

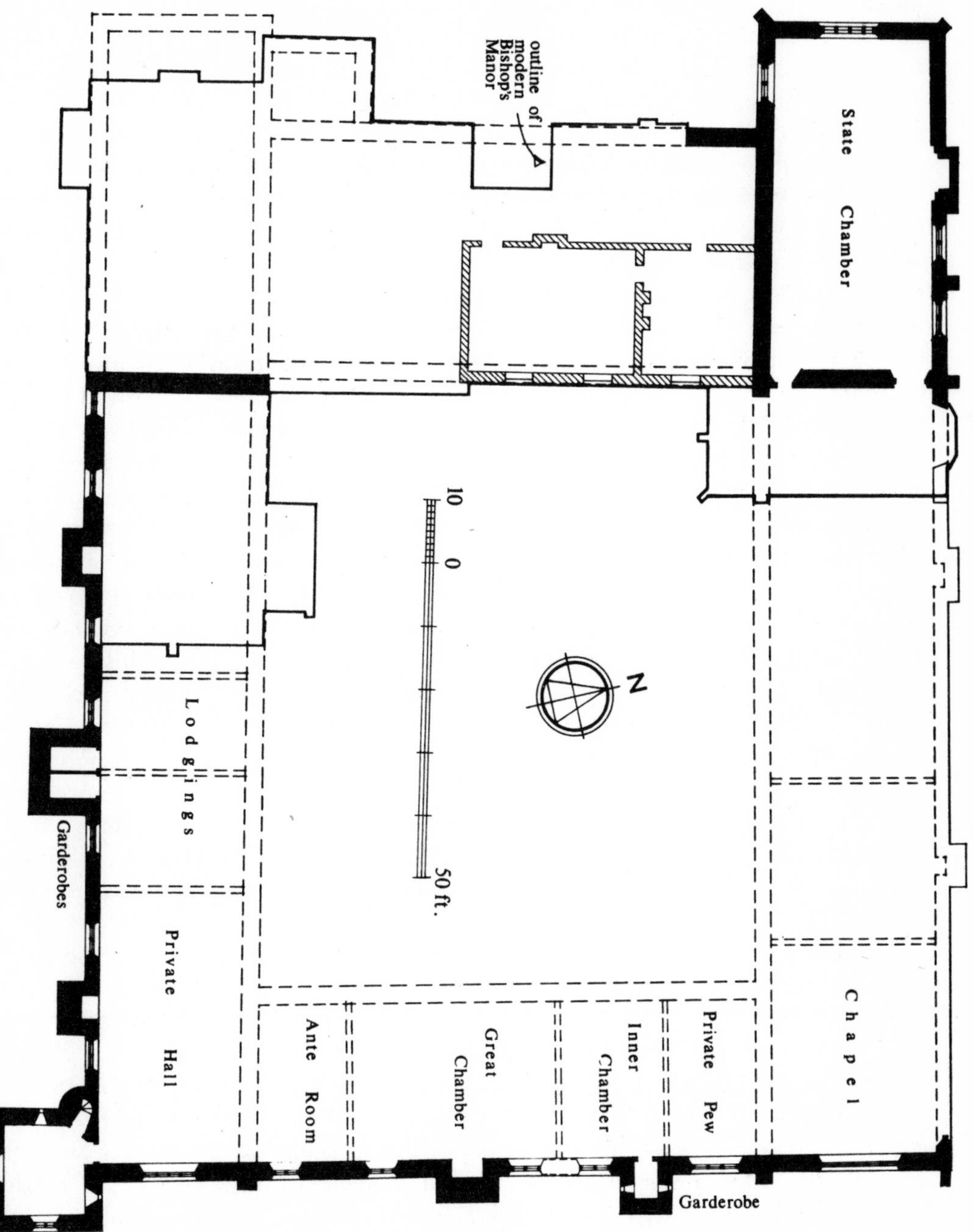

Fig 10: *First floor plan of the Archbishop's Palace*

Neville as the possible builder of the Palace. In 1383 he obtained a licence to crenallate his palace at Rest,[4] and Godwin said of him 'this man bestowed much cost in repairing the Castle of Cawood, building divers towers and other edifices about the same'. It was he who sanctioned the building of the new college for the vicars choral at Southwell in 1379, and he may well have started work rebuilding his palace here at the same time. Finally, a date of 1379 for the earliest existent parts of the palace places it more convincingly with the similar examples of courtyard planning at Amberley and Dartington already described; it is then contemporary with, instead of ante-dating, them. It is even possible that on the slender stylistic evidence the building was still later in date, and started by Archbishop Arundel (1388-96); of him Godwin said 'while he was at Yorke he bestowed much in building upon divers of his houses . . .'.

Waldby, Lescrope, Longley, and Bowet, appear to have taken little interest in the manor of Southwell, but John Kemp, Archbishop from 1426 until he was translated to the see of Canterbury in 1452, must be credited with the major work of building the palace at Southwell, and with giving it its final form. He was unpopular at York, which he rarely visited, and at Ripon his house was demolished by bands of rioters (instigated by the Earl of Northumberland) who were angered by the harsh proceedings which Kemp had taken against some of the laity for spiritual offences. His palace at Southwell by contrast must have been a haven of peace; it was virtually complete by 1436, when William Ryke was granted, for life, a newly-built chamber over the entrance porch of the hall, with 10 marks per year out of the issue of the estate, in consideration of his services in connection with the new building of the archbishop's mansion at Southwell.[5] A Latin couplet of the time reads that Kemp 'built at Southwell a beautiful manor and decorated it with costly furnishings'.[6] The description that Kemp 'built' the palace, however, may exaggerate his achievement, and it seems more likely that he completed, or restored it. Another account runs, probably more accurately, '. . . the Archiepiscopal Palace, which the same Archbishop, at his own costs and charges, honourably restored, and enriched with furnishings and sundry books'.[7]

The full nature and extent of Kemp's work relative to the form of the palace then already in existence has never been satisfactorily explained, but it is significant that the earliest parts of the building are in the great hall and in the base courses of the courtyard walls. If a late 14th-century date for these is correct, then the work at that time may have been limited to the replacement of an aisled form of timber framed hall by a stone structure, and to the layout of a courtyard plan of service rooms with possibly a single-storied timber structure against the stone outer walls. A modest scheme of this kind, or a modest beginning to the later extensive building, would not have been remarkable enough to merit particular mention; later the ground floor windows were inserted, and the upper works completed to make the impressive mansion of Archbishop Kemp's time.

After Kemp, William Booth (1452-64) and his half-brother Lawrence (1476-80) took Southwell as a favourite residence; both died and were buried in the church. According to Godwin, Archbishop Rotheram (1490-1500), also known as Thomas Scot, built the pantry, bakehouse, and new chambers adjoining the river; these cannot now be identified, but were probably on the south side, and may have been part of the suggested outer courtyard ranges. Wolsey, in disgrace with the King, spent the summer months of the last year of his life, in 1530, at Southwell. He stayed at one of the prebendal houses until his palace could be repaired and made habitable, but by the autumn he was at Scrooby on his way to York. Archbishop Sandys (1577-88) was the last to make Southwell his principal residence, and his fine tomb in alabaster now stands in the north transept of the church.

In 1603 James I wished to make an exchange for the archbishop's manors of Southwell and Scrooby, to provide himself with residences near Sherwood Forest as a convenience for his journeys between England and Scotland.[8] This was never carried out, and the archbishops remained in possession. An inventory of the goods of Archbishop Tobie Mathew (1606-28) includes very modest furnishings at Southwell; a chapel, great chamber, withdrawing chamber, study, nursery, chambers for his chaplain, steward, and eight others are listed (App. E). Although the palace had remained unmolested during the difficult years of dissolution and re-establishment of the collegiate church in the 16th century, its destruction in the Civil War of the 17th was complete and final. The Scottish Commissioners occupied the palace, and Cromwell's troops stripped the lead from the roof and left the building open to the weather; the parishioners contributed to the destruction, carting away the stone and timber for use elsewhere. As Shilton quaintly put it later, 'were every feather stuck in its own wing, many a mansion in the town would totter at its base'. Even the archbishop's steward, William Clay, became involved, and after the Restoration in 1662 he was writing to defend himself against the accusation of taking stone and timber from the palace for his own purposes.[9]

The archbishop's state chamber was the only part of the palace then still habitable; the Hon. John Byng, on his visit in 1789 described above, wrote

> At a small distance from the church remain those ruins of the Archbishop of York's palace, wherein resides one of the Vicars (who all seem to be, with the rest of the choir, most comfortably, nay superbly, lodged). A beautiful old chimney yet endures.

Shilton later recorded

> the Great Hall has long been converted into a dwelling house, and is now occupied as a very respectable seminary for young ladies, under the direction of Mrs. Williams. In the remaining part, now called the Great Chamber, the Justices of the Soke of Southwell hold their sessions.

The great chamber was partitioned into two parts for these purposes, and the court occupied the western end with access through an external door clumsily inserted in the fine west window (Pl. XI). The house which occupied the eastern end was extended by building over the site of the original great hall (Pl. XXXVII), and the stone wall of this extension which overlooked the courtyard was later incorporated in the modern Bishop's Manor. From correspondence by Richard Becher, who was the archbishop's steward from 1757 to 1775, it is clear that the archbishops were careful not to grant leases for long periods which might commit their successors, and refused them for the usual terms of three lives.

When the diocese of Southwell was created in 1884, the problem of a suitable residence for the bishop was not immediately solved; Ewan Christian had prepared a design for a house attached to the old state chamber, but apart from this he did not attempt to relate the new building to the ruins. The Right Reverend Edward Trollope, Bishop Suffragan in the diocese of Lincoln, bought the house and ruins from the Ecclesiastical Commissioners in 1881 for £1600 and restored the great chamber, renewed the roof and windows, and built the stone staircase at the east end. Dr. Ridding, the first Bishop of Southwell, however, lived in the 18th-century house built by the Cooper family on the ruins of the Priory of Thurgarton adjoining the church there, and it was not until 1905 that an official residence was proposed in Southwell itself. The building of the present Bishop's Manor was then carried out by the Commissioners to the designs of their architect, William Douglas Caroe. The new house is an undistinguished building with the cottagey character popular in the early years of the present century. It has, however, been skilfully incorporated within the west side of the old ruins, occupying the site of the original great hall, and restoring the porch and the arches which once led to the service rooms and the detached kitchen. The house was completed in 1907.

Notes to Chapter Four

1. In Fig. 10 the description of rooms has been adopted from P.A. Faulkner, 'Some Medieval Episcopal Palaces', in *Archaeological Journal*, vol. CXVII (1970).
2. J.H. Parker, *Some Account of Domestic Architecture in England* (1853), vol. II, pp. 237 and 38.
3. G.M. Livett, *Southwell Minster* (1883), p. 135, says that Dugdale attributed the building to Thoresby in his *Monasticon*, but this is incorrect. Other historians have repeated this dating without further evidence.
4. *Calendar of Patent Rolls*, 1381-85, p. 333.5.
5. *Calendar of Patent Rolls*, 1436-41, p. 49.
5. J.F. Dimock, *Architectural History of Southwell Minster* (1869) Papers read to the Lincoln Diocesan Architectural Society.
7. Transcribed from Thomas Stubbs, continued by an unknown author in James Paine, *Historians of the Church of York and its Archbishops* (1886), vol. II, p. 436.
8. *State Papers Domestic* 16 Aug. 1603, King James I to Archbishop Hutton.
9. Borthwick Institute at York, ref: 67608.

V

Vicars' Court and the Residence

1. The Medieval College

THE REFECTORY for the canons which was established by Archbishop Ealdred before the Conquest is the first record of collegiate buildings serving the church at Southwell. In time, the canons acquired their prebendal mansions in the town, but the need for communal buildings revived with the growth of numbers of vicars choral and chantry priests, and included their lodgings and ancillary rooms. Nothing remains of the first building which Dickinson said, without confirmation from other sources, to have been on the far side of the Potwell Dyke (then called Bullivant's Dyke) which crosses Church Street east of the Minster. In 1379 Richard de Chesterfield petitioned Alexander Neville, Archbishop of York, to build a new college for the vicars choral at the east end of the church where Vicars' Court now stands.[1]

> that the Manse heretofore built for the habitation of the Vicars Choral of the said church is situated at a great distance, and the road between them muddy and deep, and the lodgings thereof are greatly threatened with destruction, so much so that the said vicars have not conveniently been able to reside there, and it is a long time since they did reside there, but they have dwellings for themselves apart and scattered in the town, whereby Divine Service in the church aforesaid is much diminished. Opportunities for insolence are afforded, evil speaking arises among the people, and scandals and perils to their souls are produced . . .

The new building was sited within the limits of the churchyard as it was at the time, 'contiguous to the Manse belonging to the Prebend of Beckyngham'; the land there was unencumbered, 'the remaining part of the said churchyard being large enough for processions and burials, and other things there to be done'. An Inspeximus of Letters Patent of Alexander Archbishop of York, John of Waltham, Official of the Court of York, and John of Caunton, Prior of Thurgarton,[2] recites the petition and the proceedings which followed; the site was studied, recommendations made and the dimensions of the area allotted were given: 146 ft. on the west side, 100 ft. on the east, by 206 ft. on the north side, and 211 ft. on the south. The present buildings of Vicars' Court by comparison occupy an area approximately 117 ft. wide by 188 ft. long exclusive of gardens.

Richard de Chesterfield was a canon of Southwell, Prebendary of Oxton I in

1365, and then of Norwell Overhall from 1370 until his death in 1404; in 1392 he made a considerable grant of property to the chapter in trust, to augment the common fund of the vicars choral. This provision of collegiate buildings was very much in line with similar foundations elsewhere. At Lincoln,[3] Vicars' Court was built as lodgings, each with its garderobe, c.1310, and at Wells c.1350 Vicars' Close was built as a complete street of houses with the chapel and common hall closing the two ends respectively.[4] Both of these were on the generous scale appropriate to the greater numbers of clergy of the wealthier endowments.

The 1379 building at Southwell was modest by comparison and consisted of a quadrangle with the lodgings on the west, north and south sides. A hall, in which the community dined in common, in the manner of the colleges of Oxford and Cambridge, occupied the east side, and access to the quadrangle was through a gateway in the west side. The arrangement was characteristic of much domestic planning in the late 14th century, both for religious and secular foundations, and the single gateway access was appropriate to the stricter control imposed on the vicars choral. It may not be mere coincidence that William of Wykeham was prebendary of Dunham at Southwell in those years; although there is no evidence of his personal involvement in the building, he may have influenced its design. It is in accordance with his principles of discipline, and there are strong similarities with the planning of his foundations of New College, Oxford in 1379, and Winchester College in 1382.[5] Dickinson described the building as having a ground floor of stone under a deep roof which accommodated an attic storey; he goes on to say that in 1485 William Talbot, at his own expense, removed the roof and built a first floor of timber framing, infilled with mortar and plaster, and roofed at a lower pitch than before, Dickinson is a valuable chronicler of his own times, but the gaps in his historical researches were filled in by his fertile imagination, and this description is not supported by other records. A drawing by Samuel Hieronymus Grimm is in the British Museum, and another from an identical viewpoint, in the Bodleian Library, is captioned 'W. front of the Vicars' houses at Southwell, Notts. as it was in 1775' (Pl. XL). The first floor framing shown is typical of the 14th century, and therefore almost certainly the original building; the stonework to the ground floor could be the facing up of framed walls to the underside of a jettied floor, and the windows are 17th-century in design. William Talbot was a canon of Southwell and prebendary of Oxton I; his grave slab still exists, and has been built into the chancel north wall; translated, it reads 'Here lies William Talbot, wretched and unworthy priest, awaiting the resurrection of the dead under the sign of the cross'. This is a very modest memorial for a man who was supposed to have done so much for the vicars choral out of his own resources, and his work, if any, was more likely to have been limited to repairs and improvements, but not on the scale of rebuilding assumed by Dickinson.

After the Reformation, when the clergy were allowed to marry, the college made only 'six indifferent houses', two on each of the south, north, and west sides, which accommodated the reduced number of vicars of the new statutes of Elizabeth's reign. In 1690 the chapter reported to the archbishop at his visitation

> several houses or habitations belonging to our vicars, singing men, and choristers. That these houses have been laid together by order of your Grace's predecessors (as we have been credibly informed) by which means what were anciently sixteen houses or apartments are now reduced to four, whereby the rest of the vicars' singing men, and choristers are forced elsewhere to seek habitations.

In 1693 the archbishop ordered that 'the buildings called the Vicarage must be divided equally for five vicars' houses (the Parish Priest to reside in the parish vicarage).' It is clear that the old building had been altered and restored several times, and was probably most inconvenient for any uses whatsoever.

2. The First Residence House, 1689

After the Restoration, the prebendal houses in the town were in poor repair and leased to laymen. In the vicars' court itself, communal living was no longer the custom of a celibate clergy, and the buildings had changed in character from lodgings for single men to family houses for a reduced number of vicars choral. The hall was no longer required, and it was this building, filling the east side of the quadrangle, which was demolished for the erection of the new residence house.

In 1689 the chapter petitioned the archbishop, Thomas Lamplugh, for permission to build a house for the canon who was undertaking his residence in rota,

> that by the Statutes of the church (made by Elizabeth of blessed memory) the Residentiaries are to keep their residence in their proper prebendal houses (if it may be done). But so it is that some of us have no such houses, some have theirs defaced during the late Rebellion, but none belonging to the whole College have such a house which he found not in lease; so that we are all destitute of an convenient place to perform our residence in (excepting onely the Prebendary of Oxton the second part) to our great discouragement and incommodity, whereby we have been plunged into great straits and inconveniences being forced to borrow or hire. To remove such inconveniences as well as to remove the scandal hereof for the future, we judge it advisable to erect one Common House for the performance of our residence. And whereas there is a certain place in the Vicaridge where stood a spacious Hall and made use of by our predecessors in former times (as we are credibly informed). We desire (with your Grace's approbation) to build in this place as most fit for such a purpose. And whereas the work will be too great to be supplied from our common Dividend we doe therefore humbly beseach your Grace to be a Benefactor in this necessary work to give us so many trees out of your adjoining park of Norwood as your Grace's generous goodness shall think fit to bestow upon us with liberty to exchange some of them . . .

By the end of the 17th century, Tudor Renaissance in the mainstream of architectural development had given way to the Palladianism of Inigo Jones and his successors. The scholarly classicism of the Queen's House at Greenwich and the Banqueting Hall in Whitehall, both by Inigo Jones in the period 1618-21, was followed in turn by the Baroque of Sir Christopher Wren. Even Oxford, almost the last stronghold of Gothic spirit, had been shaken out of its medievalism by the Civil War; but here in the backwater of Southwell, the design of the first residentiary house of 1690 still displayed the lack of order and concern for symmetry of the traditional builders of the medieval period. A drawing in the Kaye Collection at the British Museum, probably also by Grimm, shows the west front of the house before it was remodelled in 1785 (Pl. XLI); the principal floor is at a raised level to accommodate service rooms as a semi-basement, a feature first introduced in the great houses from 1575, and could have been seen at Wollaton in 1588 and also at Hardwick Hall in 1597.[6] The elevation is a series of elements arranged irregularly about the entrance; a low entrance lobby has a hipped roof, and a substantial chimney stack prominently on the external wall at one side, with a broken pattern of windows on the other. The whole composition is more appropriate to a country vicarage of 60 years earlier. The plan is not easily interpreted through the alterations and additions of the next 100 years, but it appears to have been a simple range of rooms, with services below and attics above. Two further drawings by Grimm in the British Museum show the rear of the house. One from the east shows the ruins of the palace across open ground uninterrupted by the gardens of the later vicars' houses (Pl. XLII). A three-storied wing projecting at right angles to the main range of rooms would be the additions of 1772, but against the road, and seen more clearly in a view from the north-east, were two 17th-century projections (Pl. XLIV). The accommodation provided in this original building was equivalent to that of the wealthier yeoman farmer or smaller manor house of the period, but modest by the standards enjoyed by the residentiaries 100 years later.

The building works were in the hands of William Mompesson, canon residentiary at the commencement. As a young man he had been Rector of Eyam in Derbyshire, when the village was stricken by the plague in 1665-66. He sent his children away to be cared for, but remained with his wife to attend the villagers, persuading them to remain in isolation, cut off from outside contacts, so preventing the spread of infection to the villages around. His wife died, but he lived to become subsequently Rector of Eakring, Notts., Prebendary of Normanton and Vicar General in Southwell. He recorded the expenditure on the house in 17 pages of a ledger; work started late in 1689 or early in 1690, and the progress of the work may be followed (App. A). At first he recorded items of purchase of scaffold poles, lime, sand, bricks and timber, and payments to craftsmen and labourers; then 'to the matt maker for matts to keep out the rain before the house was glazed', and for painting of doors and windows, glass and putty. In 1693 special payments were made to prepare some rooms against the coming of the archbishop, but work continued until his final summary of accounts prepared for audit in 1695. The final cost amounted to £654 9s. 2d., most of which was raised by gifts from the archbishop, prebendaries and others, as well as by the sale of timber from the chapter estates.

An inventory of 1699 shows that the house was furnished in its essentials for the residentiary; cooking equipment in the kitchens, pantry, and brewhouse, and furniture in the dining room, library, study and chambers (App. F). A second inventory, made in 1717, 'upon Mr. Laybourn's entrance' lists further chambers, which were probably not furnished earlier. Each residentiary was supposed to check the inventory when he took up residence, and again at the end of his term.

An interesting sidelight into the contortions of financial management in which the chapter operated to finance building in this period is shown in a document in the British Museum. This manuscript is not dated, addressed, or signed but appears to be a draft for a royal submission, c.1689 in date. The only heading is 'The case of Southwell'[7];

> The Collegiate church there is an ancient foundation wherein are sixteen prebendaries out of which number there are commonly four residentiaries who, by the Statutes of this Church are to performe their residence in their proper prebendal houses if it may be done.
>
> But it so happens yt cannot be done for that some of them never had such houses, others have had theirs ruined by ye late wars, but all of them yt remain are in lease to particular persons who upon discharging their respective covenants do challenge a property in them.
>
> It is therefore thought advisable to erect one common house for this purpose that as they doe successively enter upon their residence they may successively have ye use thereof. But they are altogether disabled to goe through with such an undertaking by any advantages accrueing from ye common dividend.
>
> There is also another grievance which they are most studious to remedy. There is a certain village called Halam where there are a great number of people who pay all their tithes to ye church of Southwell, but have been all along destitute of a minister to supply ye cure there, by reason whereof very great disorders have been occasioned by ye church there gone much to decay.
>
> This expedient therefore is humbly offered both to raise money for ye building of a common resident house, and for supplying ye forlorne church of Halam (if his Majestie, who by Act of Parliament is made perpetuall Founder of ye said church, shall think fit to approve of it) that the number of vicars choral who are six, as they become vacant may be reduced to four, which is as many as ye church stand in need of, at least as ye Chapter knows how to give any encouragement unto. That out of their two respective allowances which is £30 per ann., ye Chapter may provide two probation singing men who for £5 per ann. will supply their wont in ye choire, and also have a liberty to assign over the remaining £20 of ye said salaries for term of yeares to such person or persons who shall lay down ye gross sum towards ye building of ye resident

house, in consideration whereof ye residentiaries in their respective turns will preach every fortnight at Halam between ye morning and evening prayers at Southwell. And for ye other Sunday they doubt not but ye parishioners there will provide some qualified person to take care of it. And given when ye term of years are expired then may ye said £20 per ann. be given to one of ye vicars choral ever after for his better encouragement and he to supply ye cure of Halam as aforesaid.

There is no record of this extraordinary arrangement ever being finally approved or carried out, but it is an ingenious form of mortgage in which the prebendaries and vicars choral would all be working off a loan for the benefit of a provision of a new house for the canon residentiary, and this would hardly gain unanimous approval. As for ultimately augmenting the salary of a vicar choral in this way, it is clear from the decree books that they were already holding preferments to vicarages in adjoining parishes and were pluralists in a similar way, but on a smaller scale, to the prebendaries themselves.

3. The Vicars' House, 1717

Once the residence house had been completed, there was a lull in building activity, but in 1717 the chapter had declared 'All vicars' houses are in good repair, except that reserved for the sixth vicar' and in 1719 the canon residentiary, Charles Chapell, was witnessing contracts with Richard Morley, carpenter, and Richard Ingleman to repair this house. The cost involved was small — only some £20 — but the work included building new brick walls on the ground floor stonework, and replacement of windows, doors, floors and staircase, so that the old house would have been in a very poor condition.

Further interest in these documents concerns the workmen employed. A Richard Morley was mentioned in a number of payments made by William Mompesson in the 1695 residence house accounts. A Richard Morley is later contracting for joinery work at the residence house in 1772, and the vicarage houses in 1780; two men of that name in Southwell died in 1775 and 1807 respectively, so that we see at least three generations of that name working for the chapter on building projects in the 17th and 18th centuries. The family of Ingleman is also closely connected with chapter work. Francis Ingleman, son of Richard, and described variously as bricklayer and mason, appears frequently in building records of the chapter in the later 18th century; some payments made to him indicate that he was contracting for labour and materials as an employer of labour himself, as well as being employed directly as a craftsman. Francis's son, in turn another Richard, was described as a mason, but also achieved more than local success as an architect. His responsibility for the grammar school built on the site of the former chantry priests' house, and the assembly rooms which replaced the Market House have already been mentioned. He was the architect for the House of Correction on the Burgage in 1807, and extensions to it in 1817; he was responsible for the design of much of the extension to the residence in the early

19th century; he was architect to the chapter from 1801 to 1808. His work outside Southwell included the county gaol at Devizes, Wilts., in 1810, the lunatic asylum at Lincoln in 1819-20, and the church of St. Clement, Worcester in 1822.[8] He died in 1838.

4. The Residence House, 1772

There are no further records of building work in hand for some years after 1719. The chapter authorised repairs to the residence house in 1744, but no details are available; at the same time they were leasing a vicarage house to anyone who would repair it at his own expense. In the period from 1772, however, we can trace a continuing activity in building both in the residence house and in the vicars' houses which persisted right through into the early years of the 19th century with few pauses. The records are by no means complete, and are at times difficult to separate into the various projects involved, but they do throw light on the processes of building in the period. In some accounts the chapter is employing workmen as direct labour through the canon residentiary or the receiver, settling its bills individually, and at other times employing an intermediary, as a contractor, to organise the work and authorise payments of what amounted to lump sum contracts.

The work which was started in 1772 was probably the construction of the projecting wing at the rear of the residence house. This is seen as a three-storied block in the Grimm drawing, the lowest floor being a semi-basement matching up with the original house, but the topmost floor being a full storey in height instead of the garrets of the main range (Pl. XLII). It may also be at this time that the original casements of the 1690 building were replaced by the later double-hung sash types. William Handley, described as a bricklayer of Newark, was appointed to carry out the work, supplying the design as well as materials and labour, and George Hodgkinson, who had been appointed receiver to the chapter in 1756, kept the accounts. Unfortunately the drawings have been lost, but the scheme was clearly on a large scale; the chapter raised more than £900 by the sale of timber from their estates at Warsop Wood, and payments to Francis Ingleman and Richard Morley (sons of the men employed in 1717), who subcontracted for much of the work, alone amounted to some £500. By 1776 the accommodation for the canon in residence had increased so much that the allowance of coal was totally inadequate, and the chapter agreed to an increase from nine to 12 tons for the two winter quarters, and from five and a half to eight tons for the two summer quarters. Even then the work was not complete, and minor works for the provision of 'a coach road, necessary houses, and other alterations' continued for the next year or more.

5. The Vicars' Houses, 1779

The next building projects to be undertaken – the rebuilding of the vicars' houses and the new front to the residence – were the most dramatic changes in the group at the east end of the Minster since they were erected in 1379. The central gateway in the west side of the quadrangle was the cause of considerable dispute in the 18th century. Archbishop Sharpe, at his visitation of 1693, had ordered

> All private back doors and outlets of the vicars houses to be stopped up, and the only entrance to be through the gate which was to be locked at 10 o'clock, and the key carried to the Residentiary.

This was obviously aimed at what were irregular practices amongst the vicars' choral (presumably young unmarried men!), but which were not curbed for long, and from 1716 the decree books record a long series of complaints about the conduct of the college. In 1716 Mr. William Neep, the vicar choral who was also schoolmaster, was admonished by the chapter for neglect of the boys, and it was also noted that two of the back doors of the vicarage had not been stopped up (Mr. Moore's and Mr. Neep's) contrary to the archbishop's injunctions; and in 1717, although the schoolmaster had then mended his ways, he still retained his private exit from his house. In 1734 and '35 there were angry incidents over the same problem. Mr. Bugg, coming home late at night frequently made a scene to be admitted, and on one occasion with two of his fellow vicars he broke the lock to get in. He was admonished by the residentiary, but unrepentantly questioned the right of the archbishop to make such a rule, an argument which was disallowed. In spite of this the dispute continued; on one occasion he took the gate off its hinges and threw it into the street, and on another filled the lock with lead shot to prevent its use. After setting workmen to open up a doorway from his house into the street, he was finally expelled. In 1736 three vicars were admonished for not residing in their proper houses, after several warnings; one of them, Mr. Leybourne, was actually residing at Bulmer, Yorks., at the time. He too was expelled in 1737, and the chapter was proceeding against him for neglect of his other vicarages at Edingley and Morton. One can perhaps understand some of the problems of the vicars, because this strict discipline was out of touch with the times, and the chapter was clearly not devoting adequate funds to the maintenance of their houses. At a chapter in April 1744 the prebendaries decreed 'the house in the Vicarage, late Mr. Gibson's being out of repairs; Ordered that the same be let to the best tenant that can be got, who shall lay down the money for the repairs thereof, under the directions of the Residentiary for the time being'. As Dickinson described the situation:

> from that period (i.e. 1379) to the present reign, no money seems to have been expended upon these buildings, but what absolute necessity, from time to time, required. A long lapse of years had rendered them extremely ruinous, and concomitent revolutions of manners and fashions had made them appear so incommodious, as no longer to be proper places of residence for gentlemen of liberal education, and of reasonable preferments.

That a stone and timber framed building of the quality shown in the Grimm drawing should have reached this state, even as old as it was, was almost certainly the result of neglect and insufficient maintenance. However, in 1779, the chapter acted with decision;

> whereas the houses of the vicars belonging to this church have long been in a state of decay and now threaten immediate distruction to their inhabitants, and on examination of the same by experienced workmen it appears that they are incapable of repair, and to prevent mischief as well as to preserve and turn to use the present materials it is necessary to take down and re-build the same. . .

The decree then goes on to list donations promised, mainly by the prebendaries themselves, by Lord Harborough (formerly a prebendary – the Rev. Robert Sherrard), and the archbishop, totalling £584.

> and whereas there is no reason to suppose that at any other time, or by any other manner a larger sum can be collected for this purpose, but on due consideration of the premises it appears that the present is the most favourable opportunity that can be expected for carrying this work into execution.

They then authorised the work to be started and paid for out of the subscriptions, and by any other means proposed in the future by the chapter.

Although there had been only six vicars choral for a long time, the two vicars who were also parish vicar, and schoolmaster of the grammar school respectively, were living in the town. The parish vicar was probably by then living on the site still called the Old Rectory, east of the modern grammar school in Church Street. The schoolmaster, in 1785, was accommodated with the boarders in the old chantry house behind the Crown Hotel.

Dickinson states:

> the boys not being very eligible neighbours, the Chapter have lately fixed that vicar who has care of the school in the ancient mansion of the chantry priests at a distance from the college. The parish minister's house is also distant from the college and wholly independent of the Chapter.

The scheme which was adopted in 1779 for rebuilding houses only for the remaining four vicars choral therefore allowed more space in the layout, as well as limiting the cost to something approaching their budget in donations.

Designs for the houses survive in the records. One drawing, unsigned, is of a five-bay, fully three-storied house with a gabled roof; the plan is L-shaped (i.e. an incomplete rectangle) (Pl.XLV). The houses as built are also five bays wide, but only two stories in height, with a third storey as an attic within roofs which are hipped; the plans are filled out to a complete rectangle but the rooms were reduced in size from this design, to achieve an overall economy of 100 sq. ft. per floor in each house. A note on the drawing reads 'This house with old materials 180 pounds', but in the event the houses were built of new bricks and there is no evidence of re-used timber in the structures. It was probably decided, as it would be today, that the cost of new bricks is not always more than the labour charges in recovering and cleaning up old materials from a demolition, even though the latter may be on site and save haulage. The houses eventually built, therefore, represent the intention to do so within the estimate of £180 per dwelling and even to economise on this figure.

A second plan, also unsigned, shows the whole group of four houses laid out as now, in pairs, at each side of the residence house (Pl.XLVI). The disposition of rooms approximates more closely in size and layout to the houses as built, and the lines are filled in yellow. Superimposed on this layout is an alternative outline of the group, shown in dotted lines, but out of square both within the group and in its relationship with the original residence house. A note on this drawing reads 'The dotted line shows the ground plat by Mr. Ingleman's plan, & the plan shown in yellow shows how it ought to be, and how the A.B. [i.e. Archbishop] wishes it may be'. Ingleman appears to have opted for a layout which, by its irregularity, may have been based on the foundations of the north and south ranges of the old college buildings. It is interesting to see that Ingleman who, throughout this period, appears as a bricklayer and mason, sometimes contracting for materials and labour, is now being consulted in matters of design, especially since he had been dismissed in 1779 for insolence. The author of this drawing may have been William Handley of Newark, who had already been supervising the work to the residence house in 1772, although there is no record of him ever being consulted over the design: the handwriting of the note on the drawing has strong similarities with that of William Lumby who later produced the design for the new front to the residence house although the first mention of his employment is in 1785. Both drawings show considerable skill in the draughtsmanship, and education in the handwriting.

Detailed accounts for the building of the house were not retained, but George Hodgkinson, the receiver, prepared a summary (App. B). Money received for the project came almost entirely from donations, and amounted to £606; and his final balance in 1781 gave the cost as £618 16s 6½d. Some finishing work may then have been outstanding, but even so the four vicars' houses were achieved on a very slim budget, costing less than the original residence house 90 years earlier. They remain today substantially as they were in 1781, almost stark in their lack of ornament, depending for their effect on the proportions of the windows and their spacings in the walls, and on the grouping of the linked rectangular blocks around the open courtyard.

6. The Residence, 1785

When once the vicars' houses had been completed, the residence house, terminating the group at the west end, must have presented a facade sadly out of fashion with the time, and the chapter next set about the problem of bringing it up to date. John Carr of York had been working in Nottinghamshire since 1774, firstly at Newark on the design and building of the town hall and assembly rooms, and later at Colwick Hall, Nottingham racecourse grandstand, and the reconstruction of Clifton Hall. The chapter at Southwell consulted him in 1783, and he was paid 15 guineas for a survey and plans for an addition to the residence house, but by then he was probably too busy on larger schemes to deal with a small problem of minor changes to the residence house, and there is no record that he actually

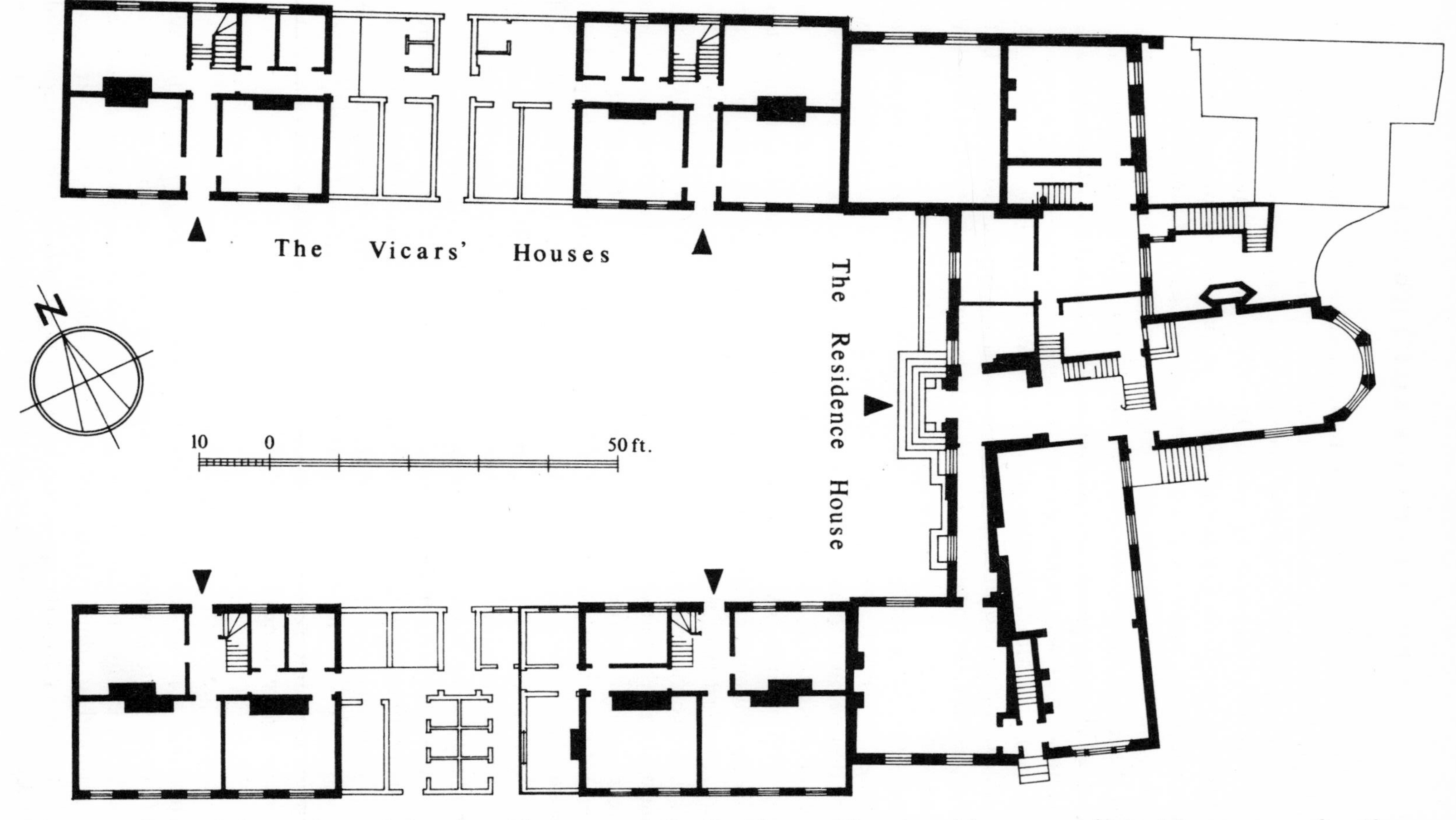

Fig 11: *Ground floor plans of the vicars' houses and the Residence. The vicars' houses are linked by groups of outhouses placed behind high walls. The west facade of the Residence House was added in front of the earlier building, in 1785, to complete the rectangular courtyard.*

carried out the work. The man eventually responsible for the project was William Lumby. Lumby, son of Thomas a master carpenter, had reconstructed Doddington Church, Lincs., in 1770, and had been appointed Surveyor and Clerk of the works at Lincoln Cathedral in 1775. In 1785 the Southwell chapter was authorising a payment of £10 to him for the preparation of plans for the choir and residence house, and it is possible that either Carr had drawn him into the project after his own survey or that Lumby was in competition with him. A similar situation had already arisen at Lincoln where Carr had prepared designs for the gaol in 1774; after delays, the scheme finally adopted was that submitted in 1785 by Lumby, who also supervised the work.

A drawing in the Minster library is signed by William Lumby and dated 1785 (Pl. XLVII). It shows two alternative elevations drawn with considerable skill, the upper one very like the facade as eventually completed, being marked 'this is the design approved by the Archbishop'; the lower drawing shows a wider elevation, having two bays either side of the central feature instead of one, and includes the return wings at the sides as eventually achieved. If John Carr himself did not inspire the designs his influence shows strongly in Lumby's work. The prominence given to the centre three bays by stepping the wall forward and capping the projection with a pediment, and the front entrance with its simple portico of two Roman Doric columns, entablature, and pediment, can both be seen in a loftier version at Langford Hall, near Newark, completed by John Carr c.1790, and the whole design has the severity characteristic of Carr's work elsewhere. When the new groups of vicar's houses had been built in 1780 the old residence house was left lying at an angle across the west end of the courtyard, and this new facade of 1785 squared it up to the strong lines of Vicars' Court, being applied to the front of the house as if it were a stage-set with very little reference to the disposition of the rooms behind (Pl. XLIII). The modern survey exposes this, and shows that the two sets of windows to the south of the entrance light only passages tapering on plan across the former front wall of the old house (Fig. 11).

Some re-modelling of the house was also planned: part of a report in Lumby's handwriting proposed enlarging the kitchen, moving the stairs, and changes in the servants' hall, butler's pantry, larder, and the chamber above. His estimate for this scheme was £578 14s. 0d., but clearly the work went further because his later statement of expenditure was £705 8s. 5d.,(App. C), and the receiver noted the total spent on the residence house in 1788 as £1,128.

7. The 19th Century.

The pattern and scale of chapter business had drastically changed from the days, only 100 years earlier, when William Mompesson was recording payments to individual labourers by the day, and his purchases of materials in great detail. The chapter returned to the problems of the residence house in 1806, 'It being absolutely necessary that the residence house be repaired'. The chapter approved plans by Richard Ingleman to raise the roof of the house; to construct a new carriage entrance through the churchyard to the west door of the house and to close that at the east side; to re-build the north-east wing; and one 'for the uniformity of the east front of the residence house and for a better disposition of the offices'. A scheme for the alteration of the south wing was deferred.

These drawings unfortunately are also missing from the records, but it is clear that the schemes went beyond the work of repairs, and entailed drastic remodelling of much of the rear part (the east side of the house), and the north wing, although Lumby's facade of 1785 was happily left intact. Thereafter the financial arrangements of the chapter combined repairs of the church fabric and the residence house into one fund, and Geo. H. Barrow, who was then receiver for the chapter, prepared a statement of receipts and expenditure for the house separately for the years 1806-09 showing a total of over £3,500 spent in this work (App. D). There is no record of further major works of building at the residence house from 1809 until modern times, when the wheel had gone full circle. The house, a rambling accretion of four stages of change and expansion since 1690, was too large to manage under modern conditions. The basement rooms had already been abandoned to storage and a kitchen installed on the principal floor; in 1956 the north and south wings were demolished, leaving only the present screen walls to link the east facade to Vicars' Court. The architect for this work was Mr. Vernon Royle, of Messrs. Broadhead and Royle, who carried out the work with skill and in sympathy with the original character of the building. His surveys of the house before alterations are the basis of the plans produced here.

Notes to Chapter Five

1. The original is in the White Book of Southwell, but is transcribed in Dugdale's *Monasticon.*
2. Copy in Notts. C.R.O., ref. DDM 105/44.
3. M. W. Barley, *House and Home* (1963), plate 20.
4. Geoffrey Martin, *The Town* (1961), plate 6.
5. Anthony Emery, *Dartington Hall* (1970), p. 114.
6. Mark Girouard, *Robert Smythson* (1966), pp. 83 and 127.
7. British Museum Additional M.S.S., ref. 28088 f46, of Index of 1854-75.
8. H.M. Colvin, *A Biographical Dictionary of English Architects 1660-1820* (1954), p. 306.

VI

The prebendal houses

The Prebendal Houses

THE MEN WHO were prebendaries in the college at Southwell varied in their aims, abilities, and achievements as men do in all walks of life. William of Wykeham has already been cited as the example of a prominent churchman and statesman of the late 14th century to whom a prebend at Southwell could have meant little more than one of many sources which made up his considerable total income. Then there was Lancelot Andrews, prebendary of North Muskham at the end of the 16th century, who was simultaneously Master of Pembroke College, Cambridge, and Prebendary (later Dean) of Westminster. He later held, in succession, the bishoprics of Chichester, Ely and Winchester, and was therefore so closely involved in high affairs in the church that he could not have been resident in Southwell frequently or for long. Nevertheless he did take up periodic residence, and some of his family remained in the town after his death. At the end of the 18th century Sir Richard Kaye, Prebendary of North Muskham and Dean of Lincoln, held no less than five livings; he was also Rector of Kirby in Ashfield, Rector of St. Marylebone, Middlesex, Archdeacon of Nottingham, and Prebendary of Thorngate, Lincoln. He was one of the most assiduous in his concern for Southwell; his attendance at chapters is regularly recorded in the Decree Book, and his generosity in the donation of books to the library is also acknowledged several times. But it is very noticeable that of the 16 prebendaries of his time, attendance at chapters was often not more than three, and the same few names recur constantly.

In contrast with these, William Mompesson, Prebendary of Normanton at the end of the 17th century, has been seen devoting his energies meticulously and almost exclusively to the affairs of the chapter, and the supervision of the work on the new residence house. Later there was John Thomas Becher, who was first a vicar choral and then from 1819 was prebendary of South Muskham until his death in 1848. He worked untiringly at putting the chapter's affairs and records in order, and at public works in the town. His pioneer work as chairman of the Incorporation of Parishes made the workhouse at Southwell an example which influenced the reform of the Poor Law about 1834. Of course there were many others who took the income of a prebendary and contributed little to church or state in return, but amongst the more conscientious the system of prebendal appointments, when there was some restraint on non-residence, worked tolerably well.

An important factor amongst the reasons for non-residence was the customary form of lease which was applied individually to prebendal estates and the mansions at Southwell alike. Rentals were based on valuations made for the tithes given by Pope Nicholas to Edward I in 1291. These provided grossly inadequate returns in later times, and in practice the real source of profit for the lessor was in the 'fines', as capital sums, which could be levied on the renewal of a lease. The successor to a prebend, therefore, might find himself with nothing more than the ground rent as his income until such times as a lease could be renewed and another fine exacted; in the event of a long lease having been granted immediately prior to his appointment he might not even live to benefit from the next fine. This then would give small inducement to take up residence. Prior to the 16th century leases of 99 or even 150 years were common, but the Ecclesiastical Leases Act of 1571 restricted leases of ecclesiastical and eleemosynary corporations to a maximum of 21 years or three lives, except in towns where 40-year leases were permitted. A further Act of 1572 gave a definition of a town which would have excluded Southwell. The prebendaries anxious to avoid mortmain and to retain personal control of their properties, preferred the lease for three lives as likely to be longer than 21 years, and so attract a larger fine for personal remuneration. The three-life leases would be valid until the death of the last of three nominees, who would naturally include children in good health; but it was also customary to renew the leases on the death of any nominee by inserting a new name on the payment of a reduced fine. The value of the fine usually authorised by the chapter was 1½ year's income; a property valued at £2,000 would produce, at five per cent interest, an income of £100 per annum. In the first case the property would be leased at its full value, i.e. £2,000 for 21 years or three lives, and ground rental which would be based on Pope Nicholas' valuation and therefore nominal. If renewed during that time, either by an extension equivalent to the lapsed period or by the insertion of a fresh nominee, the fine due to the lessor would be one and a half years' income, or £150. At times the renewals occur every few years, but even so, over a very long period of time in the succession of prebendal appointments, the total income was far below that which would have been received from a realistic rental without the complication of fines. In practice, therefore, the real beneficiary was the lessee who held the property over a long period, possibly sub-letting as a whole or in parts at rentals based on contemporary values. An example of this is shown in the Rent Book of Sir Richard Sutton of Norwood for 1788;[1] he held the Manor of Halloughton from the Prebendary, the Rev. R.P. Goodenough, at that time, at a rental of £10 7s. 6d. p.a., plus an annual payment of £10 to the curate. On the other hand the rentals he received from individual tenants of the farms totalled £722 14s. 0d. p.a., and even with Land Tax at £42 0s. 6d. p.a. he was left with a handsome profit. Leases of prebendal properties were often retained in families for several generations, and renewal was assumed as a right; William Edge in 1765 bequeathed his leasehold estate of Sacrista Prebend to his wife

Elizabeth, with a proviso in his will to take money from his personal effects to add another life to the lease. It is small wonder that a lessee with such security of tenure was often prepared to rebuild and enlarge the prebendal house to a substantial scale and at his own expense, since it was a form of leasehold tenure with no realistic time of expiry.

The negotiation of prebendal leases was carried out individually by the prebendaries, and was at no time a function of the chapter, and although they were required to be recorded in the chapter lease books very few were written up. As one would expect documentary evidence, although very incomplete, indicates a very mixed pattern of management. The archbishop, at his visitation of 1484, censored the chapter for 'the want of repair of prebendal houses, some of which have fallen down'. In 1592, the act books of the archdeaconry of Nottingham record a number of meetings of the court in the prebendal house of North Muskham at Southwell, so that at that date it would have been occupied by clergy, even if the prebendary himself may not have been in residence. In 1650, the parliamentary survey of church property includes references to the prebendal houses of North Muskham, Rampton, and Norwell Palishall, all in lease to private individuals. Forty years later the prebendaries were still using the Civil War to excuse the condition of their houses; at Archbishop Thomas Lamplugh's visitation in 1690 they reported:

> Some of the prebendal houses are in decay, at least not so decently kept as they ought to be. For instance the house of Norwell Overhall belonging to the best prebend is some part of it (lately) thatched with straw, and some of the windows thereof instead of being filled with glass are stopped with clay. The house of North Muskham is most of it demolished, suffering damage (as is said) during the late Rebellion. The house of Oxton the first part is in miserable decay as many of the materials embezzled but few years ago.

At the visitation in 1693, the prebendaries reported 'the prebendal houses are some of them in good repair, others in bad, and others are not to be found at all in being'. But the archbishop this time was John Sharpe who did so much to restore good order and discipline to a chapter which was in 'distraction and animosity'. His criticism was strong and specific.

> furthermore whereas in our late Visitation of the Church of Southwell we found several of the prebendal houses to be much dilapidated and fallen to decay through want of timely and necessary reparations, most particularly the house belonging to the Prebend of Norwell Overhall, North Muskham, and the two Oxtons. And though we do not doubt that the Prebendaries of these prebends had at that time notice given them of these dilapidations they have already at that time given orders for the repairing of these houses. Yet nevertheless we do think it fit that they should again be put in mind of this matter to the intent they should quicken their tenants or those persons they employ to a speedy dispatch of this affair. And therefore we do enjoyn that the repairs of these houses be begun as soon as may be, and the longest time we

> give for the finishing them is till our next visitation, and if by that time all the houses be not in full and good repairs we shall think ourselves obliged to prosecute those that are faulting in such matters as the law allows us to direct.

The archbishops in their subsequent visitations do not concern themselves unduly with the state of the prebendal houses; either the prebendaries were left in undisputed control of their estates, or John Sharpe's admonition of 1693 had its desired effect. It is certainly possible that the older parts of Sacrista, Norwell Overhall, North Muskham, Normanton, and Woodborough prebends may date from that time, and it is also significant that Sharpe instructs the prebendaries to put pressure on the lessees to undertake the necessary improvements, showing that it was expected of a tenant on a lease of three lives to do so. William Rastall, writing nearly 100 years later, gives an account of the houses in his time which shows that they had been improved greatly in recent years. Only Woodborough and Palishall are then described as 'decayed' and 'in very poor condition'; by the time of R.P. Shilton's account in 1818, Palishall had been demolished and new houses had been erected on the site; Woodborough received this treatment soon afterwards.

The pattern which emerges from the records is one of houses which had originally been established for the residence of the prebendaries themselves, but which were old, and frequently in lease, even at the Restoration. They had been allowed to fall into disrepair by neglect, and in some cases by vandalism, undergoing partial restoration at least, at the end of the 17th century. They were finally drastically remodelled, extended, and even rebuilt, in the last years of the 18th century by lessees who were then gentlemen of sufficient means to provide themselves with a substantial residence, even if it was leasehold, providing the security of tenure was over a reasonable period. The houses were finally sold out of the church under an Act of 38 Geo.III and a revising Act of 39 Geo.III, which entitled corporate bodies to dispose of property for the sale and redemption of Land Tax; the monies thus received were applied to clear the tax on the rest of the prebendal estates. Commissioners appointed under the Acts were party to the conveyances; in this way the Rev. William Smelt, Prebendary of Norwell Palishall, sold his prebendal mansion to William Revill, joiner, in 1802, and the Rev. Charles Harcourt, Prebendary of Norwell Overhall, sold the messuage of the prebend in 1837 to Robert Forster, surgeon. The chapter, too, as a body carried out these transactions; in 1799 it was

> decreed that a certain number of decayed cottages and small parcels of land in Southwell be sold, and the money arising by sale thereof be appropriated for the purchase of the Land Tax payable by the Chapter for the Residence House, Church Yard, Chantry House, House in occupation of Samuel Sandaver, and Warsop Wood.

Rastall identified 11 of the prebendal sites (Fig.3) – Norwell Overhall, Norwell Palishall, North Muskham, Oxton I and II, Dunham, Normanton, Rampton, South Muskham, Woodborough, and Sacrista – and his accounts are, in most cases, supported by the title deeds of existing houses. Only in the case of Woodborough is he mistaken in locating it in terms identical with those of Oxton II; but then he goes on to say that Norwell III had been sited between Normanton and Woodborough. That would place Woodborough Prebend on the site now occupied by the modern house 'Ashleigh', and Norwell III where 'Edgehill' now stands. Beckingham was probably on the other side of Church Street, east of the Residence and on the land now occupied by the Minster Grammar School; this would conform to the record of the building of the common house for the vicars choral by Richard de Chesterfield in 1379 'next to the prebendary of Beckingham's mansion'. Only the mansions of Halloughton, Eaton, and Leverton remain completely unidentified in printed or documentary sources; and the Certificates of the Chantry Commissioners in the 16th century do not record houses for the prebends of Eaton, Norwell III or Woodborough. It is significant that these last five prebends are, with the exception of Sacrista, the poorest endowments; the Sacristan had his special responsibilities in the church, but the others were unlikely to have maintained houses of any substance in the town, and were probably early losses.

Norwell Overhall

William Clay, who had been steward at Southwell for the Archbishop of York before the Civil War, leased the mansion house of Norwell Overhall in 1668, and it remained in the hands of his descendants until the early years of the 19th century. In 1758 the messuage was divided to provide marriage settlements for the children of John Clay, but by that time it was already sublet in two parts. Although singled out for mention as in a ruinous condition in 1690, the family improved the property during their tenure, so that Rastall could describe it as 'a very large pile of building. The major part of it very old but in good repair'. It seems at that time to have reverted to single occupation because it was Susanna, widow of Augustus Clay, who built the range of rooms across the front about 1784, probably for her own occupation.

The house was sold out of the church in 1837 and both parts were subsequently subject to several periods of change. The two parts today are represented by the National Westminster Bank, with Minster Lodge adjoining it on the east side (Pl. IV). The bank premises have been rebuilt, except for a small part of the front range of rooms, but a survey made in 1961 shows it to have had a wing extending to the rear, i.e. at right-angles to the front, similar to the form of Minster Lodge (Fig.12). The oldest portion of the early building on the site still existing is the north-east corner of the east wing (Minster Lodge), the east and north walls of which are rubble masonry up to first floor level, minimum 2 ft. 3 in. thick. In the east side is a 14th-century two-light window at ground level, which appears to be contemporary with the stonework around it, and during recent years, when part of the ground floor boarding was lifted, rubble foundations appeared to continue the line of this wall forward to within five feet

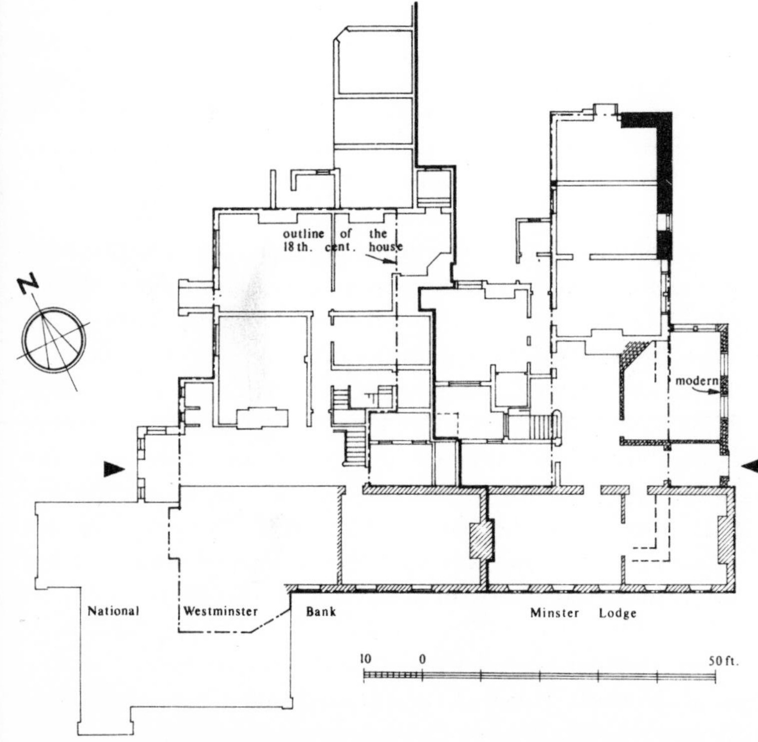

Fig 12: *The prebendal house of Norwell Overhall*
(a) *The National Westminster Bank and Minster Lodge seen from Church Street.*
(b) *Ground floor plan of the Bank House and Minster Lodge, prior to the demolition of the former, c.1960. The whole propperty has undergone several periods of re-building since 1785, but the late 18th-century range of rooms across the front remains intact in Minster Lodge. The only remaining medieval masonry is shown in black. The outline of the 18th-century house is assumed from only fragmentary evidence, but indicates a possible persistence of a late medieval plan.*

of the inside of the front (south) wall of the present house. Other walls are later constructions in brickwork, but the west wall of this wing has the remains of one timber framing post built in from first floor to eaves level.

Nothing more is known of the form of the house before the 17th century, so that interpretation cannot be conclusive, but the combined form of two wings at right angles to a central range may have been the persistence of a late medieval H-plan which incorporated an earlier range as an east wing. The central hall would have been rebuilt in the subdivision of the house in the 18th century, and in turn covered by the additions across the front made by Susanna Clay.

North Muskham

The strictures of Archbishop Sharpe on the condition of certain prebendal mansions may have had some effect, so that the house of North Muskham, which had been amongst those singled out, was probably rebuilt at the end of the 17th century in some acceptable form. It was certainly in lease again by 1722, and in 1769 was taken by Thomas Falkner, a surgeon of Southwell, who improved the property so much that Rastall described it as 'a handsome new brick house, lately rebuilt by the present lessee . . . Contiguous to the house is a good garden, as also an orchard and yard with stables and other outbuildings in good repair'.

No parts of the medieval building exist, but the centre of the rear wing which extends at right angles to the road is comparable with other 17th-century buildings in the area and may be part of a single range of rooms built c.1700, added to later, with outbuildings by Falkner. His four children inherited the property at his death in 1794, and purchased the freehold in 1809 under the Land Tax Redemption Act from the prebendary, then Sir Richard Kaye. They raised a mortgage of £700 in the following year, and it was probably at this time that the present imposing facade and range of rooms across the front were added. (Pl. IV & Fig.13).

The house later became a school. This venture may have been started by Falkner's two remaining daughters, Catherine and Susannah, who raised a further charge on the mortgage in 1827, but they sold the property two years later to the Rev. Charles Fletcher, who built it up to a considerable size. The Rev. George Elliott purchased it in 1850, and the preliminary agreement listed the property as 'all that freehold school, mansion house, playground garden and premises . . . plus forty boys' bedsteads, and hangings, and all the desks and forms of the schoolroom'. Elliott, however, was not so successful; he raised £2,300 by mortgage for the purchase but was unable to pay his debts. The property was taken over by his creditors in 1865, and was sold the following year to John Kirkland who founded the firm of solicitors still occupying the premises.

Norwell Palishall

The prebendal mansion of Norwell Palishall, sometimes called Palacehall, was mentioned in the certificates of the Chantry Commissioners in 1546 and in the

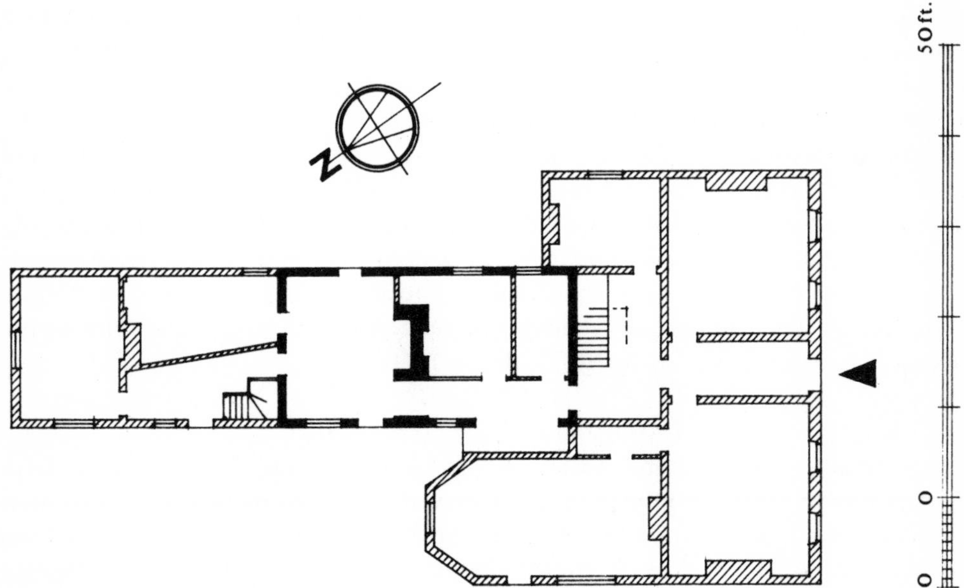

Fig 13: *The prebendal house of North Muskham*
(a) *The frontage to Church Street*

(b) *Ground floor plan. The oldest part of the house is shown in black, and is probably late 17th century in date. Additions were made in the late 18th century and the range of rooms built across the front c.1809.*

Parliamentary Survey of 1650, but nothing more is known of its early history. Rastall saw it as 'a large house but extremely old and in very bad condition', and it had then been occupied since about 1765 by Francis Ingleman the mason. A Grimm drawing of the time, shows it to have been a hall of late medieval type, with a cross passage, and with cross wings at the ends (Pl. XLVIII); one wing had a jettied first floor in timber framing, and the front wall of the hall appears to have been raised, probably late in the 16th century, to accommodate an attic storey, capped with four little gables.

In 1788 the house was divided into two parts; three-fifths, consisting of the east wing and hall, was leased to Thomas Falkner who at that time also leased, and probably resided at, the adjoining prebendal house of North Muskham; two-fifths, which comprised the west wing, was leased by William Revill a joiner. The indentures of lease are of particular interest in that each has a plan of the portion of the prebendal property involved in the transaction, which provides an accuracy of identification rare in legal documents of the period (Pl. XLIX). When Falkner died Revill took over his lease also, demolished the whole house, and borrowed £900 from Richard Barrow on mortgage to build three new houses on the site. One house, against the east boundary (now Willoughby House), was purchased by William Wylde; a second, against the west boundary (now Palishall House), was retained by Revill (Pl. IV); and a third house was built for his own occupation to the rear of the prebendal site. The latter has been demolished, but the land included an orchard and croft at the rear, a timber yard, a shop, and a narrow garden running down to the road frontage, between the other two houses. In 1802 the prebendary, the Rev. William Smelt, sold the freeholds to Wylde and Revill respectively, for the redemption of land tax, as in the cases of Norwell Overhall and North Muskham. The indentures of sale, dated 1796, between Wylde and Revill is also accompanied by a sketch plan of the house; it had two rooms at the front, arranged symmetrically about a central entrance, with a staircase in a projecting wing at the rear, very similar in general layout to the final form of the Falkner house on the site of North Muskham prebend.

Oxton and Cropwell (Oxton II)

The prebend of Oxton and Cropwell, or Crophyll, was the second to have endowments of land in Oxton, and also received part of its income from Cropwell and Hickling. It was also recorded as Oxton Altera Pars, or Oxton Second Part; and the mansion in Southwell stood within extensive grounds between Sacrista prebend on the south and the *Saracen's Head* Inn on the north. The site was divided down its length by a public footpath, which still exists as a right of way, from Westgate on the eastern boundary, to the open land on the west, linking up with paths into Barlane (the modern Queen Street). As we have already seen, the chapter petition to the archbishop in 1689, mentions Oxton II as the only house available for residence of the prebendaries, but on his visitation in 1693, the archbishop included it amongst those urgently needing repairs; either its condition was not so ruinous, or its mention was an error at the latter time. Lessees of the 18th century exploited the site thoroughly, sub-letting the house in tenements and building along the frontage in Westgate. Finally in 1803, the Land Tax Redemption Acts were again evoked and the prebendary sold the freeholds of the subdivided property.

The changes of the next few years resulted in the complete and permanent disintegration of the prebendal property. In 1811, William Hodgson Barrow, nephew of the Rev. Dr. Barrow, built the large house on the section of garden south of the footpath which is now the office of Dowson, Wadsworth and Sellars, solicitors. The croft at the rear (west) of the site changed hands several times, and was ultimately purchased by the *Saracen's Head* to form the present inn yard. The remainder, including the prebendal house, was partitioned in 1804 by R.P. Shilton [2] who retained the house and land immediately around it; a small part of the road frontage was sold to complete the site needed by the trustees of the new assembly rooms in 1805, and two shops were added to complete the road frontage (Fig.4). Also in 1805 Shilton purchased a right of way across the land at the rear to give vehicle access into Queen Street, and when the Methodist chapel was built in 1839 on leased land behind, this access was maintained in the cross passage of the portico-type front entrance. Shilton then raised money by mortgages – £400 in 1808, and a further £200 in 1810 – which would have provided the resources for improvements to the house at that time. The front of the house (to the east) was re-fenestrated with double-hung sash windows, roughly symmetrically placed about a semi-circular headed doorway, and the external walls were rendered; the layout of rooms was changed by the insertion of new cross partitions, and new fireplaces and flues were built in. Some notes of 1823 attached to the deeds describe the premises as 'a remarkably substantial brick and tiled house', and list two tenements built under the back roof, with four others adjoining nearby.

The end of the mansion house came in 1970; by then all its land had been alienated, the Methodist chapel had been built close to its west side, and extensions to the *Saracen's Head* to the east; the principal ground floor room had been converted to a Memorial Hall by driving a new entrance off the public right of way at the side. Only at the north-west corner was there any external evidence of an earlier building in parts of timber framing in the gables, and in the English bond of the brickwork exposed (Pl.LI). The significance of the house had been forgotten, and it had escaped listing as a building of architectural and historic interest, so that its destruction to make way for further extensions of the *Saracen's Head* was unopposed.

The house had been the earliest brick building in Southwell and consequently became known as the Red Prebend, and even identified as such in deeds and records; the earliest reference is in the grant of the prebendal mansion with other properties of the dissolved chapter to Sir Henry Sydneye in 1553, where it was called 'Le Reed Prebende',[3] External walls were 21 in. to 22 in. thick at the

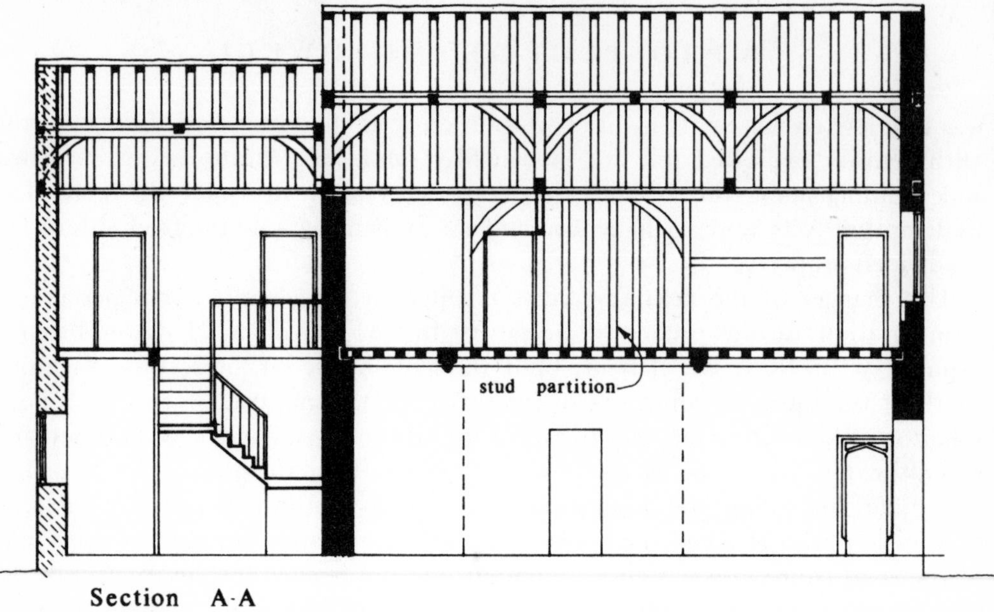

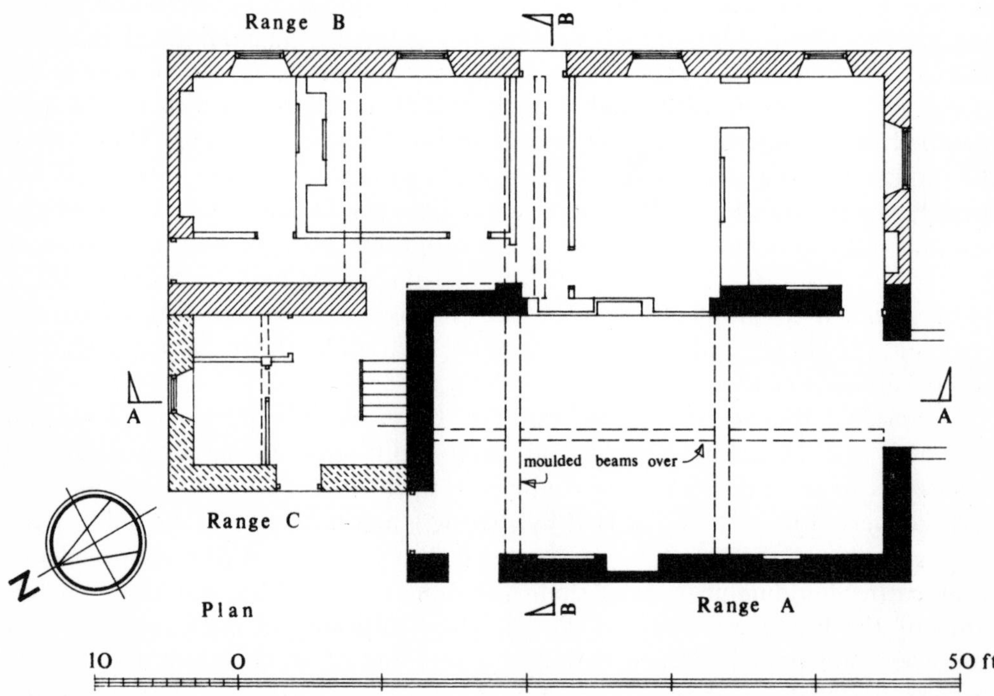

Fig 14: *The prebendal house of Oxton II*
(a) *Section A-A*
(b) *Ground floor plan. The internal partitions and fireplaces in Range B, and the windows in the external walls, were all part of the remodelling of c.1810. The first floor over Ranges A and B was originally open to the roof; Range B had been divided into four rooms by stud partitions at the three trussed frames.*

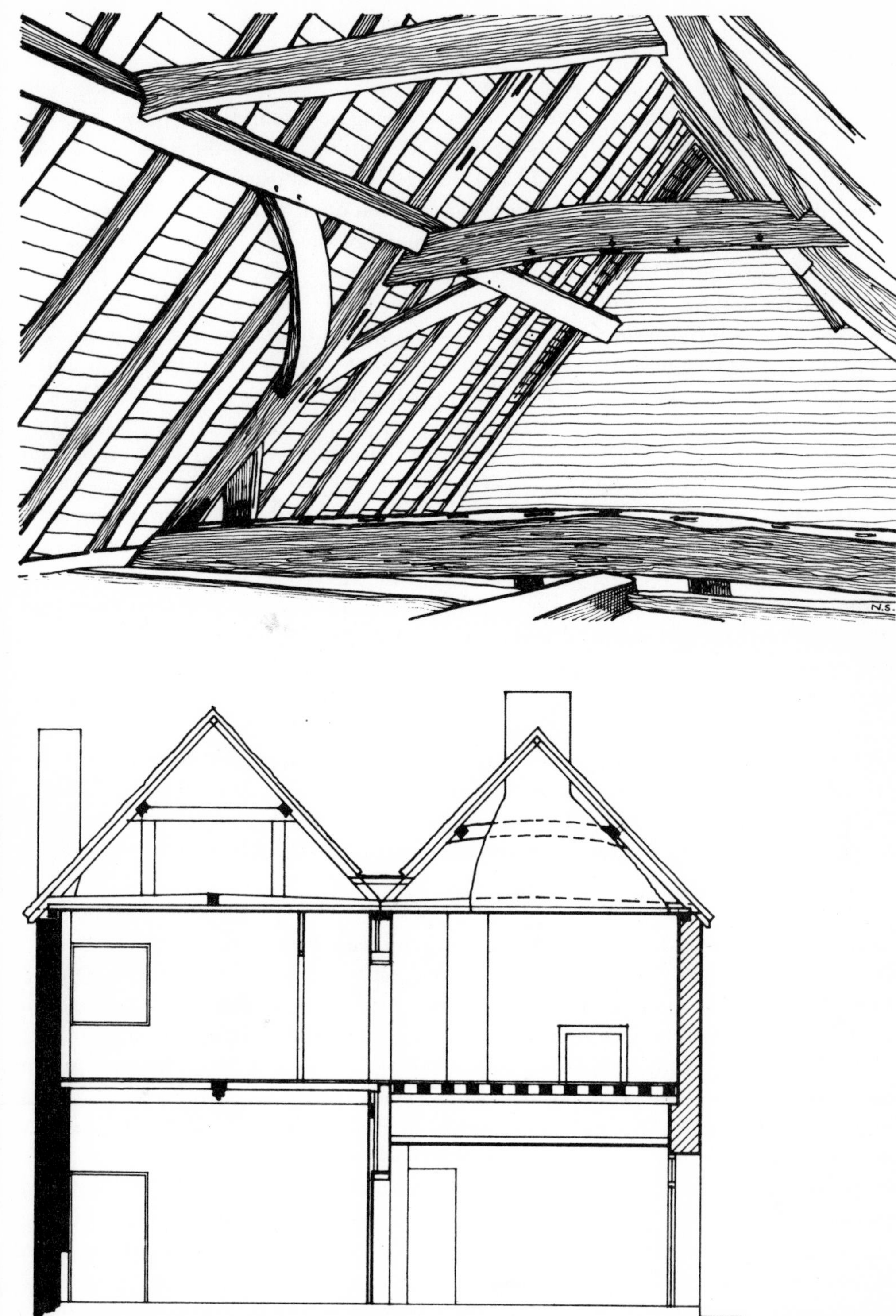

Fig 15: *The prebendal house of Oxton II*
(a) *Sketch of the construction of the roof over Range B*
(b) *Cross Section B-B*

ground floor, and 15 in. thick above first floor level (Pl.LXII). It had been constructed in three stages, the final result being a 'double pile' house (i.e. two parallel ranges of rooms, roofed separately, with a long valley gutter on the central spine wall) (Figs.14 & 15).[4] Range A had consisted of a large ground floor room, with a chamber above which had been open to the roof. Alternate roll and hollow mouldings on the transverse main beams, and on the longitudinal subsidiary beams supporting the first floor were early 16th-century in character. Against this ranges B and C had been built later, although the type of roof structure over those parts could not have been much later than 1630 in date. The original internal arrangements at ground and first floor levels in ranges B and C were impossible to interpret accurately in the light of the drastic remodelling in the 19th century.

Range A, being the earliest part of the whole structure, is difficult to place in the chronology of medieval house types, but it may be explained as a cross wing built against an earlier, and timber-framed Hall, which had stood at right angles to the road frontage. The placing of the hall with its gable end to the road would have been dictated by the narrowness of the site, bisected as it was by the footpath; and the stud partitioning in the east side of range A would then have been internal. Ranges B and C would have replaced the hall, turning the axis of the house, but the similarities in the parts were such that they could not have been constructed at widely separated intervals of time. The thickness of the brickwork is too great to have been a replacement of an earlier timber framed structure, and was therefore contemporary with the beams built in to support the first floor of range A; the beams to the cloister walk roof of Jesus College, Cambridge, are similar in section and are dated 1510.[5] The Red Prebend takes its place as one of the earliest uses of brickwork in the County.

Dunham

The mansion house of the prebend of Dunham was situated in Westgate, south of the Minster yard (Pl. V). The present building is the property of the Rural District Council, and in recent years suffered the indignity of the addition of a two-storied office extension at the side. The oldest part of the house remaining is a range of rooms across the front, consisting of two lofty stories with attics above, built in the late 16th or early 17th centuries; it was built of brick, and is only one room deep, except where a small room projects to the rear at the north end, and was described in the 1650 Parliamentary Survey of Livings as

> All that mansion house in Southwell aforesaid, commonly called the Prebend House of Dunham containing a hall, two parlour, a buttery, with seaven chambers and closets over them, a stable, outbuildings, a yard, orchard and gardens.

The seven chambers referred to would have included four attic rooms, and a Grimm drawing in the British Museum shows this house, seven bays long, each bay capped by a steeply pitched gable on the front wall against the line of the

Fig 16: *The prebendal house of Dunham*
(a) *View from the houses across Westgate. The 19th-century additions to the house, on the left, have now been hidden by a new wing of offices.*

(b) *Ground floor plan. The 17th-century building is shown in black.*

main roof on the axis of the building (Pl. LII). The 17th-century windows still remained at that time in the first floor and attic rooms, but the ground floor windows, and one at first floor level, had been replaced by 18th-century double-hung sash types. It was probably a rebuild of an earlier house on the site, and the roof today is still framed with timbers of irregular sizes (Fig.17), many bearing halvings and mortices from previous use, and some having mouldings of medieval section worked in their length.

After the Civil War, and until the early part of the 19th century, the house was in lease to the Lowe family who also resided there; they were prominent in the county and were allied by marriage to the Sherbrookes of Oxton, and the Clays of Southwell. An inventory of 1723, taken on the death of Samuel Lowe, shows him to have been a man of considerable wealth, leaving over £3,000 loaned out at interest and due to him in rents; the goods in his house included a harpsichord in the parlour, clocks, mirrors, pictures and £100 worth of plate in the hall and chambers, and in his barn stood two coaches with horses (App.J).

The accommodation of the house at that time had not been increased from the Survey of 1650. It was improved by Sherbrooke Lowe c.1780 who inserted the double-hung sash windows, and who was probably responsible for removing the

Fig 17: *Dunham prebendal house: roof structure. The form is typical of the late 17th century, but many timbers are re-used from an earlier, late medieval, building.*

little gables and attic windows across the front and substituting the roof parapet; it may also have been he who stuccoed the walls. George Hodgkinson Barrow married Elizabeth, widow of Edward Richard Lowe in 1805, and subsequently purchased the freehold of the property. He added the rear range of rooms which have semi-circular ends overlooking the garden, and plaster and joinery decoration of a Regency flavour (Fig.16); some remodelling of the front range would have been carried out at this time, including the addition of the porch, and the re-building of the staircase.

Oxton the First Part (Oxton I)

The visitations of 1690 and '93 show the prebendal mansion of Oxton I to have been in a state of ruin not only through neglect, but also by the robbing of its materials for use elsewhere. The house had stood in Church Street to the north of the east end of the church (Pl.LV), between the prebends of North Muskham and Woodborough and, assuming that it conformed to the pattern of other prebendal houses there and in Westgate, it had been sited 40 to 60 ft. back from the present road line. The new house, known today as Cranfield House, would therefore have been built behind the earlier one, and is stylistically 1700-1720 in date. The simple four-square plan (Fig.18); the *correct* proportions of the facade; the mixture of brick walls with stone dressings to quoins, string courses, and window openings; the neat composition of the central entrance with the window above; and the dormers in the hipped roof resting on an overhanging cornice, are all in the very latest fashion of the period (Pl.LIV). It is an exquisite exercise in classical design which has no equal in the town, all the more remarkable in following so closely upon the completion of the first residence house which conceded nothing to post Restoration ideas of architectural elegance. The Palladianism of Newdigate House in Nottingham's Castle Gate may have shown the way in the later years of the 17th century, but the lesson was a long time in reaching sleepy Southwell.

George Mompesson was prebendary of Oxton I from 1688 until his death in 1732, and it seems certain that he built the house for his own occupation. George was the son of William Mompesson who had supervised the building of the first residence house 1689-95, and who had in his earlier days been chaplain to Sir George Savile of Rufford, later Lord Halifax. It was from his patron that William obtained the preferments of Eyam and later, Eakring, and George undoubtedly benefited by his father's connections. He could not have been more than 27 or 28 years old when he was appointed to Oxton I, and soon held other preferments; he was Rector of St. Martin, Micklegate, York, from 1691 to 1699, Vicar and then Rector of Mansfield from 1698 to 1721, and Rector of Barnborough, Yorkshire (in the gift of the chapter of Southwell) from 1715 until his death. It seems that Mansfield was his principal residence from 1699 but he spent much of his time in Southwell attending chapter meetings regularly until 1722, the probable date of his retirement to Barnborough. Existing leases of the prebend do not begin until 1718, and the most likely date for the building of his house at Southwell is c.1709, when his father died. William had disposed of most of his property to his children some years before and George was the sole beneficiary of the residue of his estate. George's own will, dated 1731, shows him to be a man of some wealth, with an estate and manor at Waddingham, Lincs., a house and land in Southwell, and leasehold estates at Greenwich, Kent, and Tibself, Derbyshire (App.K). A codicil varying the disposition of his property is dated 1732, just before he died, but he was then a sick man and his signature pathetically illegible. William appears to have been a humble parson, content to bury himself in the work in hand, and actually refused the deanery of Lincoln when it was offered him in later life, but George had been brought up in the atmosphere of the patronage of Sir George Savile, and he could have possessed the necessary aspirations to achieve the status of a completely new prebendal mansion of high fashion in the town. Restoration of the old house would not have been good enough for an ambitious man, although he does not seem to have had the ability or opportunity to rise ultimately to higher preferments within the church.

The architect of the new house is not known, but the similarities between the design and that of Mompesson House in the Close at Salisbury are too great to be accidental.[6] Mompesson House is on a grander scale, and much more elaborate in its detail; the entrance hall is wider, allowing narrow windows to be placed to light it either side of the doorway, but the main elements of plan and facade are identical in the two houses. The Mompessons originated at Bathampton, on the river Wylye, 10 miles north-west of Salisbury, and members of the family are recorded at Maydon Bradley, and at Corton in the parish of Boyton.[7] Mompesson House was built in 1701 by Charles Mompesson; Sir Christopher Wren has been credited with the design, and indeed of many other small houses of this character but, although there is no documentary evidence to support his involvement in any of these, his work at Hampton Court in 1690 undoubtedly stimulated the style now known as Queen Anne. The Corton branch of the Mompessons had settled in Yorkshire in the 16th century, and William himself came from Thorne Park, Seamer;[8] when George was planning to build in Southwell, where better could he find his exemplar than in the more fashionable house of his relations in the Close at Salisbury?

William Becher, prebendary of Woodborough, occupied the house from 1771 and purchased the freehold in the early years of the 19th century; it was from his son, Cranfield Becher, that the house was given its present name.

Normanton

The prebendal house of Normanton presents an impressive, three-storied facade to Church Street (Pl. III). The double-hung sash windows were renewed in Victorian times to eliminate the glazing bars which would have been part of the original design, but the openings are unaltered, and the excellent Georgian proportions are intact, with the central porch of Roman Doric columns supporting a flat entablature which is also characteristic of the period (Fig.19a).

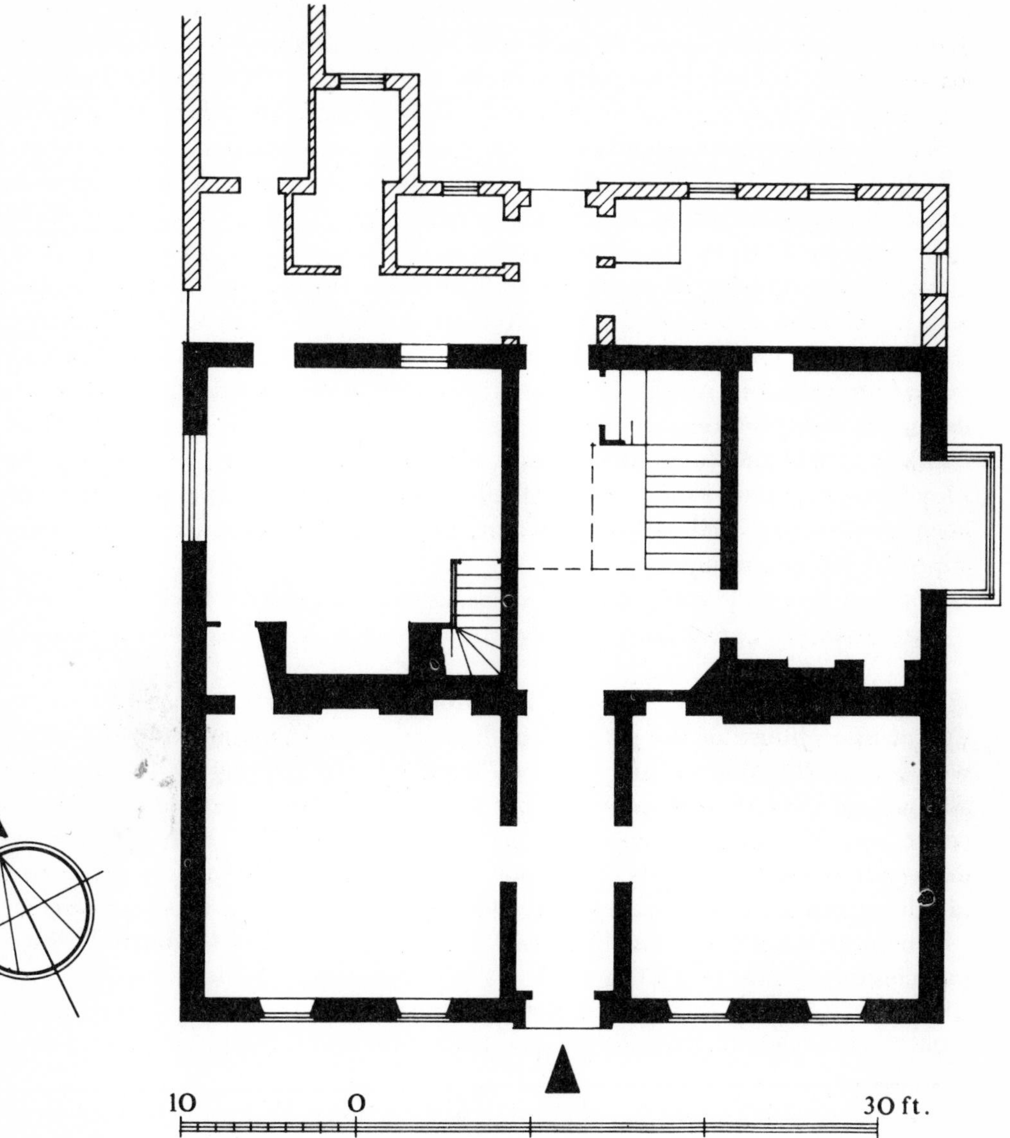

Fig 18: *Ground floor plan of prebendal house of Oxton I (now Cranfield House). A new building c.1709. See also Plate LIV.*

William Mompesson, after his harrowing experiences at Eyam, was appointed to the living of Eakring by his patron in 1670, and became Prebendary of Normanton in 1671. He seems to have divided his residence between these two livings, and probably kept the prebendal house for his own occupation, because his attendance at chapter meetings was also regular until 1703, and the building of the residence house certainly received his undivided attention. He may have retired to Eakring permanently in 1703, when he leased the prebendal mansion to Elizabeth Lloyd of Halam, together with the outhouses and land, and a farmhouse and tithes in Normanton, for 99 years, which was an unusually long period for that time. By 1746 the house was again in the hands of the prebendary. Rastall attributes the building of the house to Margaretta Tibson, who took the house on lease from 1766 and resided there until her death in 1795, and the character of the lofty front range is certainly consistent with a date of 1765-75. The rooms behind are probably earlier, although alterations in recent years prevent accurate dating or interpretation of the original plan (Fig.19b); they may be part of a building of William Mompesson's time, or more likely to be the work of Elizabeth Lloyd who negotiated such a profitable lease in 1703. The property seems to have been consistently well maintained and supported by extensive outhouses, the lease of 1766 describing it as

> Mansion house . . .with edifices, yards, orchards, gardens, backsides . . and all that gatehouse, great barn, dovecote, yard stable, and close thereto adjoining.

Rampton

The mansion house of the prebend of Rampton stands immediately opposite the west gate of the Minster, and is shown framed in the gateway to the churchyard, as it was in the late 18th century, in a drawing by Grimm in the British Museum collection (Pl. LIX). It was then a house of the early 17th century, with diaper-patterned brick walls on a stone plinth, and with three steep gables to the facade against a main roof across the building; the windows were wood casements with mullions and transoms, filled with leaded lights; against the north wall was a tall chimney stack (Fig 20 and Pl. LVIII). The form of the house had strong similarities with the Red Hall at Bourne, Lincs., built by Gilbert Fisher in 1633, although it is smaller than the Bourne house and avoids the necessity of a double pile roof.[9]

Soon after the Restoration the house was occupied by Elizabeth Rippon who died c.1679. The inventory of her goods lists the rooms substantially as they are today, and included a hall, buttery, great parlour, kitchen and larder, with chambers over; there was also a brewhouse, vat house, a dyers room, and a gatehouse chamber, but all these have how been replaced by the later outhouses (App.9). The house was well furnished with beds, tables, chairs and carpets, and generously supplied with sheets, napkins of diaper and huckaback, and pewter ware. The total value of her goods was £117, but apart from a silver bowl and 12 silver spoons, there were no luxuries of furnishings. By 1713 Gervas Rippon held

Plate I: *A general view of the town from the south, on the approach road from Brackenhurst, via Thurgarton.*

Plate II: *The Minster, and houses in Westgate, taken from the higher ground of Lowes Wong. Modern housing has been built over much of the open land but this view, taken in 1960, could not have changed much since 1800. The generating station at Staythorpe can be seen four miles away, to the east.*

Plate III: *Vicars' Court and the Residence, with (left to right) the prebendal houses of Woodborough, Normanton, and South Muskham behind, taken from the crossing tower of the Minster. Much of the housing in the distance on the right is modern but, apart from this, the built up area along Church Street and Easthorpe can still be seen to be linear development.*

Plate IV: *The prebendal sites along Church St. opposite the Minster Yard. On the left are the National Westminster Bank and Minster Lodge on the site of Norwell Overhall. On the right is North Muskham. The houses either side of the entrance to the modern car park were built on the site of Norwell Palishall, when the prebendal house was demolished at the end of the 18th century. The prebendal gardens extend back to the rear of the properties along King St.*

Plate V: *The prebendal houses along Westgate: left to right Dunham, Rampton and Sacrista.*

Plate VI: *The Chantry Priests' house, which was on Church St. at the west end of the Churchyard, behind the Crown Inn. It was demolished early in the 19th century to make way for the Grammar School built by Richard Ingleman.*

Plate VII: *The market building with a maltings behind, in King Street, prior to demolition in 1967. The old buildings had been converted to motor car workshops and showroom in modern times.*

Plate VIII: *The roof structure over the workshops, originally a malting, in King Street.*

Plate IX: *The late medieval roof structure left exposed over the showroom in front of the workshops in King S*

Plate X: *Manor Farm, Halloughton, originally the prebendal house. The 13th century stone tower house w extended by a timber framed structure built against it in the 16th century, and the house was again enlarged la in the 18th century by a range of rooms built of brickwork.*

Plate XI: *The west front of the Minster, 1775, with the Booth chapel (demolished 1784) still standing against the South West tower. The ruins of the former palace of the Archbishops of York are on the right; the state chamber was the only part left habitable. A door was inserted into the partially blocked west window to give access to one end which was used as a court for petty sessions.*

Plate XII: *The Minster from the N. W., from a drawing by Richard Hall, engraved by William Hollar, c.1672.*

Plate XIII: *The Minster from the S.E., from a drawing by C.J. Greenwood, printed by C. Moody, Holborn, and published by J. Whittingham, Southwell c.1835. The spires to the western towers were removed in 1801, when damage to the masonry was attributed to the weight of the roofs. The low pitched roofs to nave and transepts had been built after the fire of 1711, but the marks of the steeper original roofs can be seen on the walls of the crossing tower. The raised structure between the western towers had been necessary to accommodate the tall west window against the lower nave roof.*

Plate XIV: *The Minster from the N. W.*

Plate XV: *The Minster from the S. E., c.1913. The existence of the park adjoining the palace had restricted building development on this side of the church, much of it being leased as farm land.*

Plate XVI: *The Minster from the S. E., in the late 18th century. The ruins of the palace stand in front of the western towers.*

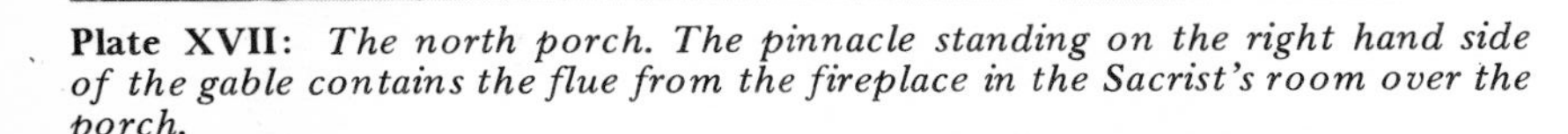

Plate XVII: *The north porch. The pinnacle standing on the right hand side of the gable contains the flue from the fireplace in the Sacrist's room over the porch.*

Plate XVIII: *The doorway into the north aisle of the nave from the porch.*

Plate XIX: *The nave, looking towards the great west window.*

Plate XX: *The south transept, showing the small doorway which gave direct access from the Archbishop's palace on that side of the church.*

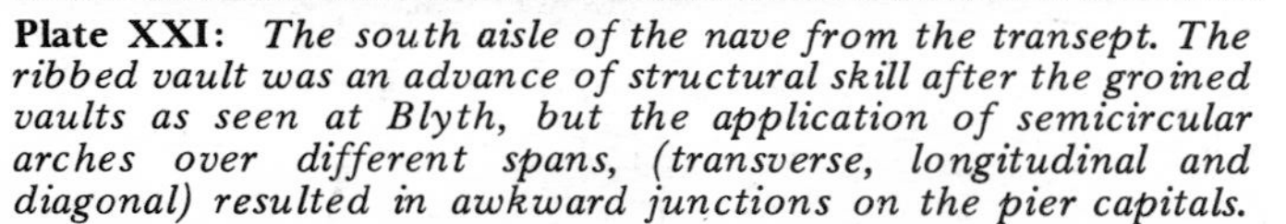

Plate XXI: *The south aisle of the nave from the transept. The ribbed vault was an advance of structural skill after the groined vaults as seen at Blyth, but the application of semicircular arches over different spans, (transverse, longitudinal and diagonal) resulted in awkward junctions on the pier capitals.*

Plate XXII: *Looking into the nave from the south aisle. In the triforium opening can be seen the corbels at the springing of the arch, and the stump left to receive a shaft at the crown; an incomplete design. The date of the font is 1661, and the design of it is similar to that in several Nottinghamshire churches which were refurnished at the Restoration.*

Plate XXIII: *The choir, looking east.*

Plate XXIV: *The Minster from the N. E. The buttress of the Chapter House was built against the corner of the little eastern transept, making a small enclosed courtyard off the cloister. This was roofed over in recent years to make the present vestries.*

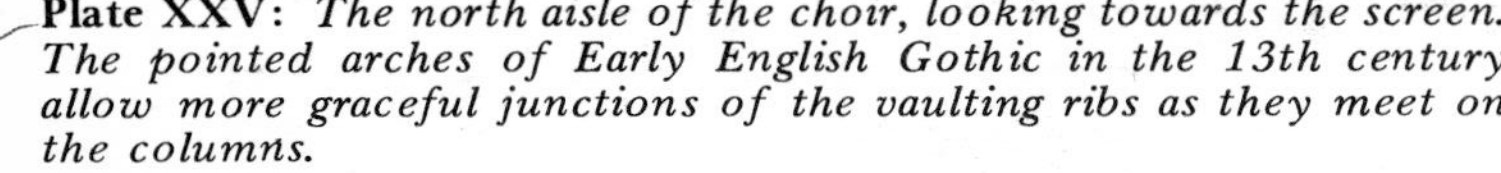

Plate XXV: *The north aisle of the choir, looking towards the screen. The pointed arches of Early English Gothic in the 13th century allow more graceful junctions of the vaulting ribs as they meet on the columns.*

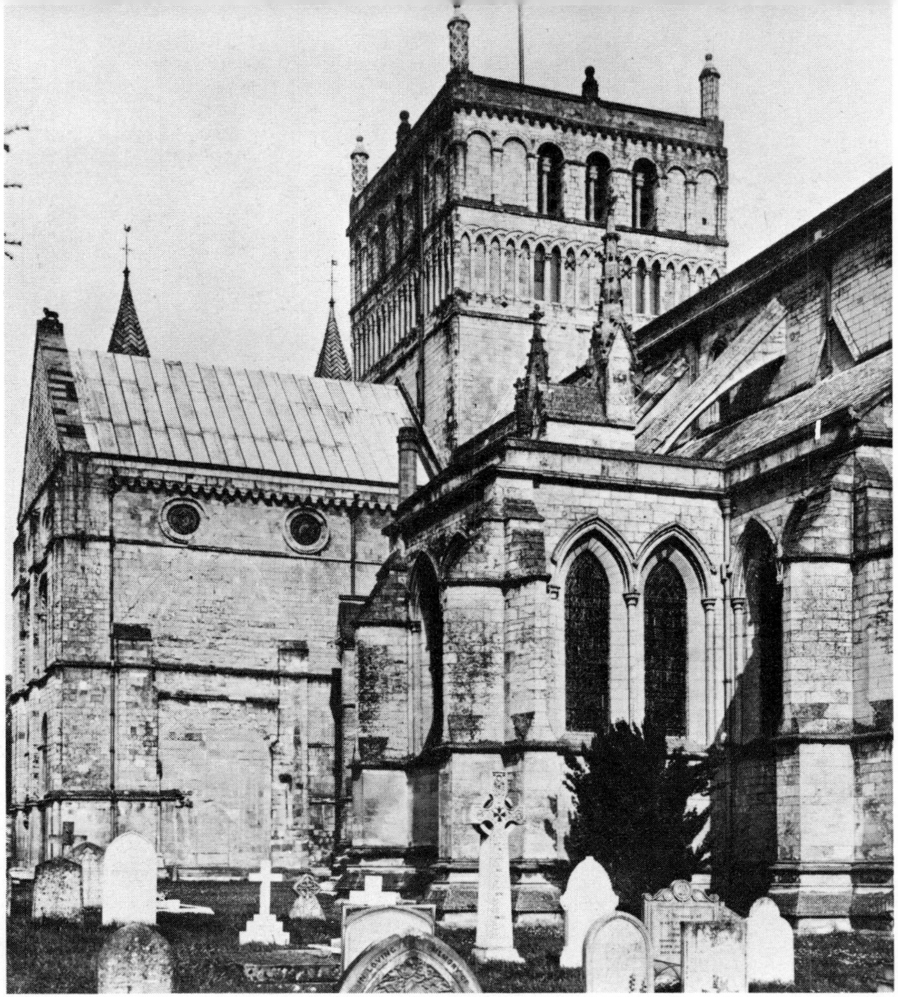

Plate XXVI: *The transept and crossing tower from the S. E. The flying buttresses over the aisle roof were a 14th century addition.*

Plate XXVII: *The doorway into the Chapter House, one of the finest examples of late 13th century carving. The attached shafts in the jamb recessions are in polished Hopton Wood limestone from Derbyshire.*

Plate XXVIII: *The interior of the Chapter House roof. This is the only polygonal chapter house in England vaulted in stone from wall to wall without the support of a central column.*

Plate XXIX a: *Late Saxon carved tympanum, now built into the west wall of the north transept as a door lintel.*

Plate XXIX b: *The early Norman carved capitals on the piers between crossing and choir.*

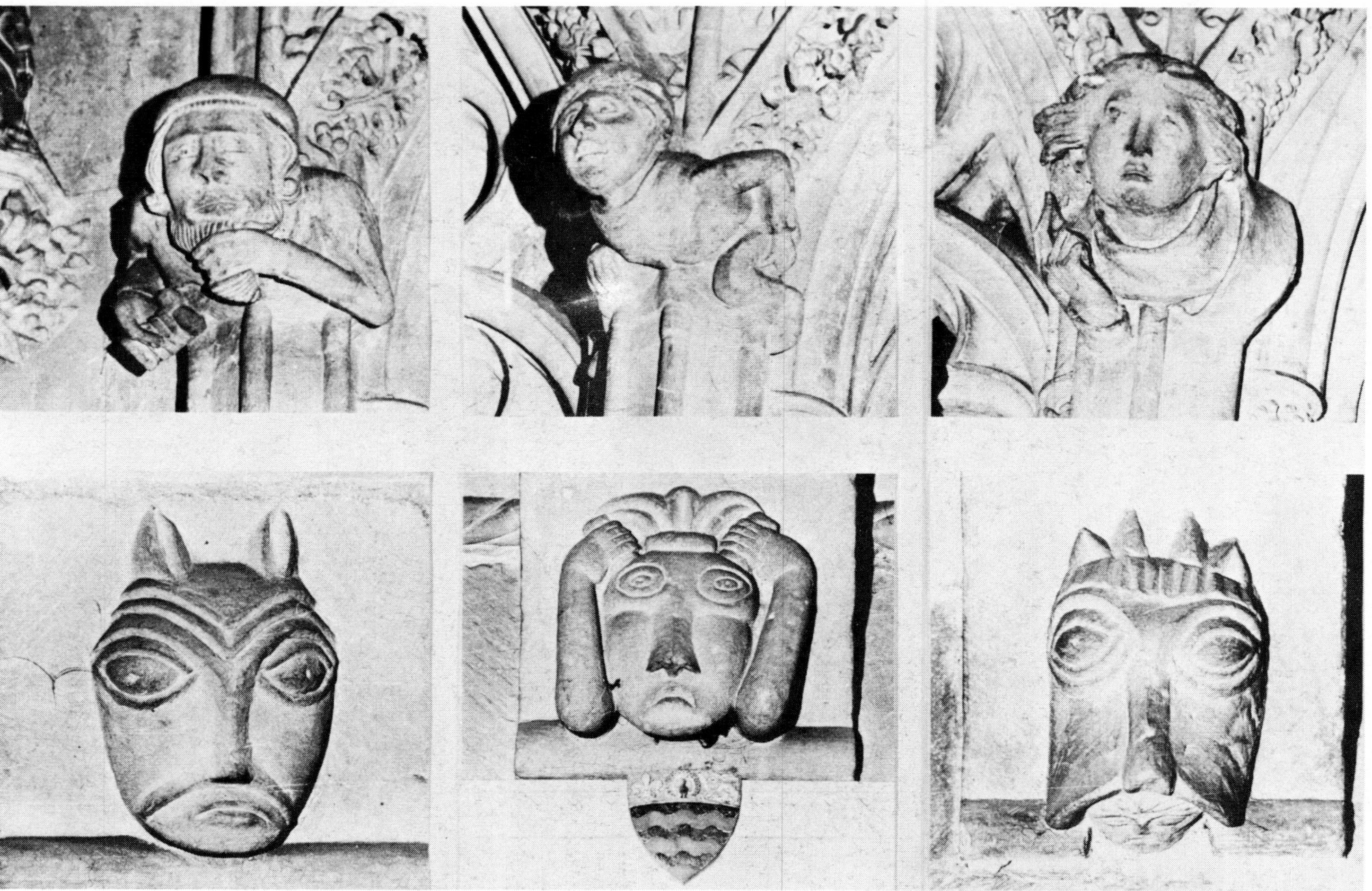

Plate XXX: *Sculptured heads. (a) to (c) Norman carvings on the aisle walls. (d) and (e) 14th-century carvings on the east side of the choir screen. (f) 19th-century restoration on the choir screen.*

d	e	f
a	b	c

Plate XXXI a: *Detail of vaulting ribs in the vestibule on the west side of the choir screen.*

Plate XXXI b: *Detail of the blind arcading in the cloister leading to the Chapter House.*

Plate XXXII: *The modern Bishop's Manor built in the ruins of the medieval palace of the Archbishops of York, seen from the crossing tower of the Minster. The garderobe tower is situated at the far corner of the ruins; smaller garderobes can be seen projecting out from the external walls indicating that the east and south sides of the courtyard were originally occupied by lodgings for members of the Archbishop's household.*

Plate XXXIII: *The east wall of the palace ruins taken from outside the courtyard. (This wall is on the left of Pl. XXXII) The garderobe tower is on the corner at the extreme left, and the smaller single garderobe is on the right. The projection from the wall between the garderobes is a chimney stack.*

Plate XXXIV: *The garderobe tower and a chimney stack viewed from the south (the far wall in Pl. XXXII). The projection corbelled out from the internal angle contains the newel stair from the first floor to the roof of the tower.*

Plate XXXV: *Sketch of the inside and plan of the garderobe tower, dated 1787.*

Plate XXXVI: *The palace ruins looking out (S.W.) from the courtyard c.1900 (before Bishop's Manor was built on the site of the great hall). The large archway on the right is the opening from the entrance porch, and the smaller arches originally led into service rooms and passage; these were incorporated into the new building.*

Plate XXXVII: *The house which was built on the site of the great hall in the 18th century, seen from the palace courtyard; this was incorporated into the Bishop's Manor built in 1907. The gable on the right marks the end of the range containing the Archbishop's state chamber, and the only part of the palace to have survived the Civil War period.*

ate XXXVIII: *The palace ruins at the end of the 18th century, seen from the N. E.*

ate XXXIX: *The palace ruins from the S. W., reproduced from Rastall Dickinson's History of Southwell. his is the opposite viewpoint from Pl. XXXVI; the arches to service rooms and passage are shown, as well the doorway in the external wall on the south side. The garderobe tower is on the extreme right.*

Plate XL: *The college of the Vicars Choral built in 1379 at the east end of the churchyard, where Vicars Court now stands. This view is of the west side; the central gateway led into a courtyard, on the opposit (east) side of which was the hall later replaced by the Residence House.*

Plate XLI: *The west front of the first Residence House, built in 1689. This drawing was made b S. H. Grimm between 1779 and 1785; the new Vicars' houses are shown, left and right, but the new fror to the Residence had not then been added.*

Plate XLII: *The rear (east side) of the Residence House, 1787. The window at the extreme right is part of the original house of 1689. The projecting wing and other rooms at the rear were remodelled in 1772 and the whole was enlarged in 1806. The ruins of the palace can be seen across the open ground at the left of the view.*

Plate XLIII: *Vicars' Court and the Residence House c.1787, seen from the W. This view has remained almost unchanged into modern times.*

Plate XLIV: *The Minster from the N.E., showing the Vicars' houses and the rear of the Residence House, at the east end of the churchyard. The drawing is dated 1761 but cannot be earlier than 1780 when the Vicars' houses were built. The dovecote and barns of Normanton prebendal house are shown on the right.*

Plate XLV: *A design for a vicar's house. The houses finally built were reduced in size from this proposal.*

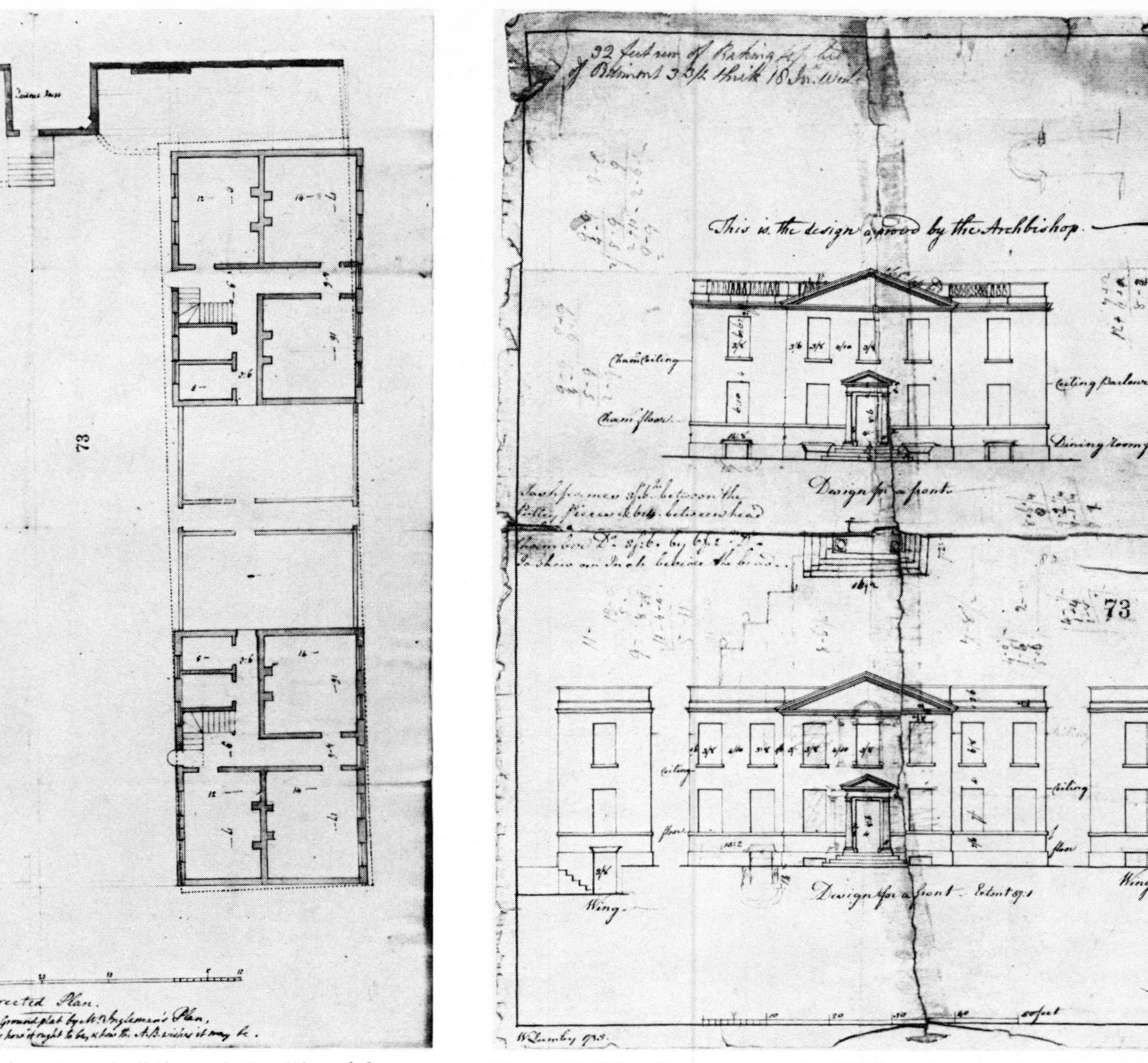

Plate XLVI: *The approved plan for the rebuilding of the Vicars' houses c.1779.*

Plate XLVII: *Two designs by William Lumby for the new front to the **Residence House**, 1785. The upper drawing was the one approved by the Archbishop, but short projecting wings were eventually added*

Plate XLVIII: *The prebendal house of Norwell Palishall c.1788. This was demolished c.1795 when the present Palishall House and Willoughby House were built on the site.*

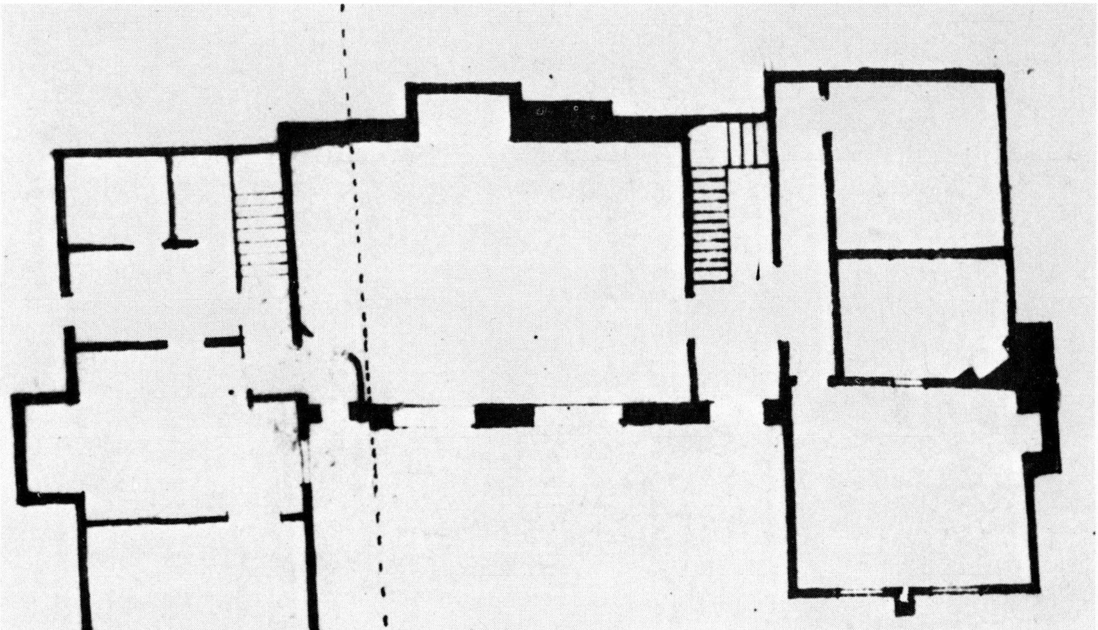

Plate XLIX: *The prebendal house of Norwell Palishall, reproduced from plans in leases of 1788 (Notts. C.R.O. DDSP 42/47 and 48).*

Plate L: *The east front of the prebendal house of Oxton II. The late medieval house had been remodelled c.1808 to produce a roughly symmetrical facade which successfully masked its original character and form.*

Plate LI: *The prebendal house of Oxton II from the rear (west). The English bond of the brickwork, and the timber framing exposed in the gables of the external walls, were the only indications of a possible early date for the house, until demolition allowed a more thorough examination.*

Plate LII: *The prebendal house of Dunham before it was remodelled by Sherbrooke Lowe c.1780.*

Plate LIII: *Sacrista Prebend. This is the only house in the town in which the Gothic Revival style was methodically applied for alterations and additions in the late 18th century.*

Plate LIV: *The prebendal house of Oxton I, built c.1709, now Cranfield House.*

Plate LV: *The Minster from the north c.1785. Standing in front of the north transept is the prebendal house of Oxton I, seen from the rear; to the right of it is North Muskham, with Norwell Palishall and Norwell Overhall partly hidden in the trees extreme right. On the extreme left are the new Vicars' houses and the side of the Residence House. Woodborough prebend had been reduced to a small tenement by that time and is hidden in the trees on the left.*

Plate LVI: *The prebendal house of Rampton.*

Plate LVII: *The Minster from Lowes Wong (west), with the rear of the prebendal houses on Westgate in the foreground.*

Plate LVIII: *The 17th century staircase in Rampton Prebend; a detail at first floor level, showing the balusters and handrails on the flights rising up from the ground floor and continuing to attic level.*

Plate LIX: *Rampton Prebend seen through the west gate of the Minster Yard, c.1780. The windows were still the leaded sashes of a late 17th century type; a diaper pattern is shown on the brick walls which at that time had not been stuccoed.*

Plate LX a: *South Muskham Prebend. Detail of a King post, in the roof structure, with a castellated cap supporting the arched braces.*

Plate LX b: *South Muskham Prebend. A general view of the roof structure looking towards the gable end of the north wing.*

Plate LXI: *South Muskham prebend. The early 18th century staircase, with cut string and moulded balusters.*

Plate LXII: *A brick recovered from the demolition of the prebendal house of Oxton II. Early 16th century. When first moulded the wet clay was laid on a layer of hay and straw to dry in the open air; the paw-mark of a dog, impressing the hay into the clay surface, was preserved when the brick was later fired in the kiln or clamp.*

Fig 19: *The prebendal house of Normanton*
(a) *The frontage on Church Street*
(b) *Ground floor plan. The front range of rooms, shown hatched, comprises the improvements of the late 18th century. The house behind is probably older, but has undergone several additions and alterations so that its original plan cannot be defined.*

the house in lease; he died in 1714, and the inventory taken in the same year was valued at £341 (App.H). His household goods were only summarised in the rooms, and were worth only £64 8s. 4d., but the remainder of the valuation, in farm stock and equipment in the yard and barns were those of a yeoman farmer of some substance.

Rastall described the house as one of the best prebends in the town, having been improved by the lessee, who was then William Smith, so that the present stucco on the walls and the replacement sash windows must date from that time (Pl. LVI). William Smith also built a new brewhouse and coal shed, but after his death c.1830, his widow remained in occupation, and a survey made by the Church Commissioners in 1848 records that 'the house and rest of the premises are much out of repair, the great age of the tenant having probably prevented any material repairs from being entered upon'. In 1852 the freehold of the house was sold to the then lessee, W.A. Cotton, but purchased back by the Commissioners in 1934.

South Muskham

Church Street east of vicars' court takes a double bend to pass by the site of the prebend of South Muskham. The house, therefore, stands across the straight line of the road to face the *Saracen's Head* Inn at the far west end, and although the present building is in brickwork, stuccoed white, with Georgian-type sash windows, its form is medieval in origin (Fig.21). It consisted of a central hall with projecting parlour and service ranges at the ends. The hall is now two-storied throughout but the entrance, at one end of the hall range, is consistent with an earlier cross passage at this point. The house has been extensively remodelled in at least two periods; the present staircase by the entrance is an excellent example of work of the first quarter of the 18th century, with a cut string and moulded balusters, and probably dates from the insertion of the first floor over the hall (Pl. LXI); and Rastall records that it was 'a large house, in good repair, and much mended in appearance by a new front'.

The later brickwork of the walls replaces a timber frame, all traces of which are now hidden or removed, but evidence of the original house still remains in the roof structure. The roof covering is now modern, blue Welsh slates, and the structural framing over the hall is contemporary with this; the roof over the cross wing at the south end accommodates a generously coved ceiling to the first floor rooms, probably 18th-century in date; the roof over the north cross wing, however, contains two trussed frames, and a gable frame, of a type prevalent in the 13th century. The tie beams are slightly arched, and carry short, octagonal king posts with moulded bases and castellated caps; two arched braces from each king post support a collar purlin running the length of the roof, and two more spread transversely to the junction of collar and rafters. The soffit of the eastern of the two tie beams is pegged for arched braces which would have sprung from wall posts, all traces of which have disappeared except for a short centre section

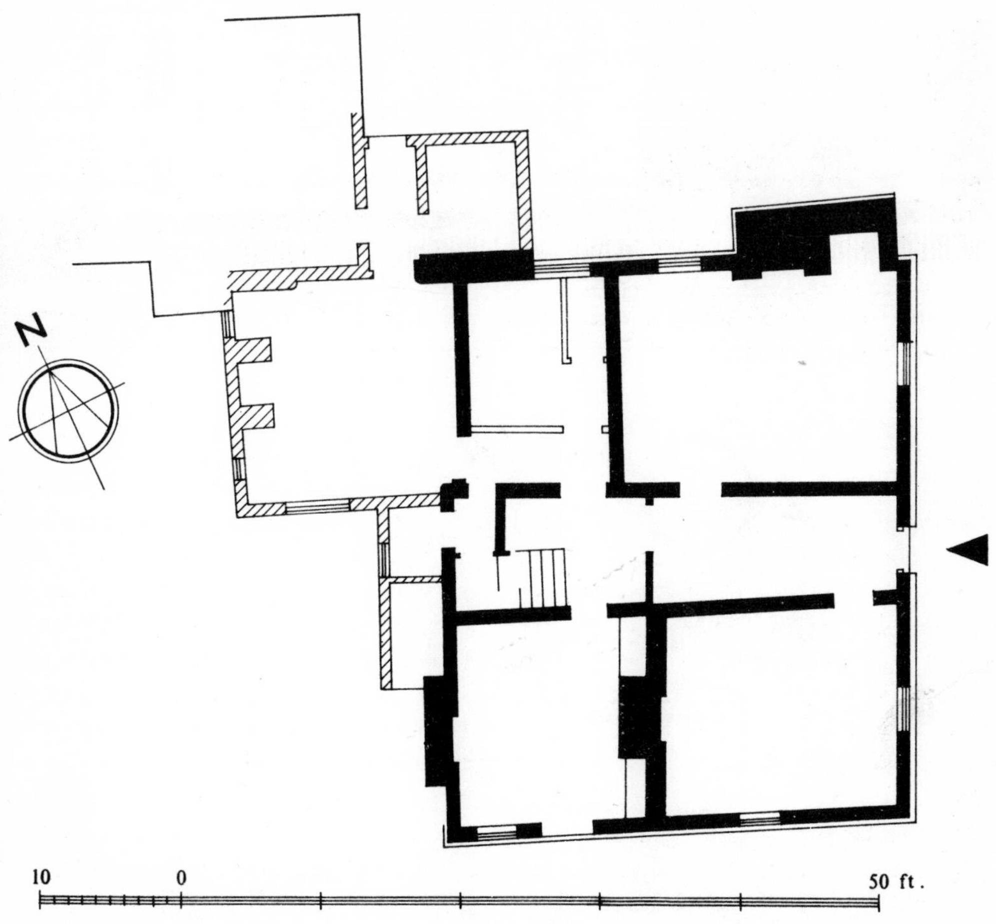

Fig 20: *Ground floor plan of the prebendal house of Rampton. The 17th-century house is shown in black. The outhouses were rebuilt in the late 18th, or early 19th century, parts of which are shown hatched. See also Plate LVI.*

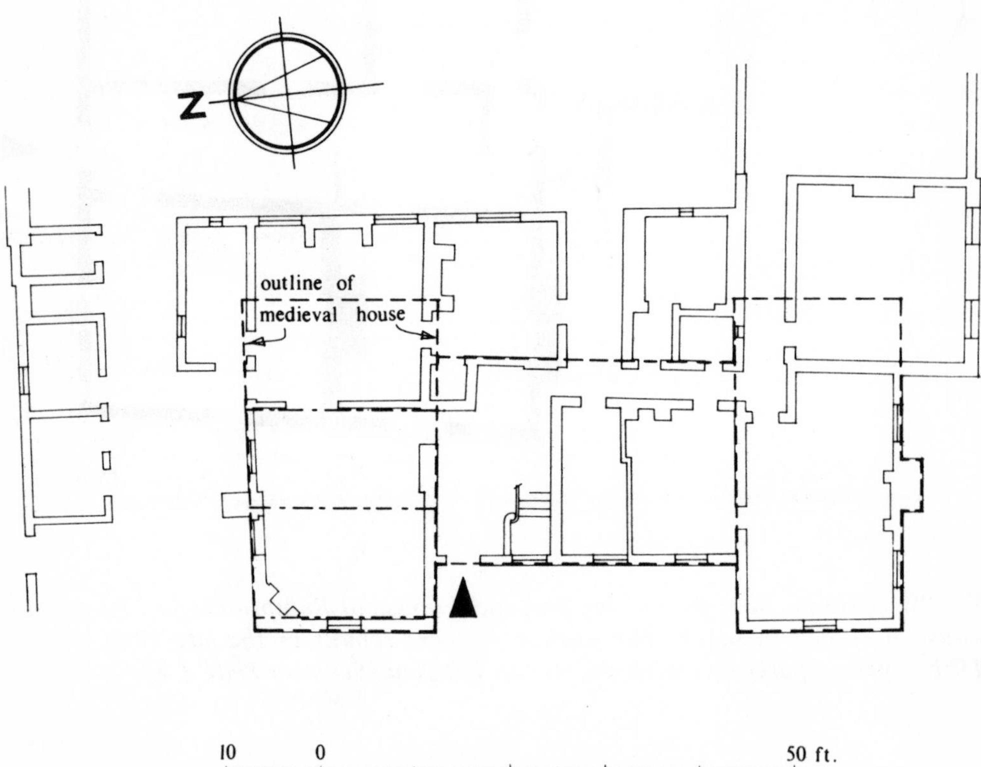

Fig 21: *The prebendal house of South Muskham*
(a) *General view of the house from Church Street*
(b) *Ground floor plan. The house was largely re-built in the 18th century on the late medieval plan, although enough of the roof structure remains to define its earlier form.*

of the arch (Pl.LX a and b). Part of the wall framing remains of the west gable of the cross wing; this consists of a tie beam tapering from the centre, and supporting a tapered post which in turn carried the end of the collar purlin (fig.22); studding remaining in the frame is infilled with plaster reinforced with pieces of plain roofing tiles. The whole structure is of high quality, and of a type for which no parallels can be found in the East Midlands; comparative examples however exist in the 15th-century roof of the *Woolpack* Inn at Coggeshall, Essex, in the roof of Barking Church, Suffolk, and in Dixter Hall at Northiam in Sussex (1450-66).[10]

Richard Becher leased the house from the end of the 18th century and carried out many of the improvements; his son purchased the freehold in 1814 and, except for a short break between 1829 and 48, the house remained in the Becher family until 1916.

Woodborough

There are no records to be found which throw light on the history of the prebendal house of Woodborough. Rastall described it as 'much decayed' and Shilton wrote that the house had 'dwindled into a small tenement'.

Fig 22: *The prebendal house of South Muskham; a sketch of the medieval roof structure, which was originally open to the first floor. Holes for pegs, along the bottom edge of the tie beam below the king post, indicate that arched braces may originally have stiffened the tie beam on to the wall framing.*

During the extensive rebuilding of the vicars' houses, and the alterations to the residence house in the 18th century, the chapter had considered the provision of a suitable coach house for the residentiary. In 1779 the stable, coach house, and yard, occupied by Mrs. Tibson and part of Normanton prebend had been taken on a lease of 21 years, but in 1788 the chapter authorised expenditure on a new coach house, which was built, together with a cottage, at the rear of the prebendal house of Woodborough. In 1819 Richard Ingleman purchased the front portion of the premises facing Church Street, together with a small area of land for a garden, and built for himself the house known today as Ashleigh, occupying it until his death in 1838 (Fig.23).

Ashleigh was therefore, in effect, a re-fronting of the earlier prebendal property, as has already been seen at North Muskham and Norwell Overhall. The survey of the present house shows the front range, parallel with the modern road line, but adapted to the angle of layout of the earlier buildings. The elevation is well proportioned and carefully detailed, but the outstanding feature of the house is the graceful stone staircase cantilevered out from the wall of the entrance hall. The buildings behind are also in brick, but of the cottage type characteristic of Nottinghamshire after the middle of the 18th century, and lacking in features to assist more accurate dating.

Sacrista, or Segeston

The mansion house of the prebend of Sacrista stood in Westgate, between Rampton and Oxton II; the house today presents a facade of the Gothic Revival to the street. The rooms of the front range are disposed either side of the central hall and entrance, and project forward as short, gabled wings; the windows are in bays at the ground floor, but flush with the walls above; stone mullions divide the windows into lights, capped with four-centred arches, the upper ones enclosed below hood moulds which are returned down the sides; the projecting entrance has a flat roof hidden behind a pierced parapet (Pl. LIII). The facade has the straightforward symmetrical regularity of classical building of the 18th century, gothicised in the emerging fashion, as by the country gentleman aided by his book of designs, but the effect is charming and wholly restrained. Inside, the pretence is abandoned; the rooms, with their corniced ceilings; and the cut-string stair curving around a narrow well in the hall, are simple, but elegantly, late Georgian. The date is c.1775, but the source of the design is not known. The symmetrical assembly of Gothic parts is reminiscent of William Kent's work around the middle of the 18th century, and Sanderson Millar, in the same spirit introduced the pierced parapet into the symmetrical facade of his new hall at Lacock Abbey, built in 1753;[11] James Wyatt imparted a Gothic flavour to the classical composition of Sheffield Place, Sussex, which he built c.1776 for John Baker Holroy, later Lord Sheffield,[12] but Wyatt was not consulted by the chapter at Southwell until 1792, and there is no record of him having other connections with the town. The prebendal house was sold under the Acts for the Redemption and Sale of the

Fig 23: *Ashleigh; built on the site of the prebendal house of Woodborough*
(a) *The front on Church Street*

(b) *Ground floor plan. The front range of rooms was built c.1819 across an older house on the site.*

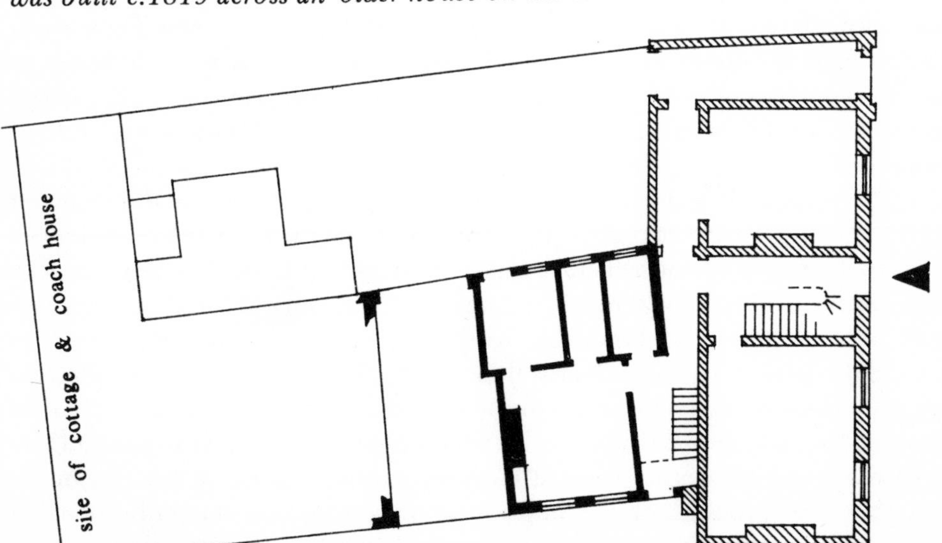

Land Tax, in 1836, but purchased in 1939 by John Player and presented to the Ecclesiastical Commissioners to provide a house for the choristers of the cathedral. It is now leased to the Minster Grammar School on these conditions.

Rastall described the house as 'Formerly a small ordinary house, but of late much improved and made not only convenient but pretty, by the present lessee and occupier . . .'. This would have been Nicholas Hutchinson who leased the house from 1774 until 1798, and his improvements included the range of stuccoed Gothic Revival rooms across the front. Behind these, and at right angles to the road, a single range of rooms also in brick but standing on part of a stone plinth, and having an eaves cornice of projecting brick courses, may be the remains of the earlier house noted by Rastall (Fig. 24). According to Shilton later (1818) the house had been 'rendered still more commodious' by William Barrow, referring to the later parts of the present extensive wing at the rear.

Summary

Of the original 16 prebends of the collegiate church, these 11 provide written or physical evidence of the standards of accommodation, and of the varied management, in church endowments over a long period of architectural history.

Apart from the church, no buildings exist in the town which can be said to be wholly medieval in character, but the remains of the masonry in the walls of Norwell Overhall, the outstanding structure in the roof of South Muskham, the details of Oxton II, and even the moulded timbers incorporated into the roof of Dunham, show that the earlier houses of the prebendaries had been of high quality in materials and workmanship. The scale of accommodation and layout of rooms in the late medieval period is evidenced in South Muskham, and in the recorded plan of Norwell Palishall, where the central hall with cross wings occurs in houses of manorial status; characteristics surviving in the plans of Norwell Overhall and Oxton II support a hypothesis that this form may have been standard at least for the wealthier prebends. Norwell Overhall is the only house to include substantial evidence of stone construction, and for the rest, timber framing with an infill of mud and stud, or plaster reinforced with stone or tiles, was most likely.

The earliest use of brickwork occurred in Oxton II, but Rampton and Dunham provide the 17th-century examples of design employing it in mass construction. The plan of Rampton is one which became the double pile house elsewhere, but Dunham adhered to the single range, although it is a singularly lofty and spacious example of the type. The houses suffered most from destruction, added to neglect, in the period 1630-60; Norwell Overhall, North Muskham, and the two Oxtons were singled out for mention in the records, but the parts of these, and of Normanton, Sacrista, and Woodborough, which might be ascribed to building by lessees in the late 17th century, are in all cases modest in scale. A stranger in the town at that time would have the impression of comfortable but unfashionable affluence in the prebendal houses lining the churchyard, probably mixed with a

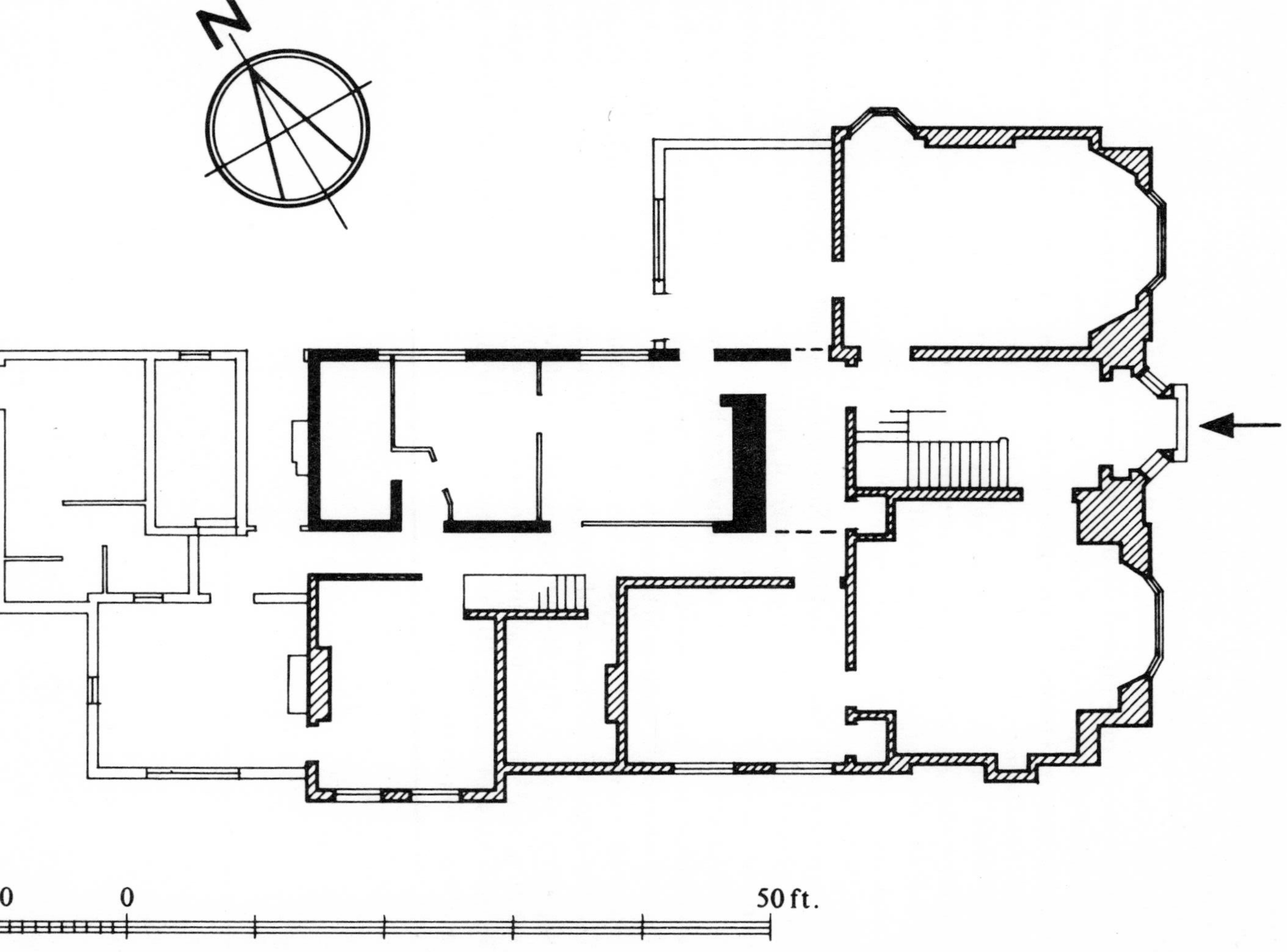

Fig 24: *The prebendal house of Sacrista. The oldest remaining part of the house is shown in black. The front range of rooms was added in the late 18th century, further additions made behind in the 19th. See also Plate LIII.*

certain amount of picturesque decay. In such a setting the elegance of the new house of Oxton I must have been a startling contrast in the early years of the 18th century; this is the only house which can be positively identified as built by the prebendary for his own occupation after the Restoration, when leasing of properties was universal practice.

By the late 18th century Norwell Palishall, Norwell Overhall, and Oxton II had all deteriorated into divided occupation, but in contrast Dunham had long been maintained by the Lowe family, who, helped by their liaison with the Sherbrookes of Oxton, could claim to be classed amongst the gentry of the county, and Rampton was the home of a prosperous farming family. The period from 1780 into the first quarter of the 19th century, however, saw the most dramatic changes and intensive activity in building. Norwell Palishall was the only house to be completely demolished, and the site was re-developed for three comfortable dwellings; South Muskham was re-fronted, Oxton II remodelled, Rampton improved, and Dunham enlarged by the addition of rooms at the rear. Norwell Overhall, North Muskham, Normanton, Woodborough and Sacrista, were all improved by the addition of a range of rooms across the front to present a new and fashionable, facade to the street. With the exception of Oxton II and possibly Woodborough, all this work was carried out by lessees who were by then too well established for the houses ever to revert to being the residences of individual canons who might wish to settle in the town. These men provided for themselves, like John Thomas Becher, prebendary of South Muskham, who built Hill House on the edge of the manor of Burgage. The new and enlarged residence house supported the dignity of the canon who took up his quarter's residence in rotation, and when the legal means for disposing of church property was provided in the Acts of George III, the houses, one by one, passed into the hands of gentlemen of private means.

Notes to Chapter Six

1. Notts. C.R.O. DDM.103/17. I am indebted to Mr. Lawrence Craik who drew my attention to this reference from his work on the Halloughton records.
2. Richard Phillips Shilton, described as a Schoolmaster, who was author of the *History of Southwell* (1818).
3. *Calendar of Patent Rolls 1553,* Ed. VI, vol. V, p. 60.
4. M.W. Barley, *The English Farmhouse and Cottage* (1961), p. 218.
5. Royal Comm. on Hist. Monuments, *City of Cambridge* (1959), vol. II, p. 396.
6. Mark Girouard, 'Mompesson House, Salisbury', in *Country Life,* 25 December 1958.
7. Walter C. Metcalfe, ed., *Visitation of Wiltshire 1565* (1897), p. 33.
8. K.S.S. Train, ed., *Nottinghamshire Visitations 1662-64* (Thoroton Society, Record Series, vol. XIII, 1950), p. 16.
9. M.W. Barley, 'Rural Housing in England', in *Agrarian History of England and Wales* (1966), vol. IV, ed. by Joan Thirsk, pp. 716-17.
10. Coggeshall – see Royal Commission on Historical Monuments, *North-East Essex (1922),* p. 118-9, and plate p. xxxvii.
    Barking – see Fred Crossley, *Timber buildings in England* (1951), pp. 56 and 134.
    Northiam – see Olive Cook, *The English House through Seven Centuries* (1968), p. 24.
11. Sir John Summerson, *Architecture in Britain 1530-1830* (1953), pp. 240, 244, and 283.
12. Anthony Dale, *James Wyatt* (1956), pp. 128-30.

Bibliography

The principal printed works consulted placed under appropriate chapter headings. (Page references to these works are given only where necessary to amplify points of special importance; notes to the text are generally restricted to works of specialised interest not listed below.)

Chapter One: Introduction

The Town:

Beresford M.W. and J.K.S. St. Joseph, *Mediaeval England* (1958).

Chambers, J.D., *Nottinghamshire in the eighteenth century* (1932).

Everitt, Alan, 'The Marketing of Agricultural Produce', in *Agrarian History of England and Wales,* vol. IV, 1500-1640, (1966) ed. Joan Thirsk.

Gover, J.E.B., Allen Mawer and F.M. Stenton, *The Place-names of Nottinghamshire* (1940).

Martin, G.H., 'The Town as Palimpsest', in *The Study of Urban History* (1968), ed. H.J. Dyos.

The Vernacular Tradition:

Barley, M.W., *The English Farmhouse and Cottage* (1961).

Barley, M.W., *The House and Home* (1963).

Barley, M.W., 'Rural Housing in England' in *Agrarian History of England and Wales,* vol. IV 1500-1640, (1966) ed. Joan Thirsk.

Firman, R.J., 'Gypsum in Nottinghamshire', in *Bulletin of the Peak District Mines Historical Society,* vol. 12, pt. 4 (1964).

Firman, R.J. and P.E., 'A Geological approach to the study of Mediaeval Brickwork', in *The Mercian Geologist* vol. 2, No. 3 (1967).

Lloyd, Nathaniel, *A History of English Brickwork* (1934).

Smith, J.T., 'Mediaeval Roofs: A Classification', in *Archaeological Journal,* vol. CXV, (1958).

Summers, N., 'Manor Farm, Halloughton', in *Transactions of the Thoroton Society,* vol. LXIX (1965).

Chapter Two: The Collegiate Foundation

Beaumont, R.M., *The Chapter of Southwell Minster* (1956, revised 1971).

Dickinson, William Rastall, *Antiquities Historical, Architectural, Chorographical, and Itinerary in Nottinghamshire and the adjacent Counties.* Part 1, vol. 1 (1801). (A revised edition of Rastall, under his assumed name).

Dimock, Rev, James F., 'The fortunes of the Church of the Blessed Mary the Virgin of Southwell through the troubles of the sixteenth century' in *Associated Architectural Societies,* vol. III, Pt. 1. (1854).

Dugdale, Sir William, *Monasticon Anglicanum* (1655-73), (and edited and re-published 1817-30 vol. VI, Pt. III).

Leach, A.F., 'Visitations and Memorials of Southwell Minster', in *Camden Society* (1891).

Page, W. (Ed.), *The Victoria County History of the County of Nottinghamshire* (1910).

Raine, James, *The Historians of the Church of York and its Archbishops* (1857-94).

Rastall, W., Dickinson, *A History of the Antiquities of the Town and Church of Southwell in the County of Nottinghamshire* (1787).

Shilton, R.P., *A History of Southwell* (1818).

Stenton, Sir F., 'The Founding of Southwell Minster', in *Thoroton Society Transactions* vol. LXXI (1967).

Thompson, A. Hamilton, *The Cathedral Churches of England* (1925).

Thompson, A. Hamilton, 'Certificates of the Chantry Commissioners for the College of Southwell in 1546 and 1548' in *Thoroton Society Transactions* vol. XV (1911).

Thoroton, Robert, *The Antiquities of Nottinghamshire* (1677).

Throsby, John, *Thoroton's History of Nottinghamshire* (1797).

Chapter Three: The Minster

Dimock, Rev. Arthur, *The Cathedral Church of Southwell* (1901).

Dimock, Rev. James F., 'The Architectural History of the Church of the Blessed Mary the Virgin, Southwell', in *Journal of the British Archaeological Assn.* vol. VIII (1853).

Dimock, Rev. James F., Architectural History of Southwell Minster, in *Lincoln Diocesan Architectural Society,* (1869).

Killpack, W.B., *The History and Antiquities of the Collegiate Church of Southwell* (1839).

Livett, G.M., *Southwell Minster* (1883).

Thompson, A. Hamilton, 'The Cathedral Church of the Blessed Virgin Mary, Southwell', in *Thoroton Society Transactions,* vol. XV (1911).

Chapter Four: The Palace of the Archbishops of York

Chapter Five: Vicars' Court and the Residence

Chapter Six: The Prebendal Houses

Emery, Anthony, *Dartington Hall* (1970).

Faulkner, P.A., 'Domestic Planning from the twelfth to the fourteenth centuries', in *Archaeological Journal,* vol. CXV, (1958).

Faulkner, P.A., 'Castle planning in the fourteenth century', in *Archaeological Journal* vol. CXX (1963).

Faulkner, P.A., 'Some Mediaeval Episcopal Palaces', in *Archaeological Journal,* vol. CXXVII (1970).

Godwin, Francis, *A Catalogue of the Bishops of England* (1615).

le Neve, John, *Fasti Ecclesiae Anglicanae* (1854).

Lloyd, Nathaniel, *A History of the English House* (1934).

Parker, J.H., *Some Account of Domestic Architecture in England* (1882).

Raine, James, *Fasti Eboracenses* (1863).

Richardson, A.E. and H. Donaldson Eberlein, *The smaller English House of the later Renaissance 1660-1830* (1925).

Wood, Margaret, *The English Mediaeval House* (1965).

The principal documentary deposits consulted:

Bodleian Library, Oxford
The Gough Collection of Maps and Drawings.

Borthwick Institute of Historical Research, York
The Bishopthorpe Papers.

British Museum, London
Kaye Collection. Add. M.S.S. 15537-48; Notebooks of Sir Richard Kaye. 18551-571 Harleian MSS 6826.

Southwell Minster Library
The White Book of Southwell; Chapter Decree Books, Lease Books, Chapter Accounts.

Notts. County Record Office
Indentures of lease and sale, Wills and Inventories, Tithe Award 1841, Land Tax Assessment 1780, etc.

Public Record Office
State Papers (Domestic), Calendar of Patent Rolls (published by H.M.S.O.)

York Minster Library
Torre M.S.S.

University of Nottingham Library MSS Dept.
W.A. James Collection.

Also indentures of lease and sale of chapter and prebendal properties in private ownership and in solicitors deposits.

Appendix A

The Residence House, 1695

(from Southwell Minster Library)

An account of expences and disbursements upon the Resident house, Library and other places belonging to the said house.

Imprimis these following bills of Mr. Bensons were allowed and paid by Mr. William Mompesson then Canon Resident.

Mr. Bensons first bill

Paid to Will Dove a Labourer 6 days	00	03	06
John Wareing Labourer for the like	00	03	06
Hugh Noble Labourer 2 days	00	01	08
Will Eggleston Labourer 6 days	00	03	08
Tho: Fleeman Labourer 5 days	00	03	04
Rob: Hall Labourer 4 days & a half	00	03	00
Paid for 2 Weelbarrows	00	10	06
For 4 Skeps	00	02	00
For 5 loads of Lime and Carriage	02	06	08
Paid John Dawbene for 4000 Bricks	02	08	00
Allowed in drink to those that brought ye Lime	00	01	08
Allowed in drink when the bricks were lead	00	01	00
for leading those bricks	00	09	00
Mr. Bensons charges when he went to bespeak Lime	00	02	00
Paid John Parnell for mending the pump	00	03	00
Nails, Tallow and allowance in drink	00	01	00
For a new spout to the said pump	00	01	06
John Wareing Labourer as before 6 days	00	03	06
Will. Egleston Labourer 6 days	00	03	06
Hugh Noble Labourer 4 days	00	02	08
Tho: Fleeman Labourer 6 days	00	03	06
Rob: Hall Labour 6 days	00	03	03
Simon Reddish Labourer 6 days	00	04	00
John Wareing Labourer 4 days	00	02	04
Rob: Hall Labourer 4 days	00	02	00

Hugh Noble Labourer 4 days	00	02	04
Simon Reddish Labourer 4 days	00	02	08
Tho: Fleeman Labourer 3 days & a half	00	01	09
To Rob: Pettinar Mason for repairing the wells	00	06	00
For mending the Weelbarrows	00	00	06
Sept. 23 spent then in Ale of the workmen	00	02	10
To Charles Harp for leading stone from the Lady House	00	05	06
For uncovering the said house given to this work by Mr. Butler	00	13	00
To John Biggins Carpenter for taking it down	00	12	06
To Labourers for layeing by the materials	00	09	10
To John Lilly for leading the same to the woodyard	01	04	00
To Edward Crofts for the like	00	08	06
Then spent in drink	00	01	06
A pick Ax	00	01	06
Spent on Mr. Johnson imployed in surveying the work	00	03	06
For makeing a Saw pit	00	00	08
Spent more on the said Mr. Johnson	00	03	04
And also on John Biggins, Francis Butcher and Tho: Robinson when the came to give directions about this work	00	01	00
More to John Dawben[e] for Brick	02	00	00
Wood bought of Tho: Huthwait	00	13	00
A Ferne rope	00	09	08
Laid out for cutting and loading wood as above said	00	08	06
For leading 12 loads of wood	02	05	00
To Charles Harper for a load of Lime & Carriage	00	10	00
More for 10 loads of sand	00	11	06
Expended when Norwood-wood was sold	00	04	02
For leading of brick by several persons	00	18	00
For laying them up against Spring	00	02	00
More to John Dawben[e] for Brick	04	12	00
For leading Deals and in drink to those that brought them	00	17	04
For laying them up	00	00	04
To John Biggins Carpenter for 17 days	01	05	06
To Ric. Morley for 23 days and a half, Carpenter	01	10	08
	£	s	d
Sum tot	29	18	04

Mr. Bensons 2d Bill Sep: 2d. 1690			
To Will Hall & Rob Sargenson Labourers	00	02	08
To Couling, Salmon & Willington Labourers	00	03	04
To John Johnson for carriage of a load of lime & a load of stone from Mansfield	00	10	00
For drink for the Labourers	00	00	04
To Tho: Wilson for a soc & a Kitt	00	03	04
To John Wareing & John Jenkinson Labourers for 4 days	00	04	00
To Hu: Noble 2s 8d. & Wm. Beckit 2s. Labourers	00	04	08
To Wm. Hall 2s 8d. & Wm. Simpson 2s. Labourers	00	04	08
To Tho: Willington 4s & Ric: Ward 1s. 8d. Labourers	00	05	08
To the Men that fetched Sand, in drink	00	01	06
To Rob: Parker Smith for plateing hods and trunks	00	04	07
To Hu: Noble 4s. & Jo: Wareing 4s. Labourers	00	08	00
To John Jenkenson 4s. & Wm. Hall 4s. Labourers	00	08	00
To John Naul, Joyner, for six Hodds	00	01	08
For 4 Trunks	00	02	08
To Ric: Naul Joyner for making 4 windows	00	07	06
For 5 Deals each 4 yards long	00	08	04
To Ric: Borrodale 11 days Wm. Simpson 6. Labs.	00	11	04
To Ric. Borrowdale 3s. 4d. & Wm Hall 3s. 4d. Labs.	00	06	08
To Wm. Beckit, John Wareing, Hu: Noble and Tho. Wittington each 4s. for 6 days Lab.	00	16	00
For Beefe 6s Eggs 2d Bread 6d to entertain Eackring Booners	00	06	08
To Charles Harp for 3 loads of Lime & fetching	00	16	00
For Butter 4d Carrot 3d and flower 1d Entertain booners	00	01	01
To Oxton men that brought Brick	00	07	06
To Francis Gun for 20 load of sand	00	17	06
To Sam Savadge for the like	00	17	06
More to them for fetching 8000 Bricks	00	16	00
More to them for 2 load of Lime fetching	00	10	00
Allowed them in drink	00	02	00
Paid to the Nailar for a parcel of nails	01	05	10
To Wm. Hall 3s4d & Hu: Noble 3s4d Labourers	00	06	08
To Tho: Wittington 4s and Wm Beckit 4s Labs.	00	08	00
To John Jenkinson 3s4d & Tho. Wittington 3s4d Labourers	00	06	08
To Ric: Borrowdale 3s4d Wm Simpson 3s4d & Beckit 3s4d	00	10	00
Spent on the Mansfield workmen	00	03	08

To John Dawbene for 14000 Brick and some Tile	08	18	00
To Farnsfeild Men that led Brick	00	04	06
More To Rick: Stenton on the same acct.	00	01	08
To Leywood for pileing up Brick	00	00	06
To Rob. Watson, Carpenter at the rearing	00	17	00
To the Labourers then	00	04	06
More to the Nailar for Nails	00	18	06
Borrowdale 4s Beckit 4s Simpson 4s Jenkinson 4s Noble 4s Wittington 4s Labourers	01	04	00
To Tho: Woodhouse for Scaffold poles	00	18	00
To Tho: long for the like 6s. Carrinton 1s4d	00	07	04
To Simon Reddish labourer omitted before	00	03	04
To Rob: Groon for fetching 2 load of Stone and 1 load of lime from Mansfield	00	16	00
To Wm Hudson labourer	00	03	04
To Wm Simpson 3s4d Noble 3s4 and John Jenkinson 3s4d Labourers	00	10	00
To To: Wittington Labourer	00	03	04
To Chr. Beckit 8d and Wm Beckit 8d Labourers	00	01	04
To John Coup for leading 2 days Sand and one day Stone	00	12	00
For 12 Ridge tiles	00	01	06
Mr. Bensons horse hire to Oxton & spent there	00	00	10
To Will. Addamson Mason	00	13	00
For 2 bunches of Reeds	00	01	03
	£	s	d
Sum tot	30	10	09

Mr. Bensons 3d Bill. Oct. 71:90

To Wm Beckit 4s. Ric Borrowdale 3d4d and Chr. Beckit 3s4d. Labourers	00	10	08
To Rob. Pettinar Mason	01	00	05
To John Phillips for mending the copper	00	18	00
To John Lilly for fetching a load of lime	00	05	00
To Mr. Mores men that brought bricks	00	01	00
To Simon Reddish for goeing errands on this account	00	01	06
More to him for 5 days & a half as Labourer	00	03	08
To Wm Savadge for 12 bundles of reeds	00	04	00
To Ric: Ward for five bottles more	00	03	00
Spent on the pewterers man and horse	00	01	00
To Edward Crofts for 2 load of lime 10s 2 loads of wood from Norwood 4s and more for lime and sand 4s	00	18	00

More to him for 5 load of brick leading	00	04	00
More to him for leading stone 2 days from John Gibsons, & one load of brick from Hockerton	00	08	00
To Mr Blanthorn to buy colours & oyle	00	15	00
To Rob: Parker, Smith for the Copper grate and other work	00	16	00
To Jo: Wilson for fetching of several materials	00	10	00
To Mr Fowler for glew & to the matt maker for matts to keep out rain, before the house was glazed dureing winter 9^s^	00	09	07
Paid more for reeds to several persons	00	14	11
To Hu. Noble labourer 11 days	00	06	11
To Tho: Wittington Labourer 11 days	00	06	05
To Will. Simpson labourer 10 days	00	05	10
To Will Hall Labourer 10 days	00	05	10
To Hu: Noble Labourer 6 days	00	03	00
To Wm Hall 3^s^ and Wittington 3^s^ labourers	00	06	00
To Ric. Borrowdale labourer 13 days	00	06	10
To Wil. Simpson labourer	00	03	00
To John Jenkingson labourer 12 day	00	07	00
To Edward Harvey for leading the wood from Bellowpark 2^ll^10^s^ & spent 4^d^	02	10	04
To Rob Watson to pay the nailar	00	09	04
To Leywood for helping to fill sand	00	00	04
To Hu: Nobles boy for serving the matt maker as before	00	01	09
For Straw to make them	00	06	00
To Will. Adamson Mason	01	12	00
More fore 37 bundles of Reeds	01	01	07
To Ric Naul. Joyner for makeing the great door	00	04	00
To Ric Reddish for work done by his brother a labourer	00	09	03
To Ric Borrowdale 2^s^6^d^ Wm Simpson 2^s^6^d^ and Wm Hall 2^s^6^d^ labourers	00	07	06
To Wittington 2^s^6^d^ & Noble 2^s^6^d^ Labourers	00	05	00
More to Wittington 5^s^6^d^ Simpson 5^s^6^d^ and Wm Hall 5^s^6^d^ Labourers	00	16	06
More to Hu: Noble 5^s^6^d^ and to Ric Borrowdale 5^s^6^d^ Labourers	00	11	00
More to Mr Blanthorn for paint	01	05	00
To Tho: Reynold for a load of lime	00	05	04
A load of Brick from Oxton	00	03	00
To Sam Savadge for 3 loads of lime & 2 loads of Brick from Oxton	01	02	00

To Fran: Gun for 2 loads of lime & 2 loads of Brick from Oxton	00	16	08
More to him for fetching one load of tile & 5 loads of sand	00	05	00
More to him for a load of Brick	00	01	00
To Rob Pettinar for Mason work done at the Brewhouse etc.	00	02	08
To Rob Green for 2 loads of lime 10^{s}8^{d} and 2 loads of Brick 4^{s}	00	14	08
To Rob Watson for Reeds paid by him	00	01	06
To John Haughton Glazier	05	00	00
To Noble 3^{s} Wittington 3^{s} Hall 3^{s} and Simpson 3^{s} labourers	00	12	00
More to Jo. Wilson for work done by his team	01	04	06
To Edward Gervas and Jo. Randale for sawing by the foot	01	07	09
To Tho. Wittinton Labourer	00	03	06
Noble 3^{s}6^{d} Hall 3^{s}6^{d} and Simpson 3^{s}6^{d} Labourers	00	10	06
To Charles Harper for five loads of Brick from Hockerton	00	10	00
More to him for two loads of Stone from Mansfield	00	11	00
To Wittington 3^{s} Hall 2^{s}6^{d} Noble 3^{s} and Simon Reddish 3^{s} Labourers	00	11	06
To Fran: Stenton for fetching a load of Lime	00	05	04
More to Mr Blanthorn for painting the doors & windows	01	00	00
To Rob Parker, Smith	01	10	00
To M$^{rs.}$ Thornton for Ale & Bear allowed the workmen at several times	04	10	00
Mr. More for Bricks	03	00	00
To Jo. Carrinton for 1 load of lime and carriage	00	10	00
To Rob. Watson Carpenter	03	00	00
To John Biggins Carpenter	01	00	00
Fran: Butcher Carpenter	04	00	00
To Sam. Baily, Smith	00	05	00
To Peter Jackson Mason	05	00	00
To Randale and Gervas	00	02	00
	£	s	d
Sum tot	58	15	01

Mr. Bensons 4th Bill

Tho. Robinson, Mason, 3 days	00	04	00
To John Simpson Mason	01	00	00

To Tim: Stamford Joyner	01	00	00
To Jo: Wilson	00	13	08
To Edward Gervas the Sawer	00	02	06
For 6 locks	00	08	06
To Ric: & John Naul Joyners	00	06	00
For Glue	00	05	03
To Ric: Robinson Gardiner	00	03	00
More to Mr Blanthorn, ut Supra	01	00	00
To Will Hudson, Labourer for a 11 days	00	05	06
To Wm Hall & Hu: Noble Labourers	00	11	00
To Will Simpson, Labourer	00	05	06
Allowance in drink to the Labourers	00	05	00
More to Ric and John Naul Joyners	00	13	00
To Simon Reddish Labourer	00	03	00
To Joseph Wilson	00	06	00
To John Blundy for a Ladder	00	06	06
To Tho: Robinson Mason	00	17	04
To John Biggins Carpenter	05	00	00
To Ric. Reddish for Simon as Labourer	00	15	00
To Mr. Wells for Kiln drying a parcell of deal Bords	00	05	00
To John Coup for work done by his team at several times	01	06	00
To John Kitchin for a 11 Bales	00	02	09
To Sam. Baily Smith	03	00	00
To Rob: Kitchin	00	00	06
To Tho: Woodhouse for Setts in the 2 Gardens	00	02	02
To John Randale the Sawer	00	01	00
To Mr Garner for lime	00	10	10
To Will Kemp for nales	03	12	09
To Ric: Robinson for fruit trees	00	07	00
To Hu: Noble for 3 days as labourer	00	01	06
To Ric: Robinson ut supra	00	05	00
To Simon Reddish Labourer	00	04	00
To Simon Reddish for White Leather	00	08	06
More to him to bespeak deals at Newarke	00	00	08
To Wm. Hall Labourer for 4 days	00	02	00
To Hu: Noble labourer for the like	00	02	00
To John Caley for fetching one load of lime	00	05	04
More to Rich: Robinson for fruit trees	00	11	03
To John Haughton for mending ye Copper	00	00	02
For fire Shovel, Tongues and other things	00	03	00
	£	s	d
Sum tot	26	04	02

Mr. Bensons 5th Bill

To Mark Keep for tialls for scaffolds	00	10	00
To Wm Hall Labourer for 4 days	00	02	00
To Wm Simpson for the like	00	02	00
To Robinson the Gardiner for trees and work	01	14	00
To Cornelious Tyrril for drawing the last account	00	04	00
To John Biggins Carpenter	02	00	00
Peter Frignal for his encouragement was promised grass for his horse and for wch Mr Thornton had	00	06	00
To Will. Stenton for 16 strike of lime	00	05	04
To Mr Benson for 20 strike	00	05	06
For one load of walling stone and two pavers	00	02	06
To Will. Hudson labourer for 2 days	00	01	00
More to Rob. Parker, Smith	01	09	07
To streighten accts wit Ric: Robinson Gardiner	00	04	10
To Mr Wilkock for a horse which he lent Rich. Robinson to bring trees	00	00	08
To Simon Reddish Labourer	00	04	03
To Hu: Noble 3 days and Wm. Hall 3 days labourers	00	03	00
To Rob: Pettinar and his man, Masons	00	05	06
To Francis Hall Labourer	00	03	00
To Tho. Woodhouse for more setts	00	02	06
To Ed: Crofts for work done by his team	00	15	00
To Wm Hall 3 days 1s6d. Hu: Noble 3 days 1s6d labourers	00	03	00
To Wil. Simpson labourer 1 day	00	00	06
To the Glazier	01	00	00
To Wm Simpson 1s4d Wm Hall 8d Labourers	00	02	00
To John Randale for one day and dressing the sink	00	01	02
To Ric. Naul Joyner 4 days and a half	00	06	00
To Mrs Jackson	02	01	06
To Ric Naul Joyner 7 days and a half	00	10	00
More to Ric. and John Naul Joyners	00	13	04
More to John Naul Joyner 5 days	00	06	08
To the Glazier for plumbers work	05	00	00
To John Naul Joyner	00	05	04
	£	s	d
Sum tot	19	10	02

Mr. Bensons 6 Bill

Paid to Wm Hall and Simon Reddish Labourer	00	03	10
For fetching Wood	00	03	02

To Wil. Randale for Reeds	00	02	06
Expended on the workmen w^{n} they thrashed plaister	00	01	00
More by order to them	00	00	06
To Wil Adamson Mason	00	04	00
Will. Savadge labourer 3 days	00	02	04
Wm Eggleston labourer 4 days	00	02	00
Wm Simpson, labourer	00	02	00
To Rob. Wittington labourer	00	02	00
To Ric: Naul & Tim: Stamford, Joyners	01	00	00
To John Biggins Carpenter	00	09	04
For allowance in drink to the sawers	00	00	08
To John Naul	00	10	00
To Wm Simpson labourer	00	04	02
To Ro: Wittington labourer	00	04	02
For allowance in drink	00	00	10
To Ric & John Naul Joyners	01	00	00
More to them & Tim: Stamford Joyner	01	15	00
More to Tim: Stamford	00	10	00
To Wittington Labourer	00	00	08
More to Ric Naul Joyner	00	05	11
To Tho: Reynold for fetching stone from Linbey	00	05	06
To Tho: Robinson for helping to load	00	00	06
To Jo: Adams for Nails	00	19	08
To Wm Hall labourer	00	02	00
More to Ric: Naul Joyner	00	07	01
Allowance in drink to the Masons	00	03	04
Paid Tim: Stamford Joyner by Mr Mompesson's order	00	10	00
To Ric: Naul to buy deals at Newarke	00	02	00
To Tho: Robinson Mason	01	10	00
To Ric Robinson Gardiner as appears by bill	00	12	09
For 77 deals and some oak boards	05	17	06
	£	s	d
Sum tot	17	14	05

Mr. Bensons last Bill Aug: 7. 91

For carriage of wood out of Norwood	00	06	00
To Ed: Crofts for a load of lime & sand	00	11	00
To Jo: Blundy for Nails	00	02	00
To Ric Jenkinson for laying up brick and lime	00	01	00
To John Adams for 2 pair of joynts	00	01	00
To Will Simpson Mason to be acc^{ted} for in his work	00	02	06

To M[rs] Hall for some old boards	00	10	00
To Ric: Naul Joyner	00	18	00
More to him by M[r] Mompesson	00	10	00
More to W[m] Simpson Mason	01	00	00
For 2 large scutles to carry rubish in	00	01	00
To Simon Reddish for reeds	00	06	00
To Rob Parker Smith	00	10	04
To M[r] Aslin for 7000 bricks	04	04	00
To Widdow Thornton for some bricks	00	05	04
for a Riddle for the lime	00	00	08
For Stone from Linbey	00	05	00
For leading Bricks from M[r] Aslins	00	12	00
	£	s	d
Sum tot	10	05	10

1[t] Bill	29	18	04
2[d] Bill	30	10	09
3[d] Bill	58	15	01
4[t] Bill	26	04	02
5[t] Bill	19	10	02
6[t] Bill	17	14	05
& Last Bill	10	05	10
tot. of M[r] Bensons Acc[ts].	192	18	09

Other accounts given in by M[r] George Mompesson dureing his Residence at Southwell on the Acc[t] of the Resident house, Library, etc. allowed and paid by M[r] Mompesson.

For 3 Plaister thrashers	00	03	00
To Ric & John Naul Joyners	00	08	00
To W[m] Randale for 6 Bundles of Reeds	00	03	00
To M[r] Blanthorn to buy Oyle	00	05	00
For 3 Locks	00	02	09
To M[r] Andrews for Brick	07	07	08
To Rob: Parker, Smith	00	03	04
To Ric. Naul Joyner for 2 days work	00	02	08
To Tho: Robinson 10 days work and his man 9. Masons	01	00	06
To Will. Hudson his Labourer	00	06	10
To Ric. Robinson for Apricock trees and other plants	00	10	09
To W[m] Simpson for Ale allowed to workmen & his own work	00	12	02

For the carriage of deals from Newark	00	03	06
More to Rob: Parker Smith	00	12	00
Drink to workmen when plaister floors was shot at a 2d time	00	01	00
To Wm Keep Labourer	00	00	06
To Tho: Robinson Mason	00	10	00
To Ric: Naul & a Stranger Joyners that made the Cornish in the dining room chimney	00	12	00
To Ron: Parker Smith for Casements	01	04	00
To men who brought Lime	00	01	02
More to Tho: Robinson Mason	02	12	10
A Bill from Sam: Baily smith for Casements & other work	04	00	00
To Wilson for leading Sand & Clay	00	05	00
For an Iron Ceive	00	03	06
For cleanseing the well & pump	00	07	00
To. Mr Kemp for Nails	01	18	00
More to Tho Robinson Mason	03	00	00
To Ric: Naul Joyner	00	05	00
To a Smith for hinges	00	02	00
More carriage of deals from Newarke	00	03	09
More to Tho: Robinson Mason	01	16	06
To Wm Simpson Mason	01	00	00
To a Joyner who turn'd ye Banisters	00	05	00
To Simon Reddish Labourer	00	10	00
To Ric: Naul Joyner	00	05	00
To Wm Hudson Labourer	00	01	02
To John Abbot for Sand	00	02	06
To Charles Harp for leading Brick & Lime	00	16	08
For Nails used in the wainscot	01	01	06
To Simon Reddish Labourer	00	05	00
To Fra: Hall Labourer	00	10	00
To Rob. Parker Smith	00	08	04
To Ric. Naul Joyner	00	07	04
More for 2 Iron Hinges	00	02	04
To John Haughton Glazier	00	02	06
To Ed: Crofts for leading Brick & Lime	00	08	04
More Brick bought at Oxton	01	10	00
To Wm Hall Labourer	00	02	09
To John Adams A Smith	00	07	00
For 2 Riddles	00	01	00
To Ben Willcock for writeing Mr. Bensons accounts	00	02	00
For 2 pair of gimmers from Nottingham	00	01	04
To Clear accts with Rob: Parker Smith to Ap: 28.91	00	10	10
And to Clear accts with John Haughton Glazier at the same time	01	12	00

To Mr Rippon for fetching a load of deals from Mansfield	00	05	00
To Mr Fowler for more glue	00	02	06
6 pair of small Gimmers from Newarke	00	01	06
For a strike of critch Lime	00	01	04
For 6 loads of Lime to Mr Garner	01	06	00
More for 2 loads of critch Lime	00	10	00
To John Gibsons man for drying Deals	00	05	00
Sum tot	42	07	04

This sheet is attested by me
Geo. Mompesson

These following sums where disbursed by Mr William Mompesson

Paid by Rob: Busfield to workmen in Bellow Park on acct of the Resident house	00	10	00
To the Mansfield men as follows:			
To Geo: Balm for Free stone	03	08	00
To Isaac Milner	01	10	00
To Rob: Watson	05	08	06
To Mr Garner for lime	04	11	06
To Peter Jackson & his men	10	00	00
To Peter Frignole & his men	03	00	00
To Streighten accts with these men	07	14	00
To Fra: Butcher to buy deals	10	00	00
More on his brothers acct for work	05	00	00
And to streight accts with him	00	06	09
To John Biggins Carpenter to buy deals	08	00	00
For the materials of Sr Ric: Loyds old house	05	00	00
To Mr Girton of Newark for deals	03	18	00
To John Haughton the plumber	02	00	00
To Dan: Clay Joyner towards ye Wainscot	06	00	00
To Mr Blanthorn for painting the dineing room with one shilling earnest	06	01	00
For lime at Warsop and the carriage of it by Eakrin & Bilstrop draughts	04	18	00
To Jo: Palethorp ye 2 Jones & Wm Peck for felling & breaking up wood in Bellow Park	01	09	00
And 100ll was borrowed towards the building ye bond commenceing May 20th 1690, the interest in May 91	05	00	00

More in extraord: Charges for 2 Journeys one to London another to York by Mr M-Son all which was to raise contributions to this work, when 100ll was got from my Lord Cornish Rawlinson, and the Norwood trees from the Arch:Bp of York & 10ll from Dc Holder	00	00	00
Wood in Bellow Park wch was allowed ye Earl of Kingstone in his fine for Kneesal Lease. Two parts of which belongs to the accountant a 3d part to Mr Cudworth when the accounts are ballanc't.	10	00	00
To Rob: Petinar Mason	02	10	00
A large Wiskit to carry Rubbish	00	00	06
To John Dawbene for 4000 Bricks	02	08	00
John Biggins Carpenter haveing wholely undertaken the double roof of the Brewhouses May 14 92 pd him yn	08	00	00
Expended on the workmen when the roof was reared	00	08	00
Paid Dan: Clay Joyner on Acc't	00	10	00
More to him by bill, by Mr Burbidge	06	00	00
To Rob: Petinar Mason. May 28. 92	00	15	00
He rec.d on this acct of Ric Inglesbys	01	06	00
Allowed the workmen May 30. 92 in Ale	00	01	00
Paid Ric: Naul Joyner Nov: 28. 91 for 33 days work omitted in the preceding accounts	01	18	00
To Wm Simpson Labourer at the same time	00	03	00
And then allowed in drink	00	02	00
To a Cooper for mending the common Tub	00	01	00
To Mr Rippon for bringing a load of deals from Mansfield	00	05	00
Paid Rob Pettinar Mason who undertook all the mason work in the last building yt was in 1692	06	01	06
Paid more to John Biggins Carpenter to be accounted for	04	00	00
To Hu: Noble Labourer for prepareing the Kitchin for paveing	00	01	00
To Mr Blanthorn for layeing some windows in Oyle in ye last Building	00	05	00
A Bill from Mr Girton for Deals	05	00	00
Paid more to Rob: Pettinar Mason	03	18	04
Paid more to Mr Blanthorn	01	00	00
92. July 3d Paid to John Haughton Glazier for lead work & to be accted for	03	00	00
Aug. 13. 92 paid to Ric Naul Joyner	00	08	08
Paid Rob: Silvester of Mansfield for paveing work	04	13	01
To Ed: Crofts for bringing a load of these pavers	00	05	04
To John Dawbuck for 1000 Bricks	00	12	00
Oct. 13. 92 paid Wm Turner his bill for leading several materialls to this work	04	13	00

To Ric: Stenton for some ridge tiles	00	02	00
To Rob: Parker Smith for mending some locks	00	00	06
To Phil: Harrisson for some scaffold ropes	00	11	00
Mr Kemp bill for nails	03	05	03
Mr Burbidge for deals	11	09	07
To streighten acc^{ts} with John Haughton Glazier for lead & glass work	03	01	09
Allowed a bill of Mr Hesledens which he paid to several men imployed in this work	13	12	11
A years interest in May. 92 for the 100^{ll} that was borrowed	05	00	00
To Clear accounts with John Biggins Carpenter, to Nov. 3. 92	22	08	04
Bills paid for the resident house within Mr Chadwick's Residence:			
Ap. 22. 93 Paid to R. Watson to discharge. To Ketton of Mansfield for hair before omitted	01	00	00
Copeing stones bought of Mrs Silvester before omited to be paid	00	12	00
Paid Mr Blanthorn for drawing some black below ye hangings in the best chamber after charg'd			
Dan: Clay Joyner, who made the Wainscot in ye dineing room brought his bill Ju: 4. 93 when to streighten all accounts with him, was paid	20	11	01
Mr. Hesleden discharged several bills to prepare some rooms agst they comeing of the Arch BP. whose bills where allowed & paid	06	14	00
Paid Mr Blundy for Nails	00	13	00
More for Reeds	00	03	00
Given the workmen to drink	00	01	00
To Tho: Reynold for leading lime & sand	00	14	02
Paid Mr John Cartwright for the interest of 50^{ll} borrowed on this Acc^{t}	02	10	00
Paid Mr Burbeck of Newark the interest of the other 100^{ll} in 93	05	00	00
July 21 paid a bill to George Vessy of Eakrin for leading several loads of Lime from Warsop	01	16	00
Paid to Wm Hurst on the same account	00	05	00
Nov: 3. 93 paid to John Croup for sand	00	02	00

Bills paid by Mr Low as follows

To Rob Parker, Smith	00	11	09
Ric: Stathem Carpenter	01	16	00

To Mr Burbidge for Norway planks	01	05	06
To Mr Kemp for Nails	01	02	03½
To John Haughton Glazier for glass	01	07	06
To Mr. Garner for lime	00	17	08
To John Biggins Carpenter	01	00	00
Mr Flowers Stable being pull'd down and the materials used in this work allowed him to hire another	00	10	00
To John Alcock Labourer	00	01	00

The accounts for the Resident House dureing the time Mr Brearey should have kept Residence.

To Rob Parker Smith	00	05	06
Paid the Cooper for Setting 2 Garths on the common tub	00	01	00
Sep. 29. 94 Paid to Ric: Morley Carpenter	01	10	00
To Mr Kemp for Nails and 2 bunches of Reeds	00	07	00
To John Dawbene for 2000 and a half of bricks	01	10	00
To: Tho: Reynold for Carriage of Brick	00	11	04
To Ric: Naul, Joyner for a dore in the new passage	00	04	00
For a load of Lime	00	04	08
To Mr Fowler for glue & other things abt ye best Bed	00	03	00
To Mr Gee on the same account	00	05	07
To Mr Law for allowance in Ale to the workmen, before ommitted	00	07	06
To Rob: Pettinar Mason to be accted for	01	10	00
33ll 9'5½			

To streighten all accounts with Rob: Pettinar Mason	00	17	08
Allowed a Bill to Mr Benson Oct. 8. 94, for what he had laid down for work aboute the Resident House	04	09	01
The interest of 100 & 50ll before mention'd and borrow'd on this acct. in May 94 and paid to the fore mention'd parties	07	10	00
To Francis Butcher, Carpenter	05	00	00
Mr Benson hath laid out these following sums as appears by his Bills			
For fetching good from More house which now used in ye best Chamber towards its funiture	00	06	00
To Mr Cross the upholster for setting up the bed	01	05	00
To Blundy for Nails	00	13	10
For Reeds	00	03	00
To John Biggins for makeing the Staircase & other work	05	16	04
To John Haughton Glazier	01	07	06
6 deals & a slitt one to the Vicaridge	00	07	00

To Ric. Ward for reeds	00	02	06
To Ric Naul for 4 days	00	05	04
To Ric. Morley for 3 days	00	04	08
Ale for Ric: Naul & Ric Morley	00	00	09
To John Biggins for 3 slitt deals	00	03	00
To Ric. Naul, Joyner for 26 days	01	13	00
To him for makeing the new doore	00	03	00
To Will. Simpson a labourer	00	01	03
To Rob: Pettinar Mason	00	14	00
For drink to the workmen	00	01	02
For wood to burn the plaister	00	03	00
To John Biggins for 8 bunches of laths	00	04	00
To Tho. Reinold for lime & sand	00	16	00
To Mr Blanthorn for blacking the Chamber	00	01	06
June 7th to Rob Parker, Smith	00	04	02
June 16th to Wm. Kemp	01	07	00
To Mr Collinson	01	09	10
May 9th to Mr Collinson	03	19	03
Mr Benson hath laid out in Mr Chadwicks Residence as appears by his bill	09	10	00
He likewise paid to Mr Fillingham on the acct of Norwood park wood for damage pretended to be done	05	00	00
To Mr Benson for his care aboute the Building & the payment of bills	02	00	00
To John Haughton, Glazier	00	03	00
Paid to Wm Turner Sep. 27. 92	01	08	06
The interest of 150ll before mention'd one in May 1695	07	10	00
To James Nicholson for writeing the accounts & other Services done	00	10	00
A Bill to Ric: Morley before forgot	01	17	09
To Gregory Balm of Mansfield for the last Stone he sent	02	07	00
To Mr Johnson of Nottingham for surveighing the grownd	2	0	0
To Rich'd Naule wch Mr Benson paid him not before charged	0	14	4
To John Biggins for stoopes & Railes about the Vicaridge	7	9	0
To Sam Bayly for altering the Range in the Kitching	4	7	6
and for mending the Sink	0	4	0
Total Sume			
Total of Mr Wm Mompessons Account	361	13	1
Total of Mr Bensons Account	192	18	9

Total of Mr Geo. Mompessons Acc^t	42	7	4
The Goods in the House	57	10	0
The Charge in full	654	09	2

April 25 1695

Alloratur per me Jer: Cudworth
Auditorem.

Mr Mompesson charges himself with the receipts following

from the Lord Rawlinson	100	0	0
for the two Chapt^r Leases made over to Mr Mompesson in consideration of	190	0	0
Arch. Bps. Lamplughs gift in wood sold for	045	0	0
for Mr Clay's Lease	010	0	0
Arch Bp Sharps gift	020	0	0
Deacon Holders gift	020	0	0
the Earl of Clares now Duke of Newcastles gift	060	0	0
the Prebendaries subscriptions for wood sold	085	10	0
part of the Kings Money	020	0	0
Recd more from the Chapter	014	0	0
Allowed for work done at Mr Chappels house	005	0	0
The charge Total	537	10	0
Total of the Discharge	654	9	2
So remains due to Mr Mompesson	116	19	2

April 25. 1695
Alloratur per me Jer: Cudworth.
Auditorem

Memorand that in these Accounts there is a mistake of four pounds over charged upon ye Chapter so that remainder bal due to Mr. Mompesson ye sums of 112 19 2.

Wm Mompesson

Appendix B

The Vicars' Houses, 1780

(from Southwell Minster Library)

1780 Vicarage Houses. An Acct. of the Monies recd. & sp^{d} in the years 1779-80 & 81 by G. Hodgkinson an acct. of re building the above houses.

1779 Monies recd. by subscriptions towards the rebuilding the houses belonging to the Vicars Choral.

		£	s	d
25. Janry.	Mr. Reckand	20	0	0
	Dr. Caryl (in part of £100)	40	0	0
1st Feb.	Lord Harborough. By a D^{rt}. dated 20 Jan. 21 days after date on Wm. Noble, Melton.	100	0	0
	D^{o} – by a D^{rt} dated 20 Jan – 10 months after date on d^{o}.	100	0	0
25th	Dr. Rastall	50	0	0
	Dr. Wanley	15	0	0
	Mr. Loverack (By Dr. Oakes)	20	0	0
	Dr. Caryl (the rem^{r} of £100	60	0	0
	Mr. Porter (in part of £30	13	15	0
	Mr. Oliver	24	0	0
	Dr. Thomas	21	0	0
	Mr. Thos. Spragging for wood @ Halam	25	0	0
19 July	Fr. Ingleman 3 ton of old plaister @ 6/8 per ton	1	0	0
	Mr. Porter (the rem^{r} of £30)	16	5	0
	His Grace the Arch Bishop of York	50	0	0
	Mr. Cayley	25	0	0
	Mr. Watkins	10	0	0
	Dr. Cooper	15	0	0
		£606	0	0

1779	Disburst	£	s	d
28 Jan	Pd. Thos. Watson for his journey & his Expences with a ltr to Lord Harborough	0	9	2
	Pd. Wm. Thompson for hors & lime for d^{o}.	0	3	0
27 Feb.	Pd. for Ingleman – Bricklayer a Bill	8	19	4
10 March	Pd. Do.	1	6	9
29 March	Pd. Do.	4	3	10
22 May	Pd. Do. for Labourers	1	2	8
	Pd. Do. for do.	3	0	4
	Pd. Do. On Account of Work	8	8	0
	Pd. Geo. Harrison a Bill for carr^{e}. etc.	0	2	0
7 June	Pd. Sam^{e}. Herod for 7600 bricks	5	0	8
14 June	Pd. Fr. Ingleman on acct. of Bricklayers work	8	8	0
3 July	Pd. Richard Morley – Carpenter on Acct.	20	0	0
25 July	Pd. S. Herod for 13400 bricks	9	3	6
27	Pd. Fr. Ingleman on further acct.	8	8	0
	Pd. Wm. Wyre for tiles	1	5	0
	Pd. Saml Wright for lime	7	16	0
	Pd. S. Herod for bricks	6	12	1
11 Sept	Pd. Fr. Ingleman on further account	10	0	0
23	Pd. do on do.	8	8	0
2^{d} Oct.	Pd. Rich. Morely on do.	20	0	0
9th	Pd. Fr. Ingleman for labourers	3	18	9
29	Pd. Mrs Dawbney for carriage of materials	25	8	6
	Pd. G. Harrison for D^{o}. of Nails	0	3	4
	Pd. Fr. Ingleman the Rem^{r} of his Bill for measured work (the whole being £49.10.11)	5	18	11
	Pd. D^{o}. – for 400 bunches of reeds	8	0	0
10 Nov.	Pd. Richd. Morley on further Acct.	13	3	5
11	Pd. Thos. Bains for bricks & tile	46	6	10
	Pd. Sam. Herod for D^{o}	7	10	0
	Pd. Richd Elsam for Carr. of Stone	1	0	0
27	Pd. Fr. Ingleman on acct. of inside work	5	5	0
24 Dec.	Pd. D^{o}. on Acct. of D^{o}.	6	6	0
1780				
12 Jan.	Pd. Mr. Royle for Carr^{e} of Goods		4	3
	Pd. Jno Yates for d^{o} of materials	19	5	0
21	Pd. Robt Taylor for Ale etc. for workmen at the rearing	1	11	6
28	Pd. Richard Morley on further Acct	80	0	0
14 Feb	Pd. Fr. Ingleman on D^{o}.	14	0	0

		£	s	d
4 Mar[l]	pd. S. Herod for Brick Pavors	4	7	0
23	Pd. Fr. Ingleman on further Acct.	5	5	0
25	Pd. Mattw. Shepard for lime	9	4	0
15 Apl.	Pd. Richd. Morley on further acct.	30	0	0
15 May	Pd. John Richardson painter on account	4	4	0
16	Pd. Wm. Wright for lime	5	14	0
	Pd. S. Herod for Bricks etc.	1	19	0
20	Pd. Wm. Raynor Glazier on Acct.	32	0	0
10 June	Pd. Antho Ince Stone Masoner	12	14	10½
19 July	Pd. Fr. Ingleman the Remr. of his Bill for measured inside work (the whole being 42.11.9)	11	18	9
	Pd. Do a Bill for Lime & Days work	4	7	11
	Pd. Jno Ricardson the remr of his Bill for painting (the whole being 13.19.0)	9	15	0
22 Aug.	Pd. Mrs. Daubrey for leading Bricks, etc.	2	8	0
	Pd. Richd. Morley on further Acct.	30	0	0
	Pd. Robt. Adams for Iron work	4	4	0
	Pd. Jno Cullen for sand	0	11	0
	Pd.S. Herod for bricks	0	13	0
	Pd. Rd. Morley the remr. of his Bill for carpenters work (the whole being 221.7.0)	28	3	7
		568	7	1½
1781				
	Pd. Mr. Oliver for Hair	3	14	0
	Pd. Wm. Raynor the remr of his Bill for glaziers work (the whole being 63.13.6)	31	13	6
	Pd. Thos. Baines for bricks	0	14	3
	Mr. Huthwaite, Ironmonger (not paid)			
	Recd. by Subscriptions as on the other side	618	16	6½
	due to Geo. Hodgkinson	606	0	0
		12	16	6½

28 April
1781 Recd. of the Rev. Wm. Becher twelve pounds sixteen shillings and 6½ in full of the above balance by me

Geo. Hodgkinson.

Appendix C

The new front to the Residence House, 1785

(from Southwell Minster Library)

General State of the Accounts relating to the Additional Alterations which have been made to the residentiary house.

	£	s	d
Mr. Ince for bricks	53	14	0
Mr. Tinley ditto	32	3	8
Timber Merchant	116	0	0
Carpenter	98	0	0
Ironmonger	14	10	0
Sawing deals, etc.	11	8	9
Lime	12	12	0
Hair	3	10	0
Plumber & Glazier	119	10	0
Bricklayer & Plaisterer	76	0	0
Mason & stone	60	0	0
Leadings	24	0	0
	621	8	5
to complete the whole Expence Surveying included, about	84	0	0
	705	8	5
Estimate	650	0	0
	55	8	5

Cellar, Stone Bannisters, work in kitchen, chamber, Projecting Portico
Alterations in Chamber Communication etc.
not included in the original estimate.

Appendix D

Alterations to the Residence House, 1806

(from Southwell Minster Library)

An account of the Receipts and Expenditure occasioned by Rebuilding a part of the Residence House and making alterations in the East and West Entrances. From May 1806 to April 1809, by Geo. H. Barrow.

Received		£	s	d
1806	By money borrowed per order of chapter of Mrs. Rooke & Rich$^{d.}$ Redman	200	0	0
1807 8 May	By monies raised per sale of stock belonging to Geo. H. Barrow in 3 p. c^{t} Cons this day at 63 3/8, agreeable to an order of chapter held 23rd April 1807 making with £500 borrowed of Mr. Keyworth & placed to the New Fabric Fund the sum of £1200 then ordered to be borrowed	700	0	0
1808 18 Jan	By money then decreed to be borrowed of Mr. James Dowland from 4 Dec. 1807	2000	0	0
3rd Aug.	By James Nicholson upon sale of an old bedstead		15	0
1809 Jan^{y}	By Messrs Ridge upon the sale of old wood by Auction	12	13	6
19th	By money then decreed out of the Rota Fines	600	0	0
	1809 1st April This Account was examined with the vouchers which were delivered up and proved to be correct. Wm Becher Can: Res.			
		£3513	8	6

	Disburst	£	s	d
1806	To Richd. Ingleman, Mason – His Bill at			
to	Sundry times	951	13	6
1809	To Wm. Nicholson & Son, Carpenter			
	do–––do–––	1128	5	3
	To John Lee, Glazier, do–––do–––	235	12	8
1806	To costs – on procuration of £100 each			
	from Rooke & Redman	3	17	8
	To Geo. Hawksley for nails etc to Oct. 1806	2	13	10
1807	To Leonard Saxby – for leadings from			
	May '06 to Jan '07	74	7	5
	To Stephen Saxby for do. do. to do.	14	8	0
	To Thomas Hunt – for Bricks as per Bill	14	5	0
	To Jno Hibbard – for lime – ,,	25	12	6
	To Jos. Hibbard – for Lime – ,,	23	15	0
	To James Adams Whitesmith from			
	April '06 to Apr. 07	18	6	11½
	To Richd Fothergill – for slates – as per Bill	61	4	0
	To 1 years Interest of £200 due 5 April 1807	10	0	0
	To Molly Adams – for carriage – as per Bill	1	5	6
	To W. Nicholson Jnir – for Ale to Workmen	2	18	8½
1808	To Thos Hunt – for Bricks – as per Bill	34	4	6
	To Geo. Ince – for Stone – ,,	7	3	5
	To Richd Fothergill – for Slates – ,,	6	4	0
	To Miss Rouse – for Locks etc. – ,,	41	15	6
	To Thos Wood – for Kitchen Jack etc. ,,	3	17	10½
	To Leond. Saxby – for Leadings from Feb			
	to Oct. 1807	69	18	0
	To Stephen Saxby – for Do. in Feb. 1807	2	15	0
	To Jno Birkett for Hair – fm June '06 to			
	Oct '07	9	7	6
	To 1 Years Interest of £200 – due to April 1808	10	0	0
	To do. of £700 due to 8 May 1808	35	0	0
	To costs upon selling out Stock	3	19	6
	To ½ yrs. Interest of £2000 due to 4th June 1808	50	0	0
	carrd. over	£2842	11	3½
	Brot. on	2842	11	3½
Disburst				
1808	To Willm. Long – Plumber – a Bill	107	0	10
	To Geo. Hawksley – for nails etc. from Oct.			
	'06 to April 1808	81	15	3

		£	s	d
	To James Adams – Whitesmith from Apr '07 to Sept. 1808	33	15	5½
	To Henry Richardson – Painter – as per Bill	95	16	1
	To Mr. Dowland - ½ yr. Interest of £2000 due 4 Dec. '08	50	0	0
1809	To Hodgkinson & Co. costs on procuring said £2000	20	17	2
	To Nicholson & Son – carpenters – for sundry repairs from Feb. to July 1808	15	17	4
	To Jer. Nicholson & Co. for Bricks etc. as per Bill	6	13	3
	West Entrance			
1806	To Mellors & Co. – as per Bill – at Sundry paym[ts]	54	9	10
	To Thos. Raynor – for getting stone	2	18	0
	To Leon[d.] Saxby – for Leadings – as per Bill	25	6	0
	To Stephen Saxby – do – do	16	12	6
	To Jos[h] Wass – for 156[t] – Gravel	7	16	0
	To Geo. Ince – for stone	12	12	2
	To Rich[d.] Ingleman – for laying pavement etc.	18	16	2
	East Entrance			
1808	To Cook & Herod – for labour at Gravel Walk	4	7	6
	To Jn[o.] Sandaver – for plants, shrubs, etc.	7	4	8
	To Leonard Saxby – for leadings – as per Bill	19	14	6
	To J & E Smith & Co. – for iron gates	21	0	0
	To Jos. Kirk – for carr[e] of do from Mansfield		7	6
	To R[d.] Ingleman – for stone coping, paving etc.	27	17	10
	To Jer. Nicholson & Son for paving stone as per Bill	14	19	3
	To the Commission upon receiving and paying £3500	17	10	0
	To Post of Lrts – carr[e] of parcels – Rec[t] Sps. Doc[ts] & C also preparing this account On parchment	7	9	11
		£3513	8	6

Appendix E

Archbishop Tobie Mathew, the Palace, 1628

(from The Borthwick Institute of Historical Research, York. Chancery Rolls, 1628)

A true and perfect Inventory of ye Goods and Cattells which late were and did belonge unto the most Reverend Father in God Tobie late Lord Archbishopp of Yorke Primate of England and Metropolitane viewed and prised at Southwell in the Countie of Nottingham by foure indifferent persons viz: George Small gent Thomas Palmer gent James Arnold and John Beedham the 23th. day of July *1628.*

At Southwell

Imp:^{ris} in the Nurserie one stand bedstead with a wooden teaster and a truckle bedstead	xiiij^{s}
It a table on a Forme and a frame for a payre of virginals	vj^{s}
It iij Presses one bigger than another, & a litle cupbord	xl^{s}
It iij Joynd Formes and iiij dosan and iiij Joynd stooles	l^{s}
It vij litle Joynd stooles	iiij^{s}
In the next Chamber a bedstead with a wooden teaster & a Livery Cupbord	xviij^{s}
In the chamber next to that a Feild bedstead a livery cupbord and a litle table on a Frame	xl^{s}
In the Lobby a table on a Frame	iiij^{s}
In the Chappell a large wainscoate seate and a deske for the Chapline	xiij^{s} iiij^{d}
It iiij Planke formes	iij^{s}
In the Chamber next the Chappell a table on a Frame and a Joynd stoole	iij^{s}
In the Chamber next the withdrawinge Chamber a Livery Cupbord, a Frame for bookes and a joynd stoole	xiij^{s} iiij^{d}
In the withdrawinge Chamber a litle table on a Frame and iiij Joynd stooles	x^{s}
In a studdy next thertoo a litle table on a frame & divers shelves	iij^{s}

In the greate Chamber, ij tables on Frames a litle draw table and a Cupbord	xx^{s}
In the Rowles Chamber a livery bedstead	iij^{s} iiij^{d}
In the Chamber above that a bedstead with a wainscote head a table on a Frame a wooden Chaire ij litle tressles and ij litle shelves	x^{s}
In the Chamber at the end of the greate Chamber a Livery bedstead and iij Joynd stooles	v^{s} x^{d}
In the Chamber within that a bedstead wth a wainscoate head a shelfe and a Planke Forme	vj^{s}
In the Chaplins Chamber ij bedsteads with wooden teasters iij tables on Frames & ij Cupbords	xl^{s}
In the Stewards Chamber a bedstead with a wooden teaster and ij tables on Frames	xx^{s}
In the Storehouse a table on a frame & ij Cupbords	xj^{s}
It in divers rooms aboute the house xvij livery bedsteads vj tables on Frames iiij stooles a turn'd Chayre and a litle safe	iiij^{li} x^{d}

Appendix F

The Residence House, 1699

(from Southwell Minster Library)

An Inventory of ye Goods belonging to ye Residence House in Southwell, April 17th, 1699.

Kitchin

Four dozen of plates
One Pye Plate
Seven pewter dishes or chargers
One deeper dish for soop
3 pewter porringers. 1 wanting when Mrs. Carie came
A pewter flaggon
A window curtaine
One pewter cup
One mustard pott
One coale pick. 10 knives
Two Rings for a table
Two pewter chamber potts
One pewter basin
A rolling pin & pudding slice
Footsteps for ye jack
6 knives. 13 forks
2 pewter dishes

Tinns

2 dripping pans. 1 fish plate
1 cullender. 2 Dishcovers
1 Dridging box
1 paire of brass candlesticks
One snuff dish & snuffers
2 kettles 3 Pott kettles
2 saucepans 1 Brass ladle
1 copper cann 1 Egg turner
1 warming pan. 1 frying pan

1 Chafing dish
1 brass stew pan

Iron
3 spitts. 2 Racks. 1 paire of tonges
1 fire shovel. 1 Tosting fork
1 Beef fork. 1 cleever. 1 Trivet
1 shredding knife. 2 Running hook
1 Double hook 6 skuers. 1 fender
1 Jack with Jack Line & chaine
1 Pig Plate. 2 Hangers. 2 Frogs
2 Iron plates. 1 paire of bellows
1 Salt box. 1 candle box
4 Bulrush chairs. 1 lazy back
1 Kitt. 2 skuers
1 iron drinkin pan.

Low Lobby
1 Table. 1 Forme

Pantry
1 Powdring tub. 2 Flower Tubs
2 Pipping potts. 6 Barrels. 1 Kimnell
A Key board

Dining Room
2 dozen of Russia chairs
2 Oval tables. 1 sideboard table.
1 Grate. Fireshovel & Tongs
1 doz. of Pictures in Ye Upper lobby, Staircase & Best Chamber.
1 Table in Ye upper Lobby.

Best Chamber
8 cane chairs. 1 large looking glass
1 table & stands. 1 Fireshovel & tongs
Grate. Bellows. Hearth brush
1 Underquilt. 1 Feather bed
1 Boulster. 2 Pillows 3 Blankets
2 upper quilts. one silk & ye other calicoe
7 curtains course Holland for the windows. Printed hangings
1 fine large . . . ider

A Press to hang clothes in the passage to Ye other rooms

Next Chamber
Feather bed wth a Matt. 1 Boulster
2 Pillows. 2 Blankets. 1 Rugg
Hangings. Side table with a cloth
2 old Turkey work stools. 1 Grate

Back Kitchin
1 Range. 1 Temms. 1 Hairsieve
Another of Tiffany. 1 Kneading Tub

Brewhouse
1 Copper. 1 Mash tub wth an Underdeck
2 Washing tubs. 3 New Fatts.
Tun dish. A thing to beat in drink
Kitts.

The Library
Folio 127. Quarto 15
Octavo 8 Large frame for
Benefactors carved & laquerd.

Ticknal Ware
2 Panshons. 1 Black Pitcher
1 Long Mugg. 2 little ones
1 White & blew Traite Dish
2 Chamber pots. 1 White chamber pot.
one flint glas

In the Closet or Study by the Lobby
4 Acts of parchment
two for land taxes one
for births and burials &
one for the capitation
Register of Leases
The White Book
A Rental 1539. Liber A
A book of admissions Institutions etc
Registrum capitale 1470
Audit Accounts 1690
To be put into the Treasury
Tabula jive Repertorium
(list of books continues over page miscellaneous Receivers Acts, books of leases, fines etc.)

Appendix G

Elizabeth Rippon, Rampton Prebend, 1683
(Notts. County Record Office PRSW/97/17B)

A true Inventory of all and Singular the goods Chattells and Creditts of E Rippon widow deceased taken and appraised at Southwell the 9th. day o 1683 by Thomas Rippon gent and William Lock as followeth

Impri's her purse and apparell 04

Item In the Hall
A fire Iron two tables and two formes one Cupboard a Lanseckle Three Chaires & other things 02

Item In the Pewter Buttery
Nineteen pewter dishes 3 dozen of Pewter plates 7 pewter Chamber potts 2 basons eleven Candlesticks six salts, one Cupboard and other things 06

Item In the Great Parlour
One Bedstead with a Feather bed bolster Curtains, & other things beloning to it, three tables, & Carpetts one stand, one Livery Cupboard 15 Chaires foure stooles and one Forme, Fire Iron & Tonge & other things 10

Item In the Kitchin
Eleven Brasse Panns three Skelletts three brasse potts, three brasse morters & 3 pestles, Fire Iron Frogs shovell tongs hooks a gallow tree, three pairs of Cobb Irons & nine spitts three Iron Dripping panns 5 tinn plates 2 brasse ladles, one wooden platter 3 chairs & 3 stooles & other od things 09

Item In the Larder
Ten pewter dishes 4 porringers a dozen pewter spoones

	one frying Pan Clever, one Safe and a Chest one powdring Tubb one Salt Tubb, one Kymnell & Tray Two wooden platters & other od things	01	13	06
	In the Brewing house One Lead Brewing Tubb one paire of Quernes one Strike a Brandrith and a fire Grate & other Lumber	02	19	00
	In the Fatt house One Guile Fatt Five washing Truncks, one Kymnell Three Serges, and other Lumber	01	02	06
Item	In the Little Roome by the Cellar One Table and Two Formes	00	04	00
Item	In the Cellar Six hoggs-heads, three Barrells, Fifteene Flagons & some other od things	03	16	00
Item	In the Dyers Roome Two Tables and one forme	00	11	00
Item	In the Room in the Court called the Rose One table and the seats about it	00	03	00
	In the Seeled Chamber One bedstead Feather bed and Bolster Curtains & vallance, and all things necessary to it, three tables and a forme, and one Truckle bed Six Chaires and two stooles one Livery Cubbard Looking Glass, Fire Iron Tongs and Fire Shovell & Nyne pictures One Cupboard Cloath and Carpett	08	08	00
Item	In the Closett next the Seeled Chamber One Close Stoole and Pann	00	04	00
Item	In the Gatehouse Chamber One Bedstead and a Feather bed and all things to it, one Table, one Livery Table, one Chaire and Stoole one Chest one dozen of Turkey worke Cussions and the Looking Glass and an old Carpett	04	00	00

Item In a roome called the Closett One halfe headed bed with Feather bed, and things to it One Chest and a Little Chaire Also in the same roome, One Rugg two Bolsters, two Coverletts, and three Pillows One Silver Bowle, twelve Silver Spoones	08	15	00
Item In the Pewter Buttery Chamber One whole headed Bedd, feather Bed and all things belonging to it, One halfe headed bed, featherbed one paire of Coverletts and a paire of Blanketts Two Chests, one Chaire and a Screene and one Quilt	07	01	00
In the Kitching Chamber One Teaster bed, one halfe headed bed, and a truckle bed & three feather bedds, with things belonging to them, Six Chests, two Trunks and a box, Six and twenty pairs of Linned Sheets One dozen and an halfe of pillow Beers, Six Dozen of Diaper Napkins, and 3 dozen of Course huckaback napkins two Diaper Table Cloathes and one other of huckaback Two Tubs of feathers, and a paire of Mattin, Eight paire of Course sheets	28	03	00
In the Yard Chamber One Tester Bed, and one Truckle bedd, with all things belonging to them, one Table, and two Carpetts one forme eight chaires five Stooles fire Shovell and Tongs one Livery Cupboard	07	15	00
In the French Mans Chamber One Tester bed, with Feather bed, and all things belonging to it, Two tables and two formes two Chaires and foure Stools, and one Chest, and one fire Iron	05	00	00
In the Inner French Mans Chamber One feather bed, with the Tester and all things to it, two Chaires One Table, on Screene one Chest and one Stoole	04	02	00

In the yard			
One horse trough, three Swyne troughs and two ladders	00	10	06

William Lock
Thomas Rippon

117	00	00	Suma total

Appendix H

Gervas Rippon, Rampton Prebend, 1714
(Notts. County Record Office 116/106)

November the 10th. 1714

A true and perfect Inventory of all and every the Goods and Chattles of Mr. Gervas Rippon of Southwell in the county of Nottingham late deceased as followeth.

	£:	s:	d
Item Purse and apparell	10	0	0
Goods in the Kitchin and pewter and brass	5	10	0
Goods in the house and best Parlor at	4	15	0
Goods in the Mens parlor at	4	5	0
Goods in the Buttreys and Sellar at	1	5	0
Goods in the best Chamber at	5	0	0
Goods in the second Chamber at	6	0	0
Goods in the third Chamber at	8	6	8
Goods in the Cheese Chamber at	2	0	0
Goods in the Stone Chamber and Wool	10	0	0
Goods in the Garrat at	2	6	8
All the Linnens at	5	0	0
Old wood and fold fleaks at	2	10	0
All the Hay and Corn in the Barns	65	0	0
Waggon and Carts and Stone troughs	8	10	0
Coales plaister tiles slates stand hecks and wood	5	0	0
Plows harrows Gears and such materials	4	10	0
Tan forkes rakes Sacks Strike at	2	0	0
14 swine at 5^{li} 10^{s} All the sheep at 64^{li}	69	10	0
Six Cows six young beass 5 Calves all at	27	0	0
All the Horses and Mares young and old	57	10	0
Corne upon the Grounds and Clots	22	0	0
Debts good and bad at	7	13	10
A hovell and mannar at	2	6	8
Poultry in the yard	0	5	0
Things unseen and forgot at	2	10	0
	341	3	10

Appraised by

Thomas Rippon
Hen: Moore
Robert Green his mk X
Rich$^{d.}$ Vincent

Appendix J

Samuel Lowe, Dunham Prebend, 1723

(from Notts. County Record Office PRSW 122/17)

A true and perfect Inventory of all and Singular the Goods Cattles and Chattells of Samuel Lowe late of Southwell in the County of Nottingham Esqr. decd. taken and appraised the Sixteenth day of December Anno. Dom. 1723 by us whose names are herunto subscribed.

	£	s.	d.
Imprimis His Purse and Apparrell	05	00	00
Moneys at Interest	2940	12	08
Odd debts good and bad	130	14	00
Arrears of Rent	91	05	04
In the Hall			
One clock and case	01	00	00
Three Ovell Tables	00	10	00
One looking glass & Barometer	00	08	00
Fire Shovell and Tongues	00	01	06
In the Great Parlour & passage			
One Napkin press	00	10	00
Twelve Caine Chairs & Couch	02	05	00
One looking glass and Table	05	00	00
One Stove Fire Shovell and Fender	00	09	00
In the Great Kitching			
Six dozen of pewter plates	03	00	00
Six pewter salvers	00	09	00
Five and Twenty pewter dishes	03	15	00
One looking Glass	00	02	06
One Copper Stewpan	00	04	00
A pasty pan Cullender and Bason pewter	00	05	00
Two Copper tanns	00	03	06
Two brass pot panns a Fish brass pan & brass morter	01	15	00

Five brass Candlesticks	00	07	00
A brass Chaifen dish	00	02	00
One Jack Spitts & Irons in the Chimney	04	05	00
Eight Chairs and one Table	00	06	00
In the Back Kitching			
Two dozen and three pewter plaits	00	16	00
Five pewter dishes	00	10	00
One Copper	01	05	00
Five pott panns	01	00	00
Three Kettles	00	06	00
Three sauce panns	00	05	00
One bedpan	00	02	00
Two Chairs	00	01	00
Irons in the Chimney	00	10	00
In the Flower House			
Som Lumber	00	05	00
In the Cellars			
Four whole Hogsheads	00	16	00
Six Firkins	00	04	00
Thralls	00	01	00
Twenty Foure halfe hogsheads	02	08	00
In the Brewhouse			
A Copper and Irons	03	03	00
A Tubb	00	10	00
One brass pot	00	06	04
Apair of Querns	00	12	00
Other odd things	00	10	00
Coales and Wood	10	00	00
In the Barne			
Foure lathers and other odd things	00	10	00
Two Coaches wth. Harness to 'em	30	00	00
Two Coach Mares, one Sadle Mare, One Foale, Bridles and sadles	15	00	00
	3261	09	10

	£	s	d
Hay	03	00	00
In the Office			
One large press	01	10	00
One Chest of drawers	00	12	00
A desk	00	06	00
Eight Chairs	00	08	00
One other press over the Chimney	00	12	00
One little desk and Table	00	05	00
A press next the great press	00	05	00
Books in the Office and Closet	05	00	00
A Chest of Drawers	01	00	00
In the Chamber over the Hall			
One Bed and Furniture	07	00	00
Nine Chairs and one Squab	01	10	00
Foot Cloth and two Cushions	00	08	00
Looking glass & two Stands	02	15	00
In the Chamber within the last mentioned Chamber			
One Bed and Furniture	04	10	00
Five Caine Chairs	00	12	06
In Mrs.Lowes Room			
Two Bedds wth. Furniture	04	00	00
One looking glass and Table	00	09	00
Two presses & one Close Stool	01	10	00
Irons in the Chimney	00	05	00
In Mrs. Betty Lowes room			
One Bed wth. Furniture	03	05	00
In the Ceild Chamber			
Six Chairs and one looking glass	01	00	00
One Bed wth. Furniture	04	00	00
In the Serv^ts. Garrot were the Men lyes			
One Bed & Furniture & one Chest	01	10	00
In the Chamber over the Parlour			
Thirteen Chairs	00	13	00
One Easy Chair	00	03	00

Two Tables	00	18	00
Two Stands	00	02	00
In the Chamber Over the Coach House			
One Corne Skreen	00	10	00
Two Strikes	00	06	00
Hopps	02	00	00
In the Chamber over the Office			
Two Cheesehacks	00	02	00
Cheeses	00	16	00
Candles	01	16	00
A Limbeck	00	10	00
Three Trunks	00	08	00
One box	00	03	00
One Wire Cive, Som old Iron & three Flower Tubbs	00	13	06
Two Sauce panns	00	03	00
One Neck & som Lumber 12 doz: bottles	00	05	06
In the Closet next the Office			
One Shoo Toar	00	18	00
Plaite Three hundred & Seventeen Ozs & 3 pennyweight	75	00	09
Linnens	15	00	00
	146	0	3

The Goods hereunder mentioned came from Norwell and was Mrs.Lowes before she was marryd to Mr.Lowe

	£	s	d
Imprimis In Mrs.Lowe's room			
One press for Cloaths	00	15	00
A Chest of Drawers	00	12	00
One other Chest of Drawers	01	00	00
A set of Drawers more	01	05	00
Foure Chairs	00	04	00
A Looking glass & dressing box	00	06	00
One Feather Bed	01	00	00
In the Ceild Chamber			
One bed and Furniture	04	00	00
One Table	00	04	00

In the Maids Garrott			
One bed and Furniture two Trunks & two Chairs	02	00	00
In Miss Lowes Room			
Foure Chairs	00	04	00
A Clock upon the Stair Case	00	15	00
In the Hall			
One Shoo Toar	02	02	00
Two & Thirty pictures	00	10	00
Nine Chairs	00	09	00
One beaufett	00	10	00
In the Entry next to the Parlour			
One Napkin press	00	12	00
In ye Parlour			
A Harpsicoard	00	10	00
In the Chamber over the Parlour			
Six Chairs	00	06	00
In the Best Chamber			
A Swing looking glass	00	04	00
In the Chamber within the best Chamber			
One Table and Stands	00	15	00
In the Garrott beyond ye Nursery			
One bed and Furniture	01	10	00
In the Kitching			
One Warming Pan & brass bason	00	06	08
One pair brass Candlesticks	00	03	06
Three pewter salvers	00	03	06
Two dozen & a halfe of pewter plaits	01	01	00
Tenn pewter dishes	01	00	00
Nine pewter plaits	00	06	00
Two pott panns, two little Kettles & one Saucepan	01	02	00
A Gun	00	07	00
Ninety eight ozs. 3 penny weight of plate	24	10	09

In the Office			
One Ovell Yable	00	06	00
A pair of Troys	00	04	00
On the Office Chamber			
One Chest bound abt. wth. Iron	00	06	00
One Still	00	08	00
In the Brewhouse			
Two Large Tubbs	01	00	00
One Strike	00	02	06
	50	19	11
	146	00	03
	3261	09	10
Tot: –	3458	10	00

Appraised by us

Richd. Vincent
Gervas Wright
Edward Dutton

An Inventory of the Goods and Chattels of Samuel Lowe late of Southwell in ye county of Nott. Esqr decd	Taken ye 16th. day of December Anno Dni 1723

Appendix K

Rev. George Mompesson

(from Borthwick Institute of Historical Research, York, Prog. Mar. 1732/33)

In the Name of God Amen. I George Mompesson Rector of Barmbrough in the County of York, being of sound and disposing mind & memory (praised be God) do make this my last Will and Testament in ma^{n}er following.

First, I recomend my Soul into the Hands of Almighty God, in hopes of Salvation through the All Sufficient merits of Jesus Christ, and my Body to the Grave to be decently and privately buried at the discretion of my Executor hereinafter named. Whereas my Eldest Son William Mompesson Vicar of Mansfield in the County of Nottingham upon transferring to him all my Right Interest and Title to my whole Estate and Manor at Wadingham in the County of Lincoln hath covenanted and agreed to pay or cause to be paid the summ of Two Thousand and Five Hundred Pounds of Lawfull money of Great Britain, within three months after my decease to such person or persons, as by my last and Testament or other disposition I should direct and appoint in pursuance of this Covenant I do in this my Willgive and dispose of the said Two Thousand and Five Hundred Pounds in this ma^{n}er. I give unto my Daughter Elizabeth the wife of Mr.John Bird one hundred pounds. To my Daughter Mary the Wife of Thomas Allen Clerk the Sum of Three hundred pounds. To my Daughter Alice Mompesson the Sum of Six hundred pounds upon her giving up the security w$^{ch.}$ I gave her for the payment of Three hundred pounds to my Executor. I give to my Daughter Margaret Mompesson the sum of Six hundred pounds. I give unto my Daughter Ann the wife of Gilbert Hall Clerk the Sum of six hundred pounds upon my Executors being discharged and released of the payment of Five hundred pounds w$^{ch.}$ I gave security for when she was married to the said Gilbert Hall. I give unto my Son Charles Mompesson y^{e} Sum of One hundred pounds and unto my Son Thomas Mompesson the Sum of One hundred pounds having setled Anu^{i}ties upon them and my Daughter Catherine out of the Estate at Wadingham, over and above ye payment of Two Thousand five hundred pounds. All which Sums amounting to Two Thousand and Four hundred pounds I order shall be punctually paid according to the Covenant and agreement with my Son William above mentioned. Item I give the remaining hundred pounds to my Executor herein mentioned towards the discharge of my Debts or legacies. It is my will and pleasure that ye respective Sums of money hereby given to my three married Daughters Elizabeth Bird Mary Allen, Ann Hall, shall be secured to them for their naturall lives and to their Children after their decease, and I desire and require that my Sons William and George to see this performed.

I give and devise unto my Son in Law Thomas Allen and his Heirs all that Close of Freehold lying in the precincts of Lamley in ye County of Nottingham containing by Estimation about 15 Acres upon his delivering up to my Executor the Bond which I had given to Mr.Chappell for his and my Daughters use, and I do require that ye said Close, or in case it should be sold, which I willingly consent to, that the moneys arising from such sale shall be setled upon my Daughter his present Wife during her life, and to the Children of their Bodies after her decease.

I give and devise unto my son George Mompesson and his Heirs all my Interest Right and Title which I have in reversion to the House and Outhouse Orchard and Premises at Southwell in the County of Nottingham which were given to me by the last Will and Testament of George Story of the same lately deceased.

I give and bequeath unto my said Son George Mompesson all my Leasehold Estates whether at Greenwich in Kent or at Tibshelf in the County of Derby (if not sold before my death) or in any other place.

I give and bequeath unto my Son William Mompesson aforesaid all that Library of Books which I left at Mansfield, and I likewise give him my great Silver Tankard with our Coat of Arms upon it, which was my Fathers, who desired that it might always go to the Eldest son of our Family, which I likewise direct and appoint.

I give and bequeath over and above the former sums charged upon the Wadingham Estate, on the account of Legacies given by Mr.Broomhead Grandfather to my Children, which have not hitherto been answered to some of them, the following sums – viz. to my Daughter Margaret Mompesson Twenty pounds, to my Daughter Hall Twenty pounds, to my Son Charles with some other Legacies that had been left him Forty pounds, to my Son Thomas Ten pounds, deducting to him the great debts which I have lately paid for him, far exceeding all his Legacies – I give my Daughter Alice Ten pounds.

I give to all my Grandchildren that shall be living at my decease Forty shillings apiece, to be paid in two years time after it.

I give to my Sister Chappell, to my Son William's Wife and to my Son George's Wife Guineas apiece to buy them Rings.

I give unto my Nephew Anthony Raworth Clerk, and his five Sisters, Guineas apiece to buy them rings.

I give unto the Poor of Mansfield Forty shillings, to the Poor of Barmbrough Twenty shillings, to the Poor of Southwell forty shillings.

I give and bequeath the Sum of Twenty pounds towards upholding the School which we have erected & set up at Barmbrough; I desire that this may be secured by purchasing a piece of land, or letting it out to use, and that the rent or Interest be constantly paid to the School Master, as a small Salary belonging to the said School. Ten pounds of the said money may be looked upon as a benefaction of my Son John Mompesson deceased, though it was in my power to dispose of it as I pleased.

I give and bequeath unto my Son George Mompesson the whole remainder of my Personall Estate Goods and Chattels (excepting such Plate Linen or Household Goods as I shall appoint to be given away and disposed of by writing under my hand) towards payment of the above mentioned Legacies, as well for ye discharge of all my just Debts and Funerall Expenses, wch I require in the first place to be paid.

Lastly I do hereby constitute and appoint my said Son George Mompesson full and sole Executor of this my last Will by me made

In witness whereof I have hereunto set my hand and seal, and published this as my last Will this Twenty eighth day of May in the Year of our Lord One thousand seven hundred thirty and one

George Mompesson

Signed sealed and published in the presence of us who set our Hands in the presence of ye Testator.

Ezra Kitchin

John Cox

William Allen

Codicil to the Will of George Mompesson

(Borthwick Institute of Historical Research, York, Prog. Mar. 1732/33)

I George Mompesson Rector of Barmbrough in the County of York do hereby make this my Codicil in manner following which I do hereby will and desire shall be taken as part of my last Will and Testament.

First I do hereby revoke the several Legacys by me in my last Will given to my Daughter Elizabeth the Wife of Mr.John Bird, to my Daughter Mary the Wife of Thomas Allen Clerk, to my Daughter Alice Mompesson, to my Daughter Margaret Mompesson, to my Daughter Anne Wife of Gilbert Hall Clerk, to my Son Charles Mompesson, to my Son Thomas Mompesson, to all my Grandchildren, to my Sister Chappell, to my Son William's Wife, to my Son George's Wife, to my Nephew Anthony Raworth Clerk & to his five Sisters, And do hereby in lieu thereof give unto my Daughter Elizabeth the Wife of Mr.John Bird the sum of fifty pounds, to my Daughter Mary the Wife of Thomas Allen Clerk the sum of two hundred and fifty pounds, to my Daughter Alice Mompesson the sum of five hundred and fifty pounds, to my Daughter Margaret Mompesson the sum of five hundred and fifty pounds, to my Daughter Anne Wife of Gilbert Hall Clerk the sum of five hundred and fifty pounds, to my Son Charles Mompesson the sum of fifty pounds, to my Son Thomas the sum of fifty pounds in and full satisfaction of all Legacys or sums of money due to them or any of them upon account of Mr.Broomhead deceased or any other person or on any account whatsoever. And whereas I have charged the Estate at Wadingham in the County of Lincoln with three Annuitys payable to my Sons Charles Mompesson & Thomas Mompesson and my Daughter Catherine Mompesson my mind & will is that the said Estate shall be wholly discharged from the payment of all or any of the said Annuitys my Son William Mompesson giving them and each of them his Bond for payment of the same.

And further my mind & will is that the Deductions by me now made out of the several Legacys by me in my last Will bequeathed amounting in the whole to the Sum of five hundred and one pounds & nine shillings shall be paid for the Discharge of my Debts and Funeral Expenses. Item my Will and mind is that the New Legacys in this my Codicil be settled to the same uses as they were settled in my Will.

In Witness whereof to this my Codicil affixed or written to the end of my last Will (being the first and part of the second side of the second leaf) I have set my Hand and affixed my seal this eighth day of February in the Year of our Lord 1732

Geo Mompesson

Signed Sealed Published and Declared
by the Testator to be his Codicil and Part of his last
Will in the presence of the Witnesses hereunder written who subscribed their
Names at the request and in the presence of the Testator.

Geo. Hurt

Wm. Astley

Mary Lindley

Index